Rethinking Preparation for Content Area Teaching

Jane Braunger
David M. Donahue
Kate Evans
Tomás Galguera

with a Foreword by
Ruth Schoenbach

Rethinking Preparation for Content Area Teaching

The Reading Apprenticeship Approach

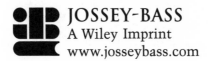

WestEd Published in Partnership with WestEd

JOSSEY-BASS
A Wiley Imprint
www.josseybass.com

Published by Jossey-Bass
A Wiley Imprint
989 Market Street, San Francisco, CA 94103-1741   www.josseybass.com

Jossey-Bass books and products are available through most bookstores. To contact Jossey-Bass directly, call our Customer Care Department within the U.S. at 800-956-7739, outside the U.S. at 317-572-3986, or fax 317-572-4002.

Jossey-Bass also publishes its books in a variety of electronic formats. Some content that appears in print may not be available in electronic books.

Library of Congress Cataloging-in-Publication Data
Rethinking preparation for content area teaching : the reading apprenticeship approach / Jane Braunger . . . [et al.].
      p. cm. —(Jossey-Bass education series)
  Includes bibliographical references and index.
  ISBN 0-7879-7166-9 (alk. paper)
1. Content area reading.   2. Inquiry-based learning.   3. Reading teachers—Training of.
4. Apprenticeship programs.   I. Braunger, Jane.   II. Series.
  LB1050.455.R48 2004
  428.4'071'2—dc22

                                                            2004014542

Printed in the United States of America
FIRST EDITION
HB Printing   10 9 8 7 6 5 4 3 2

The Jossey-Bass Education Series

Contents

Foreword

When I first heard the International Reading Association panel presentation by Jane Braunger, Dave Donahue, Kate Evans, and Tomás Galguera that led to this book, I was struck by the innovative ways in which each one of them had used and uniquely adapted the Reading Apprenticeship® framework. This inquiry-based instructional framework interweaves the social, personal, cognitive, and knowledge-building dimensions of reading through focus on metacognitive conversation—classroom talk about *how* we make sense of what we read as well as *what* the content means. The RA framework was first introduced in *Reading for Understanding: A Guide to Improving Reading in Middle School and High School Classrooms* (Schoenbach, Greenleaf, Cziko, and Hurwitz, 1999). Since its publication in 1999, the book has been used widely by teachers and literacy coaches, and in teacher education courses across the country.

By experimenting individually and together over several years with ways to use the Reading Apprenticeship framework and accompanying materials, the authors of this volume have created a new model for apprenticing preservice teachers to thinking about and working with literacy. In this new model, students begin to acquire and internalize significant new understandings through close examination of their own reading processes across varied disciplines and over time. These preservice teachers also learn to look closely at their own students, to move from thinking of reading as an activity that is the same for all students in all disciplines to one that is personal and context-specific. In this way, they are able to reframe their perceptions and questions about their students' reading in ways that help them provide more careful and informed support.

The authors have given us the voices of these young teachers-to-be as they explore their own reading identities, such as these two: *The first thing we discovered in the process of exchanging our metacognitive processes through this journal was that neither of us see ourselves as readers.* They have given us the vividness of new insights-in-process as preservice students with content expertise rethink what is "obvious" in a text: *We can ask students to reread math texts because of the nature of math, not because of their own lack of knowledge. The implication for students is that rereading math becomes a sign of a good math reader, not a bad one.*

In addition to providing a new picture of inquiry-based content area reading courses for secondary preservice teachers and providing a rich array of descriptions, classroom engagements, assignments, and preliminary research findings, the authors of *Rethinking Preparation for Content Area Teaching* have generated new questions and critiques of the Reading Appprenticeship framework as they have adapted it to their varied contexts and concerns. From Kate Evans's adaptation of Dave Donahue's assignment to meet the needs of her "nonreader" student teachers, to Tomás Galguera's exploration of the areas in which teachers of English language learners need to offer specialized support, to Jane Braunger's strong case for this model as a part of maintaining professionalism in teaching through the ongoing practice of inquiry, this volume offers both concrete tools and theoretical food for thought.

This book's contribution to the field of teacher education will be obvious to any educator or policymaker interested in providing new teachers with a richer and more flexible knowledge base about the ways of thinking, reading, writing, and speaking that are essential to their disciplines. Without such teacher knowledge, our national goals of equal access to rigorous content understanding for all students cannot be realized. But in addition to its value at the preservice teacher level, this new addition to what has unexpectedly become a Reading Apprenticeship series will be a very valuable sourcebook for mentor teachers, teacher leaders, professional development providers, and literacy coaches working with middle school and high school in-service teachers as well.

Oakland, California   *Ruth Schoenbach*
March 2004   *Codirector, Strategic Literacy Initiative*

Reference

Schoenbach, R., Greenleaf, C., Cziko, C., and Hurwitz, L. *Reading for Understanding: A Guide to Improving Reading in Middle and High School Classrooms*. San Francisco: Jossey-Bass, 1999.

Preface

> Teaching reading in our disciplines *is* teaching our disciplines.
>
> —*Strategic Literacy Initiative–WestEd*

This book grew out of both frustration and enthusiasm. As teacher educators, we had often been frustrated by our preservice teachers' view of the content area reading course as a collection of "add-ons," freestanding reading strategies to be larded into an already full middle or high school curriculum. These teachers feared that teaching reading strategies meant giving up important content and resisted seeing literacy instruction as part of their responsibility as content area teachers. However, as we organized our content area reading courses around Reading Apprenticeship®, we became enthusiastic about sharing with colleagues the impact of this approach on preservice teachers' attitudes toward and skills in content area literacy instruction.

Why Read This Book

This book offers inquiry experiences, resources, and classroom tools developed for implementation of Reading Apprenticeship in the preservice program. Readers will find here powerful ways to:

- Help preservice middle and high school teachers gain more complex understandings of the reading process.
- Help preservice teachers build awareness of the features of

text and associated demands of reading in various academic disciplines.

- Use inquiry experiences as a vehicle for preservice teachers' learning about adolescent readers' strengths and needs.
- Support preservice teachers' learning of high-leverage strategies to share with apprentice adolescent readers.

In short, readers will learn how to help preservice teachers develop the expertise to teach reading in the disciplines effectively as part of teaching the disciplines.

Audience

Although the primary audience for this book is teacher educators responsible for the preservice secondary reading in the content areas course, others charged with professional development in the school setting will find useful ideas and guidance as well. The literacy activities and engagements contained in the book were developed by members of the Teacher Education Consortium (TEC) of WestEd's Strategic Literacy Initiative. All have been used effectively in members' classrooms and continue to be revised and adapted as colleagues implement them and share results. The literacy assignments and experiences here build on and complement the work of SLI professional staff working with middle and high school teachers, inspired by *Reading for Understanding: A Guide to Improving Reading in Middle and High School Classrooms* (Schoenbach, Greenleaf, Cziko, and Hurwitz, 1999). In fact, there are many points of connection between Reading Apprenticeship in this new setting, the preservice program, and in its more established context, the middle and high school classroom. RA in the preservice experience has already proven to be a strong foundation for new teachers entering classrooms in Bay Area middle and high schools. In several instances, former students of TEC members have begun their teaching careers in schools incorporating RA. These new

teachers come well equipped to engage their students in metacognitive conversations about reading as they scaffold students' ability
to read and learn from challenging texts. Though beginners, they
are already valuable resources to their colleagues about apprenticing students to reading in the disciplines.

Who We Are and How We Wrote This Book

In 2000, we and other teacher educators formed the Teacher Education Consortium of the Strategic Literacy Initiative to explore
ways to incorporate Reading Apprenticeship into our preservice
programs. We came together to articulate a strong rationale for
content area literacy learning, and saw in Reading Apprenticeship
a promising model for that. As we began using RA as a framework
for preservice teachers' learning about reading in the content area,
we developed a number of inquiry experiences and resources,
adding to the professional development tools already in use with
middle and high school teachers in the Bay Area and nationally.
The ideas and approaches described in this book were developed by
TEC members in collaboration with one another and with our preservice students. We represent schools of education at Mills College in Oakland; University of California, Berkeley; San Jose State
University; Sonoma State University; University of California,
Santa Cruz; Stanford University; Humboldt State University; and
Washington State University–Vancouver.

We and the other members of the TEC wanted to share what
we had learned in our collaborative inquiry into preparing teachers for content area reading instruction. We also wanted to share
the evidence of our students' deeper understanding of academic literacy with RA as an instructional framework. With support from
WestEd's Strategic Literacy Initiative and a grant from the Hewlett
Foundation, the TEC designed and conducted two seminars for
teacher educators in the summers of 2000 and 2001. Over forty
teacher educators took part, subsequently incorporating RA into
their preservice programs, and joining in our ongoing inquiry into

how to support new teachers as teachers of reading. Many also joined the TEC, sharing their work and engaging in literacy inquiry activities during quarterly meetings or taking part in listserv discussions. The TEC expanded to include faculty from additional colleges and universities in California and other states.

Although the work to develop meaningful reading courses continues, a renewed sense of optimism about the content area reading course is evident among TEC members and seminar participants. TEC members continue to investigate their work with Reading Apprenticeship, and have shared the results of their course design and research at professional conferences including the National Council of Teachers of English, the American Educational Research Association, the International Reading Association, and the American Association of Colleges for Teacher Education. This is an ongoing inquiry into how to support new teachers as teachers of reading. The model of experts apprenticing adolescents to effective ways of reading in the discipline offers a powerful rationale for preparation of preservice teachers, one that capitalizes on the role of literacy in learning across the content areas.

Overview of the Contents

Chapter One frames the current context in which teacher education operates, with specific reference to the challenges posed to the preparation of teachers to teach reading in their disciplines. Various perspectives on teacher shortage, teacher quality, and the content of teacher education are described and a larger vision of literacy learning for prospective teachers is proposed. Chapter Two introduces and describes Reading Apprenticeship as a framework for teaching reading in secondary subject area classes and as the optimal way to frame preservice instruction in how to teach reading in various disciplines. In this chapter, preservice teachers' experiences learning about academic literacy via Reading Apprenticeship illustrate the four dimensions of the framework and the metacognitive conversation that animates them and supports reading to learn in the content areas. Chapters Three and Four share in-depth literacy inquiry experiences developed for preservice teachers in an RA context. Chapter Three describes a cross-disciplinary reading assignment for firsthand experience of metacognition about one's own reading process and access to others' processes in different disciplines. Chapter Four traces an inquiry project into adolescents' literacy practices and needs that helps prospective teachers become collaborative inquirers with their students about reading in their content area.

Chapters Five through Eight provide further course materials and approaches reflective of RA and developed by TEC members. In Chapter Five, instructional strategies linked to powerful learning about reading in the content areas are described; course handouts and assignment procedures are included. Chapter Six offers specifics on an alternative texts collection assignment that is designed to increase preservice teachers' knowledge of and access to extensive reading in the content areas. Chapter Seven focuses on Reading Apprenticeship for English learners, with particular advice on addressing the four dimensions and supporting the metacognitive conversation with these students. Chapter Eight addresses meeting the needs of struggling readers in an RA classroom and includes an inquiry activity into published reading intervention programs.

Chapters Nine and Ten move into life with RA after the preparation program. Chapter Nine describes a university-district collaboration in Vancouver, Washington, that pairs preservice teachers with experienced teachers in RA classrooms to enhance learning and RA practice in both groups. Chapter Ten provides data from formative studies on new teachers' implementation of RA as a framework in their own classrooms. Chapter Eleven concludes with a review of the purposes of RA in the preservice program and advice for teacher educators as they consider adopting it as an instructional framework. The book ends with two appendixes that contain classroom assignments developed by additional TEC members: a literacy autobiography to build understanding of metacognition and an inquiry into reading in mathematics.

Our aim in this book is to offer teacher educators and literacy professional development providers a productive and engaging way to frame reading in the content areas. We are eager to share what we have done and what we have learned as we employ Reading Apprenticeship both as the organizer for preservice and in-service professional development and as the instructional framework in the secondary classroom. The classroom experiences and course assignments described here are offered for readers' use and adaptation in the spirit of collegial scholarship. In our TEC group, all of us have benefited from the discussions, shared classroom activities, and resources brought to our meetings. We welcome the opportunity to widen this circle of colleagues.

Oakland, California	*Jane Braunger*
Oakland, California	*David M. Donahue*
Santa Cruz, California	*Kate Evans*
Oakland, California	*Tomás Galguera*
July 2004	

Note

Unless otherwise noted, all student names are pseudonyms.

Reference

Schoenbach, R., Greenleaf, C., Cziko, C., and Hurwitz, L. *Reading for Understanding: A Guide to Improving Reading in Middle and High School Classrooms*. San Francisco: Jossey-Bass, 1999.

Acknowledgments

The ideas and resources shared in this book owe much to the insights and collaboration of many people. We wish to thank our colleagues, the authors of *Reading for Understanding: A Guide to Improving Reading in Middle and High School Classrooms* (1999), for the solid foundation on which the Teacher Education Consortium (TEC) built its work expanding Reading Apprenticeship into the preservice teacher education program. Ruth Schoenbach, Cynthia Greenleaf, Christine Cziko, and Lori Hurwitz led the way.

Members of WestEd's Strategic Literacy Initiative inspired us as they continually developed classroom resources, professional development designs, and publications to support teachers' uptake of Reading Apprenticeship. Along with Ruth, Cyndy, and Lori, we thank SLI colleagues Gina Hale, Marean Jordan, Tamara Taylor Reeder, Cindy Litman, and former SLI colleagues Pamela Fong, Catherine Rico, and Mary Stump. Our thanks to TEC colleagues who met and shared their classroom practice in RA, joined us in ongoing inquiries into reading in the preservice program, and read and responded to drafts of chapters in the book: Jan Lewis, Cathy Yetter, Christine Cziko, Katherine Davies Samway, Jayne DeLawter, Virginia Draper, Karen Grady, Holly Gritsch de Cordova, Anita Hernandez, Susan Katz, Lucinda Pease-Alvarez, Cathleen Rafferty, Rick Sawyer, Diana Bledsoe, and Anne Watkins. A special thanks goes to Virginia Draper for excellent revision and editing suggestions on key chapters.

We thank also the Bay Area secondary teachers and their students featured in SLI videocases illustrating RA implementation:

Dr. Willard Brown, Lisa Krebs, Monica Figueroa, Rita Jensen, Dorothea Jensen, and Jill Parmeter. Our vicarious visits to their classrooms fueled spirited discussions and thoughtful learning about helping our students, preservice teachers, create Reading Apprenticeship classrooms.

Generous support from the Hewlett Foundation made it possible to convene the TEC group, support our research and writing retreats, and host the faculty summer seminars that brought Reading Apprenticeship ideas to many more teacher educators. As our outreach grew, we gained confidence in the value of what we were learning about Reading Apprenticeship to other teacher educators.

Thanks to Jana Bouc, SLI's program coordinator, for constructing our TEC listserv and updating it with new members following presentations of our work and queries from interested colleagues around the country.

Christie Hakim, associate editor at Jossey-Bass, has been an encouraging and generous supporter of the book from its inception. Sandra Beris, copyeditor, provided very helpful editing suggestions.

All of us, authors and contributors, thank our students, whose voices give life to the book and whose insights and questions inspire us to continue strengthening the work described. Our deep gratitude goes to these former students from preservice education programs at Mills College, University of California, Berkeley, University of California, Santa Cruz, Humboldt State University, San Jose State University, and Washington State University–Vancouver.

Finally, we wish to thank family and friends who have sustained us during this project: John Braunger, Robin and Mateo Galguera, and Annie Tobin.

The Sponsors

WestEd

WestEd is a nonprofit research, development, and service agency that works with education and other communities to promote excellence, achieve equity, and improve learning for children, youth, and adults. The agency focuses on what goes on not just in school but also in early childhood; in children's homes, afterschool programs, and communities; in the training and development of those who teach and guide children; and in legislatures and other decision-making bodies whose policies touch all of these. WestEd's headquarters are in San Francisco, with offices in Oakland and other cities in California and in Arizona, Massachusetts, and Washington, D.C.

Strategic Literacy Initiative

The Strategic Literacy Initiative (SLI) is a collaborative research, development, and service organization based in Oakland at WestEd. SLI works with educators and communities to develop the literacy skills of adolescents; its mission is to expand the academic, creative, career, and civic opportunities of young people through higher-level literacy development. SLI has documented gains in students' reading comprehension, with those who are second language learners and those who score in the bottom two quartiles on standardized tests of reading comprehension showing the greatest gains (Greenleaf, Schoenbach, Cziko, and Mueller, 2001).

SLI develops text and videotaped literacy case studies of adolescent readers, provides teachers with access to relevant research and resources, and studies the impact of its programs on both student and teacher learning. The conceptual and research-based core of SLI's work is Reading Apprenticeship®, an instructional framework for literacy instruction across the curriculum as described in *Reading for Understanding: A Guide to Improving Reading in Middle and High School Classrooms* (Schoenbach, Greenleaf, Cziko, and Hurwitz, 1999).

SLI conducts professional development programs for middle and high school teachers in the San Francisco Bay Area and nationwide. In addition, it offers the National Institute in Reading Apprenticeship for educators who are responsible for teacher professional development.

For more information on SLI's research, tools, and professional development programs, please visit www.wested.org/stratlit on the Web. The initiative is supported in part through funding from The Carnegie Corporation of New York, the Stuart Foundations, the Annenberg Foundation, the William and Flora Hewlett Foundation, the Stupski Family Foundation, the Walter S. Johnson Foundation, and the W. Clement and Jessie V. Stone Foundation, in addition to contracts with schools, districts, and county offices of education.

References

Greenleaf, C., Schoenbach, R., Cziko, C., and Mueller, F., "Apprenticing Adolescent Readers to Academic Literacy," *Harvard Educational Review*, Spring 2001, pp. 79–129.

Schoenbach, R., Greenleaf, C., Cziko, C., and Hurwitz, L. *Reading for Understanding: A Guide to Improving Reading in Middle and High School Classrooms*. San Francisco: Jossey-Bass, 1999.

The Authors

Jane Braunger, Ed.D., is a senior research associate with the Strategic Literacy Initiative (SLI) at WestEd, where she conducts research on professional development in literacy among middle and high school teachers; collaborates in the ongoing development of theory and practice in Reading Apprenticeship; and establishes new networks and contexts for SLI's work, especially in preservice settings. Her professional experience includes high school and college teaching, K–12 language arts curriculum development, teacher education, research, and writing. She is coauthor with Dr. Jan Patricia Lewis of a 1997 synthesis of the research on learning to read, *Building a Knowledge Base in Reading*. A second edition will be published by the International Reading Association in 2004. She is the current director of the National Council of Teachers of English Commission on Reading.

David M. Donahue, Ph.D., is assistant professor of education at Mills College in Oakland, California, where he is also codirector of the secondary English–social studies teacher credential program. Previously, he was a curriculum writer and developmental editor and social studies teacher in public schools. He has worked with Amnesty International's Human Rights Education program and the Canadian Human Rights Foundation over the past ten years and has developed and led training programs on human rights for teachers and activists in the United States, Eastern Europe, and Central Asia. He is the author of two human rights curriculum guides, *Lesbian, Gay, Bisexual, and Transgender Rights: A Human Rights Perspective*, and with Nancy Flowers, *The Uprooted: Refugees and the United States*. His research interests include learning from community service and preparing secondary teachers to teach reading and writing in subject area classes.

Kate Evans, Ph.D., formerly an assistant professor of education at San Jose State University, currently teaches at University of California, Santa Cruz. She has taught children, adolescents, and adults in California, Washington State, and Yokohama, Japan. Her book *Negotiating the Self: Identity, Sexuality, and Emotion in Learning to Teach* was published by Routledge in 2002. Her poetry, fiction, and essays have been widely published.

Tomás Galguera, Ph.D., is an associate professor of education at Mills College in Oakland, California, where he codirects the pre-K–elementary Early Childhood Emphasis and Developmental Perspectives in Education teacher credential program. He specializes in English language development methodology courses for both elementary and secondary preservice teachers and has been a certified Spanish-bilingual elementary public school teacher in Oakland. In addition to contributing to the Full Options Science System's newsletter and publishing in *The Multilingual Educator*, he has developed high school science curriculum modules for teachers of English learners and was a contributor to *Professional Development for Teachers of English Learners: A Scaffold for Change*, published by the San Diego County Office of Education. With colleagues from the Teachers for Tomorrow's Schools program at Mills College, he published *Teaching as Principled Practice: Managing Complexity for Social Change*, and with Kenji Hakuta is a contributing author to *Psychology and Educational Practice*. His research interests include the pedagogy of teacher education for language-minority students and ethnicity, race, culture, and language in education.

Contributors

Diana Bledsoe, Evergreen School District
Richard D. Sawyer, Washington State University–Vancouver
Cathleen D. Rafferty, Humboldt State University
Virginia Draper, University of California, Santa Cruz

Rethinking Preparation for Content Area Teaching

Chapter 1

Preparing All Teachers as Teachers of Reading

Challenges and Visions

Teacher educators preparing middle and high school teachers face a number of challenges. A shortage of qualified teachers, especially in urban areas, has called into question what ought to be the essential content of the teacher preparation program, how to assess quality teaching (and thus prepare prospective teachers to provide it), and how to prepare teachers to function effectively in diverse and demanding classrooms. For faculty charged with teaching content area reading, the debate about the role, method, and place of literacy instruction across the curriculum has been amplified as tests of reading achievement have become highly significant in assessing student learning and determining school success. The debate raises questions central to our work in preparing secondary content area teachers. What should teachers of adolescents learn about the nature and teaching of academic literacy? Is reading a prerequisite to advanced content learning?

The story of a fictional new teacher may serve to bring some of these challenges into focus:

Mark, an economics major in college, joined a volunteer teacher program after graduation and taught middle school mathematics for a year in a high-poverty urban school. He has stayed on in the school, earning an alternative credential through a series of district-sponsored afterschool training courses, many tied to implementation of published mathematics curricula. He has also had training in classroom management and preparing students for the

1

state's mathematics achievement tests. Mark is considered a good teacher by administrators, colleagues, and parents.

Mark is interested in what works in his classroom—for classroom management and for students' learning of mathematical knowledge and processes. He relies heavily on published programs to teach sequenced mathematical skills. His teaching style is whole class instruction, with monitored individual student practice and more practice for students who haven't shown mastery in a particular skill. He keeps a steady pace for this whole group instruction but does work with individual students during problem practice time and also invites students to get extra help from him after school. Mark does not have students work in pairs or small groups in his math class.

Mark is concerned about the poor reading skills of many of his students but doesn't know how to help, and will say that he doesn't think it's his responsibility to teach reading in a mathematics class. He wishes that students had learned to read well enough in the elementary grades to handle the reading demands of his class. He hasn't thought much about the role of reading in mathematics, other than in solving word problems, even though he studied mathematics extensively in college. He knows that state and national mathematics standards call for higher levels of problem-solving ability but finds word problems in mathematics too frustrating, especially for students who struggle with reading. Without productive ways of addressing his students' reading needs, Mark has begun to limit his use of word problems, concentrating more on mathematical operations. He worries that this low-level mathematics curriculum will curtail his students' future opportunities in math and likely rule out a college prep high school experience for many of them. He has begun to feel bored with the content of his teaching and is concerned about the students he's not reaching. However, he doesn't know how to do a better job.

Challenges for Teacher Education

Teacher Supply

Perceived teacher shortages in certain content areas and geographic locations have led to emergency credentials, most often for teachers like Mark in urban schools that serve large proportions of poor and minority students. This stopgap response to the critical need for teachers has, in recent years, lent support for an alternative route to certification, such as the one Mark took. Schools of education are being asked why prospective teachers should be required to complete a full credential program in a college or university when a less expensive and quicker route is available, one that emphasizes learning the practical aspects of teaching. Equip teachers with content knowledge and classroom management skills and get them in front of a classroom—that seems to be the idea.

Teacher Quality

Just what counts as teacher quality and how teacher quality affects student achievement and thus school performance are hotly debated issues with huge implications for teacher education programs. Adding heat, if not light, to the debate, the federal *No Child Left Behind Act* (2001) requires "highly qualified" teachers in all schools by 2005–06. The definition is left to the states, though, so we may expect an array of indicators of quality, ranging, for example, from (1) amount of coursework in the content area and grades earned in those courses to (2) amount of coursework in educational theory and practice and curriculum design and grades earned in those courses, (3) scores on credential exams, and (4) professional experience deemed relevant to teaching. Mark, our fictional math teacher, would probably do well on the first and third, and may be moving toward the fourth. However, he will probably have little chance to qualify for the second.

There are many who believe that knowledge of a subject is sufficient to teach it well. Alternative routes to certification place a high priority on subject area knowledge, and thus attract either professionals who make a midcareer switch to teaching or recent college graduates, like Mark, who sign on to teaching as a first career. Their entry into teaching is usually accomplished with a minimum of education coursework in areas such as learning theory, pedagogy, curriculum planning, research, and assessment.

A persistent theme among critics of traditional teacher education is that prospective teachers are burdened with coursework developing their pedagogical knowledge rather than focusing on their subject area disciplines. A recent report from the Education Commission of the States (Allen, 2003) that looks at teacher quality examined available research in order to address links between components of teacher preparation and teacher effectiveness in the classroom, as well as links between teacher preparation and retention in the profession. The ECS report concluded that although the research provides *moderate* support for the importance of solid subject matter knowledge to a teacher's effectiveness, it offers only *limited* support for the value of preparation in pedagogy to a teacher's effectiveness. Regarding the subject matter knowledge–pedagogical knowledge debate, the report says this:

> On one side are those who believe that solid pedagogical preparation is critical to teachers' ability to handle an increasingly diverse student population and adapt their instruction to the learning style and worldview of each student. On the other side are those who hold that teaching is much more a matter of communicating various concepts and matters of content, and that the ability to manage a classroom, evaluate students, and develop curricula are the essential teaching skills. The *No Child Left Behind Act* of 2001 (NCLB) tends toward the latter view, and the *Secretary's Annual Report on Teacher Quality* (Paige, 2002) contends that a strong grasp of subject

matter knowledge and strong verbal ability are the most important factors contributing to successful teaching. [Allen, 2003, p. 29]

We believe that this report, and other statements like it, create a dangerous false dichotomy. The omission of the role of teachers' knowledge about teaching and learning is striking here, especially given the wealth of empirical evidence and professional standards that link teacher preparation to quality teaching. In fact, the negative impact of inadequate pedagogical knowledge on instruction has been well documented (Grossman, 1990; Shulman, 1987). Reviews of research continually show that fully prepared and certified teachers are generally better rated and more successful with students than those without this preparation. And given the steadily rising bar for student proficiency, the fact that teachers who have greater knowledge of teaching and learning are more effective with students, especially at tasks requiring higher-order thinking and problem solving, is strong support for thorough preparation in teaching as well as in subject matter knowledge. (For a review of this literature, see Darling-Hammond, 1999.)

For certified teachers, National Board Certification is widely accepted as the standard of excellence—for example, satisfying the NCLB's requirements for "highly qualified teacher." Certification by the National Board for Professional Teaching Standards (NBPTS) measures a teacher's practice against rigorous standards in specific subject areas and with specific grade levels, all linked to five core propositions (National Board for Professional Teaching Standards, n.d.):

- Teachers are committed to students and their learning.

- Teachers know the subjects they teach and how to teach those subjects to students.

- Teachers are responsible for managing and monitoring student learning.

- Teachers think systematically about their practice and learn from experience.
- Teachers are members of learning communities.

Teacher educators see the teacher preparation program as the first in a continual series of professional development experiences characterized by intellectual rigor and inquiry as a stance toward learning in the profession (Ball and Cohen, 1999; Darling-Hammond, 2000). The National Board Certification process and standards offer the next step in professional development.

In contrast, the preparation that our fictional math teacher Mark received focused on subject matter knowledge and classroom management. Without the opportunity to learn about learning theory, develop habits of inquiry and reflection in action, and function as a member of a learning community, he is at a disadvantage in becoming a competent teacher and even pursuing professional development to improve. And a recent study of preservice mathematics teachers points to a more critical reason for strengthening subject matter knowledge with solid pedagogical knowledge. Researchers found that preservice teachers with high levels of mathematics knowledge were actually more likely than less mathematically knowledgeable peers to have "an expert blind spot" (EBS); (Nathan and Petrosino, 2003). That is, they were prone to assume that ninth-grade Algebra 1 students' symbolic reasoning precedes and is a necessary prerequisite to verbal reasoning and story problem-solving ability. In fact, this research showed that students move to symbolic mathematics understandings through verbal representations and procedures. The experts in mathematics actually were misled by their subject matter knowledge to predict student problem-solving difficulty inaccurately. Steeped in the discipline, they assumed that the structure of the discipline of mathematics is actually the way students learn it. Not so, say the researchers, who concluded that "the existence of EBS underscores the need to balance subject matter knowledge with well-developed pedagogical content knowledge and an understanding of how students' subject matter–specific knowledge develops" (Nathan and Petrosino, 2003, p. 923).

The ECS report calls for more research addressing the question of how best to prepare effective teachers, an inquiry already undertaken by a task force of the American Educational Research Association. In fact, there is a growing body of empirical evidence about the role of quality teacher preparation in successful teaching as measured by a number of outcomes, including student learning (Darling-Hammond, 1999, 2000). However, reports like the ECS study and the Abell report, "Teacher Certification Reconsidered: Stumbling for Quality" (Walsh, 2001), focus on what we *don't* know definitively about the impact of a teacher preparation program on a teacher's effectiveness as measured mainly by student achievement test results. We have compelling evidence of the impact of high-quality teacher preparation on teachers' effectiveness, especially the importance of knowledge of teaching and learning (Darling-Hammond, 2000, 2001). The complex connections between teacher learning and effectiveness in instruction cannot be reduced to student performance on standardized tests.

Content of Teacher Education

A growing theme in current criticisms of teacher education is that schools of education lack the knowledge base and professional validity to determine a curriculum of study and practicum experiences that prepare teachers adequately. In the case of literacy education, this belief is driven by an assumption that successful teaching can be measured by student test scores. Of course, student learning is the goal of teaching. However, the reduction of the complexity of teaching and learning to a "what works" formula of teaching as cause and test score as effect is false and damaging. One consequence of such simplistic thinking is that schools of education are feeling pressure to abandon course content that draws on constructivist, sociolinguistic, meaning-based models of reading in favor of a phonics-based model of reading with an emphasis on direct instruction, especially as represented in the 2000 report of the National Reading Panel (NRP).

In some institutions, scholarly traditions of inquiry-based learning and exploration of diverse perspectives on research as well as on literacy may be replaced with training in "what works," according to the recommendations of the NRP. A number of critiques of that report, notably by literacy researchers and teacher educators, suggest the conflict this reeducation of teacher educators will likely produce (Allington, 2002; Camilli, Vargas, and Yurecko, 2003; Yatvin, Weaver, and Garan, 2003).

The debate about preparing teachers of reading is often polarized by the false dichotomies that occur in the larger debate about teacher education: knowledge about pedagogy versus knowledge about subject matter, and preparation via coursework versus preparation through experience. Most alternative certification programs seem to capitalize on these false dichotomies, sending new teachers into classrooms with minimal preparation in how to teach and banking on their ability to learn educational practice on the job through practice, and sometimes, observation of experienced teachers. But observation of an experienced teacher without sustained mentoring and feedback for the new teacher's self-reflection and action is hardly sufficient professional development (Darling-Hammond, 2000). More important, without some guidance via frameworks of teaching and learning, how can an inexperienced teacher know what to look for in such classroom observations?

Those who argue in favor of alternative certification often disdain professional knowledge about learning theory, pedagogy, and curriculum design. In their view, teacher education is not a professional program of study but rather a credential program. As such, proponents argue that prospective teachers should have access to less expensive, less time-consuming routes to certification. Our fictional teacher, Mark, took this route, but he is struggling, and so are his students.

Underprepared Teachers

Not surprisingly, proponents of scripted programs for beginning and developmental reading instruction point to the need among alternatively certified or emergency credentialed teachers for a clear-cut, sequential curriculum to teach and assessments that are "objective" to measure students' reading achievement. For many teacher educators, this marks a stunning shift in priorities: away from teacher knowledge—for example, about reading in specific disciplines, about monitoring learning, and about pedagogy—and toward reliance on published program content and standardized tests. In such a system, the knowledge resides in the instructional program (and those who designed it) and not in the classroom teacher, who is asked merely to implement it. But can programs do the job? Can teachers who don't know much about reading and learning effectively teach children to read by relying on "teacher-proof" programs? Can teachers at the middle and high school levels who lack insight into discipline-based reading help students become effective, engaged readers? The idea that the knowledge resides in the instructional program, not in the teacher, is foreign to our best understandings of effective instruction, understandings reflected in voluminous research on teacher effectiveness.

Research by Moustafa and Land (2002) indicates that scripted programs do not improve the effectiveness of underprepared teachers and suggests that rather than shoring up uncredentialed teachers with teacher-proof curricula we would do well to prepare them adequately in the first place. The researchers, both from California State University, Los Angeles, studied the impact of scripted programs on student reading achievement. They found the percent of children scoring at or above the fiftieth percentile on California's state achievement test to be as follows:

- Lower in the schools with lower levels of credentialed teachers than in schools with higher levels of credentialed teachers

- Lower in schools with scripted programs than in schools with unscripted programs

- Lowest in schools with low levels of credentialed teachers *and* with scripted programs

Scripted programs not only fail to deliver results for students but may actually discourage inexperienced teachers from developing the professional knowledge they need to address their students' various instructional needs in reading, thus exacerbating the problem (Moustafa and Land, 2002).

Clearly, in schools staffed with committed but underprepared teachers, the teachers as well as the students are suffering. Studies consistently show that the neediest schools have disproportionately high numbers of teachers working on conditional or emergency credentials (National Commission on Teaching and America's Future [NCTAF], 1996). Also typical of trends throughout the country, these underprepared teachers leave the profession at higher rates than traditionally prepared teachers. Teach for America (TFA), one of the best-known alternative programs, has a two-year attrition rate nearly three times the national average for new teachers. In Baltimore, nearly two-thirds of the TFA corps members who began teaching in 1992 left within two years (Darling-Hammond, 2000). In contrast, retention rates in the profession for teachers prepared through fifth-year professional programs and four-year education programs are between 84 percent and 53 percent. A 30 percent retention rate for teachers trained through "alternative routes" represents lost opportunities and squandered resources both for individuals and for the profession (Darling-Hammond, 2000).

High teacher turnover exacerbates the existing problems of urban schools and brings into sharp relief the importance of building a national consensus on quality teacher preparation and effective support for new teachers. Also, given the strong evidence that teacher effectiveness increases significantly after the first few years

(Kain and Singleton, 1996), it is critical that beginning teachers be well equipped. The education system's investment in novices who leave after a year is lost (Darling-Hammond, 2003).

Literacy Education as a Flashpoint

The NCLB legislation has made reading and literacy a flashpoint for debates about teacher preparation. The national goal of the NCLB legislation for average yearly progress (AYP) measured by standardized tests in reading and mathematics has led to a focus on how best to teach reading so that scores on these tests will consistently improve for all students. In the immediate aftermath of the report of the National Reading Panel (2000), much of that focus was on elementary reading instruction, but teacher educators preparing secondary teachers have begun to feel the pressure to equip them with strategies or programs to boost the test scores of struggling adolescent readers.

In the crowded academic program for preservice secondary teachers, reading in the content areas has variously been embedded in the methods course for content area teaching or accorded its own course in the program. A separate course in reading for prospective middle and high school teachers is relatively new in some states; Washington State initiated the requirement in 2000, for example. The authors of this text teach in institutions that require secondary teaching candidates to take a one-term course in content area reading instruction. In addition, their students explore the relationship between literacy and learning in coursework, practica, and teaching placements.

Creating a Bigger Vision of Literacy in Content Area Learning

We want our preservice teachers to understand reading as larger and more complex than a basic skill acquired in elementary school and now used generically to learn from texts across the curriculum.

They must understand reading as a developmental process in which the knowledge and strategies needed to comprehend more sophisticated subject area texts develop, with appropriate support, in the process of extensive engagement with such texts. Still, we have encountered resistance in some preservice teachers to seeing themselves as teachers of reading in their discipline. We are also well aware of similar views of reading as a basic, technical skill by content area university faculty and by experienced teachers with whom our students are placed for internships or student teaching.

A number of recent studies and reports coalesce around the importance of teachers having a strong and growing knowledge base in reading. The RAND Reading Study Group (RRSG) spoke of the need to ensure that teachers "have a deep knowledge about the reading process and reading comprehension" (RAND Reading Study Group, 2002, p. 49). The International Reading Association and the National Middle School Association issued a joint statement on reading (2002) in which they called for better teacher preparation in reading and ongoing professional development to enhance teachers' effectiveness in content area literacy instruction. To accomplish this goal, the RRSG says we need to determine the knowledge base teachers need to teach comprehension effectively, the "relative power" of the different ways of accomplishing this, and an understanding of how closely "teacher preparation experiences relate to teacher practices and student performances" (RAND Reading Study Group, 2002, p. 51).

The Alliance for Excellent Education, a national policy, advocacy, and research organization that focuses on improving academic success for the nation's most at-risk middle and high school students, has published a report that echoes these calls for an emphasis on reading. *Adolescents and Literacy: Reading for the 21st Century* (Kamil, 2003) describes a developmental view of reading—specifically, reading to learn from content texts (Alexander and Jetton, 2000). The ability to learn from text changes during the course of one's education, a reality that manifests itself in a variety of ways for students. Cummins (2001) describes the documented decline in reading performance for English learners as "the fourth-grade slump" to mark the point at which simple vocabulary development and decoding skills are no longer sufficient for students to meet literacy development expectations. The instructional implications are clear: teachers must be knowledgeable about all of their students' content area literacy strengths and needs, about the demands of particular texts, and about the support necessary for particular students to learn from them. They must also know how to select accessible texts for content area learning while at the same time helping students to develop strategies and knowledge that will allow them to engage productively with more challenging texts. Students are not opening a toolbox, presumably fully equipped by the end of third grade, and using it to read their tenth-grade science text; instead, they are learning how to read this text in the process of learning high school science content, equipping their toolbox to meet the demands of content area reading in high school and beyond. This is why teachers' knowledge about literacy and learning in their disciplines is so important, with a strong foundation in the preservice program and opportunities to deepen that knowledge through ongoing professional development.

We want to help our preservice teachers see that, as expert readers in their subject areas, they are uniquely equipped to help the adolescents in their classrooms learn discipline-specific ways of reading and thinking. It is critical that they gain the insights and tools they need to help their students access and employ the complex ways of reading that each discipline requires. This is a larger vision of the middle and high school teacher's role in subject area literacy, one that our teacher Mark was not offered in his preparation that focused on "what works" to raise test scores.

We strive to help preservice teachers shift their thinking about reading to the larger vision described here, one that moves subject area reading to the center of classroom practice. But often the classroom placements for student practica or teaching make our task more difficult because of the reinforcement of the model of reading as a technical skill separate from the content. We can't assume that cooperating teachers themselves are knowledgeable about effective literacy-support practices—for example, building schema needed to understand specific texts or developing students' questioning and summarizing skills to guide their reading. And given pressures to cover the content, cooperating teachers may steer preservice teachers away from interactive strategies that help students focus on the reading process as well as on comprehension (Irvin, Buehl, and Klemp, 2003). In fact, Irvin and her colleagues note that preservice teachers are likely to find secondary content classrooms much as they were described by Alvermann and Moore in 1991, with the following features: reliance on a single text for content learning, learning facts as the main goal, little preteaching of concepts or vocabulary, an emphasis on classroom management and teacher control, and accountability via testing and emphasis on content coverage acting as limitations on reading strategy instruction.

Against this backdrop, we have been challenged to help our preservice teachers see reading as an essential mode of acquiring content area knowledge. We are committed to help these teachers deepen their understanding of reading in their discipline and develop expertise by modeling discipline-specific ways of reading that can be taken up and used effectively by their students.

Meeting the Needs of Readers Who Struggle

The prevalent idea of reading as a technical skill to be mastered in the primary grades and then consistently applied to learning in the content areas does not merely limit secondary teachers' knowledge and effectiveness in content areas. It can also lead to policy and curricular decisions that actually harm students. In this view, adolescents who struggle with literacy tasks in subject area classes need remedial intervention—for example, instruction in basic skills such as phonics or word recognition. The growing adoption of direct instruction, basic-skill reading programs in middle and high schools with substantial populations of identified "struggling readers," illustrates this increasingly dominant view of reading as a technical, generalizable skill.

This trend works against our best efforts to equip subject area teachers to embed literacy instruction in their curriculum, with appropriate scaffolding to meet the needs of individual students and make particular texts accessible. In schools that consign struggling secondary readers to basic skill instruction, content area teachers get the message that someone else will "fix" these students. In fact, students who struggle with reading may not even be in the regular content area classroom; instead, they may be spending two or even three periods a day in skill-based reading instruction that is unrelated to the curriculum. In such an impoverished learning environment, student disengagement even to the point of dropping out of school is predictable. Tragic and unnecessary, but predictable.

Meeting the Literacy Needs of English Learners

A shift away from categorical status of English learners (ELs) in schools has led to a similar one-size-fits-all mindset about meeting their literacy needs. More and more often we are seeing students who have literacy knowledge and experience in their home language, but who lack grade-appropriate skill reading English, being referred for basic reading instruction. They are identified as struggling readers rather than as readers developing literacy in English.

English learners are wrongly seen as struggling readers largely because of the persistence of deficit views of linguistic and cultural diversity. Unfortunately, knowledge and ways of demonstrating knowledge in American schools continue to be exclusively in English (Valdés, 1998). A parallel situation exists regarding the content of most remedial literacy programs. Although textbook publishers have made some progress in diversifying the cultural, ethnic, and racial content of the material used in most classrooms, the situation is quite different with remedial texts. As we discuss in Chapter Eight, the simplistic nature of such materials leaves no room for the complexities and subtleties associated with the rich and diverse cultures represented in most American classrooms. Thus, it is no surprise that English learners struggle to become literate using texts that are devoid of their own reality and experiences. It is surprising that they engage in the struggle at all.

Both native speakers of English and English learners who exhibit difficulties with academic literacy may need more experience reading texts that are engaging and more support to grapple with texts in the subject areas. Schools may confuse such inexperience with inability or a lack of basic skills. They do so to the detriment of students' reading growth, and in the case of ELs, to the detriment of their growth in oral and written English use.

Preparing New Teachers for Content Area Literacy Instruction

Our fictional middle school math teacher Mark, whose story introduced this chapter, holds the unexamined assumption that reading is a technical skill, one that his students should bring with them to his classroom, along with their school supplies. Had his teacher preparation included opportunities to investigate his own literacy history—specifically, how he became an expert reader in mathematics—he might have reexamined this belief. If he had had opportunities to ask questions about and investigate his students' reading, he might have gained an understanding of their resources and challenges as readers. If he had had opportunities to think about how mathematics is a sign system that can be "read," he might have learned ways to apprentice students into mathematically unique and important ways of reading. Ultimately, he might have understood reading in mathematics as part of teaching mathematics, and he might also have eagerly sought ways to teach reading to help his students succeed in math.

Learning how to teach involves more than learning what works to raise test scores. As the following chapters illustrate, prospective teachers also need to learn about themselves and their students as learners. In our content area reading courses, we help preservice teachers focus on their own literacy histories, particularly in academics. Focusing on learning and seeing themselves as learners also means understanding that they won't know everything they need to know upon graduation and certification. They will continue to learn through their practice, through ongoing professional development, and especially through inquiry and reflection on their instructional interactions with students. For them, and for their students, learning will not be a linear process; there will be growth spurts and lags. Elmore (2003, pp. 9–10) reminds us that learning doesn't happen in a straightforward way: "We learn in part by tearing down old preconceptions, trying out new ideas and practices, and working hard to incorporate these new ideas and practices into our operating model of the world. It takes a while for these ideas and practices to 'take,' but when they do, they often result in learning at the individual and collective level."

As teacher educators, we are committed to providing a supportive yet challenging curriculum that helps prospective teachers reexamine assumptions about literacy and learning in the disciplines. Teaching for deep understanding and ongoing inquiry is a challenge in the current "what works" education landscape. In the following chapters we explain and illustrate our choice of Reading Apprenticeship as a framework to promote in-depth content literacy learning, starting with our students—prospective teachers—and bridging to their adolescent students. In our programs, we strive to help teachers like Mark deepen their understanding of their own discipline, and particularly the ways in which literacy operates in it. Subsequent chapters describe some of the learning experiences we have designed to accomplish this.

References

Alexander, P. A., and Jetton, T. L. "Learning from Text: A Multidimensional and Developmental Perspective." In M. L. Kamil, P. B. Mosenthal, P. D. Pearson, and R. Barr (eds.), *Handbook of Reading Research* (vol. III, pp. 285–310). Hillsdale, N.J.: Erlbaum, 2000.

Allen, M. *Eight Questions on Teacher Preparation: What Does the Research Say? An ECS Teaching Quality Research Report.* Denver: Education Commission of the States, July 2003.

Allington, R. *Big Brother and the National Reading Curriculum: How Ideology Trumped Evidence.* Portsmouth, N.H.: Heinemann, 2002.

Alvermann, D. E., and Moore, D. W. "Secondary School Reading." In R. Barr, M. L. Kamil, P. B. Mosenthal, and P. D. Pearson (eds.), *Handbook of Reading Research* (vol. II, pp. 951–983). New York: Longman, 1991.

Ball, D. L., and Cohen, D. K. "Developing Practice, Developing Practitioners: Toward a Practice-Based Theory of Professional Education." In L. Darling-Hammond and G. Sykes (eds.), *Teaching as the Learning Profession: Handbook of Policy and Practice* (pp. 3–32). San Francisco: Jossey-Bass, 1999.

Camilli, G., Vargas, S., and Yurecko, M. "Teaching Children to Read: The Fragile Link Between Science and Federal Education Policy." *Education Policy Analysis Archives,* May 2003, *11*(15), 1–48. [http://epaa.asu.edu/epaa/v11n15/].

Cummins, J. "Magic Bullets and the Grade 4 Slump: Solutions from Technology?" *NABE News,* 2001, *25*(1), 4–6.

Darling-Hammond, L. *Teaching Quality and Student Achievement: A Review of State Policy Evidence.* Seattle: Center for the Study of Teaching and Policy, University of Washington, 1999.

Darling-Hammond, L. "How Teacher Education Matters." *Journal of Teacher Education,* May-June 2000, *51*(3), 166–173.

Darling-Hammond, L. *The Research and Rhetoric on Teacher Certification: A Response to "Teacher Certification Reconsidered."* Washington, D.C.: National Commission on Teaching and America's Future, 2001.

Darling-Hammond, L. "Keeping Good Teachers: Why It Matters, What Leaders Can Do." *Educational Leadership,* 2003, *60*(8), 6–13.

Elmore, R. "A Plea for Strong Practice." *Educational Leadership,* 2003, *61*(3), 6–10.

Grossman, P. *The Making of a Teacher.* New York: Teachers College Press, 1990.

International Reading Association and National Middle School Association. *Supporting Young Adolescents' Literacy Learning: A Joint Position Statement of the International Reading Association and the National Middle School Association.* Newark, Del.: International Reading Association, 2002.

Irvin, J., Buehl, D., and Klemp, R. *Reading and the High School Student: Strategies to Enhance Literacy.* Needham Heights, Mass.: Allyn & Bacon, 2003.

Kain, J. F., and Singleton, K. "Equality of Educational Opportunity Revisited." *New England Economic Review,* May-June 1996, pp. 87–111.

Kamil, M. *Adolescents and Literacy: Reading for the 21st Century.* Washington, D.C.: Alliance for Excellent Education, 2003.

Moustafa, M., and Land, R. "The Reading Achievement of Economically Disadvantaged Children in Urban Schools Using *Open Court* vs. Comparably Disadvantaged Children in Urban Schools Using Nonscripted Reading Programs." In *Urban Learning, Teaching, and Research 2002 Yearbook* (pp. 44–53). Washington, D.C.: American Educational Research Association, 2002. [http://curriculum.calstatela.edu/margaret.moustafa].

Nathan, M., and Petrosino, A. "Expert Blind Spot Among Preservice Teachers." *American Educational Research Journal*, 2003, 40(4), 905–928.

National Board for Professional Teaching Standards. *What Teachers Should Know and Be Able to Do: The Five Core Propositions of the National Board.* Arlington, Va.: National Board for Professional Teaching Standards, n.d. [http://www.nbpts.org].

National Commission on Teaching and America's Future. *What Matters Most: Teaching for America's Future.* New York: National Commission on Teaching and America's Future, 1996.

National Reading Panel. *Teaching Children to Read: An Evidence-Based Assessment of the Scientific Research Literature on Reading and Its Implications for Reading Instruction.* Washington, D.C.: National Institute of Child Health and Human Development, 2000.

No Child Left Behind Act. Reauthorization of the Elementary and Secondary Education Act, 20 U.S.C.A. sec. 6301 *et seq.* Public Law 107–110. 2001.

Paige, R. *Meeting the Highly Qualified Teachers Challenge: The Secretary's Annual Report on Teacher Quality.* Washington, D.C.: U.S. Department of Education, 2002.

RAND Reading Study Group. *Reading for Understanding: Toward an R&D Program in Reading Comprehension.* Santa Monica, Calif.: RAND, 2002.

Shulman, L. "Knowledge and Teaching: Foundations of the New Reform." *Harvard Educational Review*, 1987, 57, 1–22.

Valdés, G. "The World Outside and Inside Schools: Language and Immigrant Children." *Educational Researcher*, 1998, 27(6), 4–18.

Walsh, K. *Teacher Certification Reconsidered: Stumbling for Quality.* Baltimore, Md.: Abell Foundation, 2001.

Yatvin, J., Weaver, C., and Garan, E. "Reading First: Cautions and Recommendations." *Language Arts*, 2003, 81(1), 28–33.

Chapter 2

Framing Content Area Instruction with Reading Apprenticeship

A renewed focus on adolescent literacy poses a challenge for teacher educators. We want to equip prospective middle and high school teachers with rich understandings of literacy as socially mediated practice, the multiple literacies in which students are engaged, the specific demands of academic literacy, and high-leverage strategies to foster student engagement and agency in comprehension (Moje, Young, Readence, and Moore, 2000; Greenleaf, Schoenbach, Cziko, and Mueller, 2001). Ironically, though, the current focus on national, state, and local achievement tests may work against the goal of deep teacher knowledge about literacy and learning, fostering instead a vision of teacher as technician and reading as a technical skill.

The recently published 2002 National Assessment of Educational Progress (NAEP) results show the average twelfth-grade reading score lower than in 1998 and 1992 (Grigg, Daane, Ying, and Campbell, 2003), a statistic likely to fuel arguments for remedial reading instruction at the high school level. More and more often, new teachers are entering schools in which raising test scores, and thus removing the schools from the "underperforming list," leads to a test-centered, if not a test-prep, curriculum. Beginning teachers are entering school cultures in which reading is increasingly defined as a set of discrete skills, where literacy instruction is differentiated depending on the perceived gap between students' current reading abilities and the performance goal set by high-stakes tests. This narrow conception of reading threatens to limit prospective teachers' understandings of reading processes and of students' strengths and needs. It further constrains their effectiveness as content area literacy teachers, because reading becomes decontextualized from the diverse and differently demanding disciplines and texts in which it must be practiced.

As teacher educators we are also concerned by the current narrowing of literacy learning opportunities for the adolescents with whom we are preparing our teachers to work (Brown, 1991; Greenleaf, Jiménez, and Roller, 2002). The focus on high-stakes testing as the accountability measure reinforces a deficit model of literacy instruction. We have seen a consequent reappearance of tracking in courses with heavy reading demands—for example, English, social studies, and college preparatory science and mathematics. Such tracking represents a real step backward in equity after years of work to detrack the curriculum and help new teachers work productively with student diversity (Hull and Rose, 1989; Knapp, 1995).

Fostering Deep Understanding of Literacy

We believe that preservice teachers need to develop knowledge, skill, and a sense of efficacy about improving adolescent literacy. This will take more than a collection of strategies or classroom activities; such expertise calls for teachers to be serious learners in and around their practice. We believe that they need to develop not only content and pedagogical knowledge but also a spirit of inquiry essential to support ongoing situated decision making as teachers (Ball and Cohen, 1999). This inquiry stance also drives teachers' discoveries about how reading differs in various disciplines and about their own and their students' reading processes. Ultimately, knowledgeable teachers learn from their students the resources they bring to comprehension and learning in various content areas and then develop ways to help them become stronger readers and learners (Schoenbach, Greenleaf, Cziko, and Hurwitz, 1999).

We support an inquiry orientation to reading because it is grounded in values of equity and empowerment. New teachers must learn how to help all of their students participate in academic literacy. An instructional approach for underperforming middle and high school readers that focuses on reteaching basic skills ironically works against these equity and access goals. This approach incorrectly locates the problem as the students' failure to learn a fixed set of basic skills rather than the schools' failure to help students experience reading as the complex mental activity it is. A remedial, basic skills approach confuses inexperience with inability and often leaves weak adolescent readers even further behind their peers who are more engaged and effective readers (Langer, 2001; Ivey, 1999; Allington and Walmsley, 1995).

Ensuring that all adolescents can read to learn in various content areas is a daunting task. In the current climate of high-stakes tests and remedial interventions, teacher educators feel particularly challenged to equip new teachers with the knowledge and skill to teach reading as a developmental, discipline-specific process. Since 2000, a group of teacher educators in the Bay Area has been collaborating to prepare teacher candidates to meet challenging academic literacy demands with their urban middle and high school students. As the Teacher Education Consortium (TEC) of WestEd's Strategic Literacy Initiative (SLI), we are committed to fostering among preservice teachers a more complex notion of literacy and a confidence in their ability to help adolescents read demanding texts. We want these teachers to see subject area learning as an apprenticeship into discipline-based ways of thinking, talking, reading, and writing. In our preservice secondary reading courses, we are doing this by employing Reading Apprenticeship (RA) as an instructional framework, developed by SLI in collaboration with a network of Bay Area secondary teachers from a variety of content areas (Schoenbach, Greenleaf, Cziko, and Hurwitz, 1999). As more and more middle and high school teachers began implementing Reading Apprenticeship in their classrooms, their colleagues in teacher education became interested in the potential of RA for the preservice program.

The TEC developed as teacher educators identified RA as a robust frame for content area literacy instruction, one that could help preservice teachers develop solid understandings of and pedagogy for reading in the disciplines. Because teachers of reading in the content area courses have often expressed frustration with the lack of carry-over of their course content to new teachers' classroom work, participants in SLI's Teacher Education Consortium were eager to help preservice teachers learn that teaching reading in their disciplines *is* teaching their disciplines—reading is not a separate technical skill acquired in elementary school. In this regard, they might have been stepping up to the task implied in the frequently heard comment from teachers in RA professional development sessions, "I wish I had learned about Reading Apprenticeship in my teacher education program. I could have been a better teacher from the start!"

The Reading Apprenticeship Framework

The Reading Apprenticeship approach, described in *Reading for Understanding: A Guide to Improving Reading in Middle and High School Classrooms* (Schoenbach, Greenleaf, Cziko, and Hurwitz, 1999) is an instructional framework embedded in the process of teaching subject area content, rather than an instructional add-on or additional curriculum. RA helps students become better readers by doing the following:

- Engaging students in more reading
- Making the teacher's discipline-based reading processes and knowledge visible to students
- Making the students' reading processes, knowledge, and understandings visible to the teacher and to one another
- Helping students gain insight into their own reading processes as a means of gaining strategic control over these processes
- Helping students acquire a repertoire of problem-solving strategies for overcoming obstacles and deepening comprehension of texts in various academic disciplines

When Lortie (1975) coined the term *apprenticeship of observation*, he was describing the powerful pull of conservative teaching practices—didactic instruction, presenting facts and skills as knowledge—to shape new teachers' approach to the classroom. Preservice teachers come to schools of education with such lessons passively absorbed through their years as students from kindergarten to college and often reinforced in the classrooms they observe and the courses they take for their teaching credential (Ball and Cohen, 1999; Hudson-Ross and Graham, 2000). But Reading Apprenticeship reclaims and recasts the term: here *apprenticeship* is an inquiry-driven, theoretically sound, active, and mediated form of learning.

Basically, Reading Apprenticeship is a partnership of expertise, drawing on what teachers know and do as readers in their disciplines and on adolescents' unique and often underestimated strengths as learners. In any apprenticeship, an expert practitioner or mentor consciously models, directs, supports, and shapes the apprentice's growing repertoire of practice. The apprentice actively engages in the task, learning by doing with appropriate support, gradually moving toward skillful independence in the desired practice. It's hard to imagine learning to play baseball without stepping up to bat or learning to take good photographs without snapping a lot of pictures. In the same way, students who are expected to learn from reading in various subject areas need to have extensive, supported opportunities for sustained engagement with texts.

Reading Apprenticeship draws on the metaphor of *cognitive apprenticeship* that some researchers have used to describe a type of teaching designed to assist students in becoming more proficient at cognitive processes for valued tasks such as reading comprehension, composing, and mathematical problem solving (Resnick, 1990; Rogoff, 1990). If students are to become skilled readers of academic texts, the invisible processes involved in comprehending a text must be made visible and accessible to them as they actually engage in meaningful literacy activities (Freedman, Flower, Hull, and Hayes, 1995; Pearson, 1996). The best teachers to apprentice students to specific discipline-based literacy practices are those who have mastered them—that is, subject area teachers.

Herein lies both a key strength and a challenge for RA in the preservice curriculum. Prospective teachers can be acknowledged as experts in reading in their respective disciplines, an empowering message for novice professionals. At the same time, they need to become students of their own discipline-based reading processes and learn how to design reading-to-learn experiences for their students that build the students' expertise as readers in that discipline.

Helping preservice teachers become aware of their own reading processes can be especially difficult, because reading is second nature to most of the students with whom we work. The fluency they have poses a challenge for us in making them aware of how they read, what they pay attention to, what they do when text is difficult, and so on. Furthermore, because they have succeeded as students in their chosen discipline, the prospective teachers with whom we work believe that some of the strategies and dispositions we want them to address in their teaching are "obvious" or "natural." This is especially true for prospective teachers of English learners. In fact, some linguists have argued that nonnative speakers of a language make better teachers of that language, precisely because they are more aware of the language and what learning it entails (McKay, 2003). For prospective teachers, though, the issue is to understand that they *learned* how to read the way they do—in literature, history, science, or mathematics—it didn't just happen. Our task is to help them build on this awareness to design ways to model and scaffold discipline-based reading for their middle and high school students.

Shulman and his colleagues (1986) asserted that teachers need to develop not only *content knowledge* and general *pedagogical knowledge* but also *pedagogical content knowledge*, subject-specific knowledge about what makes some concepts or processes in the subject area hard to learn and how to help students surmount the difficulties. This last type of knowledge calls for deep knowledge both of subject matter and of students as learners. With Reading Apprenticeship as our framework for our reading in the content areas classes, we help preservice teachers develop and use all three types of professional knowledge to teach students to read in their disciplines.

The teachers develop pedagogical content knowledge largely through shared inquiry into reading in the classroom as a community. In our classes, the teachers regularly engage in reading process analysis to learn about their own and each other's ways of making meaning with text. These preservice teachers reconceptualize subject area teaching as an apprenticeship into discipline-based practices of thinking, talking, reading, and writing (see Applebee, 1996). In a Reading Apprenticeship classroom, then, the curriculum includes *how we read* and *why we read in the ways we do* as well as *what we read* in subject matter classes.

To assist preservice teachers in constructing this new conception of reading in the subject areas, we introduce them to RA as an instructional framework, derived from a view of literacy as socially and cognitively complex and drawing on the core metaphor of cognitive apprenticeship described earlier. As explained in *Reading for Understanding*, the Reading Apprenticeship framework involves teachers in orchestrating and integrating four interacting dimensions of classroom life that support reading development (Schoenbach, Greenleaf, Cziko, and Hurwitz, 1999). These dimensions are woven into subject area teaching through *metacognitive conversations*—investigations into the thinking processes students and teachers employ as they read (see Figure 2.1). The course experiences and assignments described in subsequent chapters are designed to help our preservice teachers tap the following dimensions, singly or in combination, as rich sites for developing students' academic literacy. In their own words, we include insights that preservice teachers have drawn from their experience of the dimensions and plan to apply in their own classrooms.

The Social Dimension: Building a Reading Inquiry Community

The social dimension in the RA framework involves developing a sense of safety in the classroom community and making good use of

Dimensions of Reading Apprenticeship™

Social Dimension

- Creating safety
- Investigating relationships between literacy and power
- Sharing book talk
- Sharing reading processes, problems, and solutions
- Noticing and appropriating others' ways of reading

Personal Dimension

- Developing reader identity
- Developing metacognition
- Developing reader fluency and stamina
- Developing reader confidence and range
- Assessing performance and setting goals

Cognitive Dimension

- Getting the big picture
- Breaking it down
- Monitoring comprehension
- Using problem-solving strategies to assist and restore comprehension
- Setting reading purposes and adjusting reading processes

Knowledge-Building Dimension

- Mobilizing and building knowledge structures (schemata)
- Developing content or topic knowledge
- Developing knowledge of word construction and vocabulary
- Developing knowledge and use of text structures
- Developing discipline- and discourse-specific knowledge

Figure 2.1. Dimensions of Reading Apprenticeship®

adolescents' preference for peer interactions. This dimension draws on adolescents' interests in themselves and each other as well as in larger social, political, economic, and cultural issues. As students share their confusion and difficulties with texts, they learn that confusion is a starting place for making meaning with text. They become a community of readers in which diverse perspectives and resources are acknowledged and valued (Alvermann and Moore, 1991; Moje, Dillon, and O'Brien, 2000). Through ongoing conversations rooted in text, they also ask critical questions about

content, purpose, and perspective. Our preservice teachers participate in such a community of readers with an assignment described
in the next chapter. Two prospective English teachers shared and
reflected on their reading processes as they read a novel and a collection of essays about teaching. One of them wrote: "Through our
logs, we realized that we fed off each other. [My partner] mentioned
how she was paying more attention to the images she was calling
upon once she read my journals, and I felt that I was picking up on
the issues she spoke about in [bell hooks's] *Teaching to Transgress*,
trying to make more sense of them on my own. . . . The feeding off
one another allowed me to make more sense of hooks's text and
made my marginal notes more rich."

Reflecting on these experiences with reading, preservice teachers learn that social interaction is vital as students learn to read academic texts. Social acceptance and safety are essential to support risk
taking as they engage with challenging texts, so it is important to set
norms about talking and listening. Students contribute to setting
classroom rules for discussion and norms for taking part in classroom
activities that allow everyone to participate without putdowns. A
prospective math teacher reflected on his firsthand experience of the
need for a safe, trusting learning community in a cross-disciplinary
reading assignment with a prospective English teacher:

> Building a safe community is of the utmost importance in creating
> a classroom of readers. Reading with someone we knew and trusted
> for this project lent security to the process. We are part of the same
> peer group—fellow teachers and classmates—so we were able to
> share our thoughts without fear or anxiety. Even so, there was still
> occasional embarrassment about not understanding certain refer-
> ences in the texts, such as the one to *Alice in Wonderland*. We can
> only imagine how difficult it would be for students to engage in the
> reading process if they did not feel safe. In a safe environment and
> within the Reading Apprenticeship model, students should be able
> to share "book talk" openly through their metacognitive reading
> logs, regardless of the type of text they are discussing.

In an RA classroom, interaction between teacher and students and among students is critical for learning about themselves and others as readers, about how texts work, and about various meaning-making and problem-solving strategies with texts. Group work is fundamental to learning, not just an option for classroom organization. A mathematics teacher and an English teacher who had read and reflected on their reading processes in both disciplines concluded: "In our classrooms, we would model useful reading strategies and have students themselves make their strategies explicit for their classmates. By discussing our metacognitive processes, others can become aware of our strategies, try them out, and adjust their reading accordingly."

Another mathematics teacher seemed to feel a greater sense of agency as a guide for students: "I learned how much clearer an unfamiliar text can become with the proper support. . . . I am heartened at how engaged my partner became in *The Math Gene*. This gives me hope that given the proper support, and reasonable texts, my students will be able to see reading in math class as a legitimate way to understand and enjoy the intricacies of math."

In RA classrooms teachers and students investigate the relationship between literacy and power; they examine people in our society who read, what they read, and what reading does for them. Conversely, students in these classrooms also investigate and discuss people who don't read, possible reasons for this, and its effect on their lives—personally, socially, economically, and politically. In this way, students come to see literacy as a powerful force for independence and agency, and they also see literacy as socially constructed. They learn of past and present examples where denial of literacy to individuals and groups has been a means of disenfranchisement and oppression.

In RA classrooms, the social dimension is also important for sharing talk among students and teacher about books they have found exciting or interesting. Students' options for reading expand when valued peers and teachers suggest books to read and how to choose them. Drawing on the social dimension of reading motivates students to engage with diverse texts, including those assigned in their courses.

The Personal Dimension: Creating a Sense of Agency

The personal dimension is concerned with developing a reader identity, building fluency and stamina, and drawing on strategic skills students already use in out-of-school settings. Key activities here are exploring students' identities and self-awareness as readers and setting goals and purposes for reading (Beers and Samuels, 1998). It is important to note the reciprocal relationship between the social and the personal dimensions: providing students access to each other's reading processes, preferences, and difficulties helps individuals in the group expand their own repertoire of strategies, tastes, purposes, and goals as readers. In the personal dimension, teachers recognize and cultivate adolescents' desire to become more autonomous and exercise control over their lives. When reading improvement is understood by teens as a route to this increased agency, they are more likely to take on the hard work of learning to read a range of materials, including challenging academic texts (Schoenbach, Greenleaf, Cziko, and Hurwitz, 1999).

Building a literate identity is at the core of the work in the personal dimension (Moore, 2002). Such an identity shapes whether or not an adolescent sees herself as a member of the literacy club (Smith, 1988), effective now and confident of continuing to grow, or as an outsider, convinced that she cannot read productively now or in the future. Even teachers may not identify themselves as readers, as one preservice teacher explained: "The first thing we discovered in the process of exchanging our metacognitive processes through this journal was that neither of us see ourselves as readers. . . . Once the nonreader excuses for (not) getting through the text started to vanish, we both enjoyed our books and found ourselves for the most part looking forward to what the books would offer us at the next reading."

In an RA framework, preservice teachers discover the importance of learning from their students about experiences, interests, and concerns that may drive choices about reading in various subject areas. Unfortunately, many adolescents choose not to read. For students who have decided not to read—perhaps because they have found reading to be irrelevant or because they were labeled poor readers—building an identity as a reader is crucial. As one new teacher noted, "These kids really need to have reading defanged." Consequently, preservice teachers learn ways to help students experience success in reading and learning from discipline-based texts. They learn to build students' stamina so they will not give up when text becomes difficult. With this success, students develop a sense of themselves as increasingly capable readers who can set and accomplish improvement goals, as they do for themselves in so many other areas of their lives.

Two preservice teachers, one in science and one in English, shared an insight about reader identity and agency from their cross-disciplinary reading experience: "We discovered that the stance you take as a reader coming to a text greatly affects your reading experience, from how much time you spend on the book to comprehension and how much effort you are willing to put in to gain that comprehension."

These prospective teachers are mindful of the complex and interconnected array of factors that go into developing an appropriate stance toward any given text. Background knowledge and strategies are important, of course, but their power is in the students' ownership and agency. Thinking deeply about their own agency as readers helps these prospective teachers plan to apprentice their students to confident reading in the disciplines.

The Cognitive Dimension: Developing a Comprehension Tool Kit

The cognitive dimension involves developing readers' mental processes, including comprehension and problem-solving strategies

(Beers and Samuels, 1998; Brown, Palincsar, and Armbruster, 1994; Keene and Zimmerman, 1997; Tovani, 2000). This is the area that is traditionally (and sometimes exclusively) emphasized in preservice secondary reading courses. Importantly, in a Reading Apprenticeship classroom, the work of generating cognitive strategies that support reading comprehension is carried out through classroom inquiry and includes group discussion of *when and why* particular cognitive strategies are useful. Strategies aren't learned for their own sake but rather to enable students to handle increasingly complex text, initially with support and gradually on their own (Moore, Bean, Birdyshaw, and Rycik, 1999). A preservice English teacher learned about her own cognitive strategies as she engaged in a metacognitive cross-disciplinary journal activity with a classmate: "I've become more cognizant of the reading strategies I employ when I'm stuck or unclear, especially regarding sentence structure (I break it down, and simplify to simple subject-predicate), and vocabulary (I make hypotheses about the words that I then 'test' with further information). I noticed how my use of picturing draws on images from my own experience. I've also become much more aware of how I use rereading . . . to recover fluency."

Preservice teachers are understandably concerned with equipping their instructional tool kit, so strategies loom large on their list of things to learn. We work with them to identify and incorporate appropriate cognitive strategies for reading and learning in their discipline. And although some explicit teaching of strategy components needs to occur, we want preservice teachers to engage their students in purposeful uses of selected cognitive strategies. We want the focus to be on content learning, not on the strategy itself. Key here is scaffolding students' learning so that they know not only the procedure to follow—for example, in taking part in a reciprocal teaching group (Palincsar and Brown, 1984)—but also when the strategy might help their comprehension. The goal is for their students to know when to use a particular strategy and how to do it well. In this sense, strategies in an RA class are generative, rather than applied.

A preservice English teacher saw strategies as supports to a bigger goal: "(For my students) I will emphasize that reading is about *thinking*; it is not a passive process in which we simply absorb meaning from the text. The ideas we have while we read, the pictures we form in our heads, even where our mind wanders—this is all part of the reading process."

Langer's research on "beating-the-odds" schools offers a good illustration of the generative character of strategies in RA classrooms. Langer (2001) studied middle and high schools in which students' literacy achievement exceeded expectations and schools in which students either met or fell below expected achievement levels. She found that skill and strategy instruction differed markedly in the high- and the low-performing schools that were otherwise demographically comparable. In lower-performing schools, instruction generally focused on skills as procedures, usually in isolation from content area application. Students might learn an activity for sequencing events in a story, for example, but not deepen their understanding of the concept of sequence in narrative (Langer, 2001, p. 869). In contrast, in schools that were beating the odds, teachers more often provided explicit instruction in the why as well as the how of strategies and engaged students in using them to learn from regular curriculum materials. Students were helped to think about why they were using a particular strategy—that is, what it offered them as learners from academic texts.

The Knowledge-Building Dimension: Tapping and Extending Knowledge of Content, Text, and Discourse

The knowledge-building dimension in the RA framework involves identifying and expanding the knowledge students bring to a text, including knowledge about text structure, topics and content, word structure and meaning, and discourse patterns and signals—the particular ways ideas are organized and expressed in different disciplines and various genres within each discipline (Beck, McKeown, Hamilton, and Kucan, 1997; Templeton, Beer, Invernizzi, and

Johnston, 1996; Stahl, Duffy-Hester, and Stahl, 1998; Anderson, 1994). A preservice math teacher realized the many knowledge resources she brought to reading a specific text: "I began to appreciate all of the connections the text (*The Math Gene*) brought up for me. I drew from my math training, my experiences with students, other books and articles I had read, and many mental images that I created to represent [the author's] highly technical argument. I believe one tool that I relied on heavily in understanding the book was the structure of a mathematical proof."

A prospective English teacher acknowledged the need to build those knowledge resources, saying: "I realize that, like me, students probably don't like feeling stupid when they don't have the appropriate background knowledge. Giving students context is really important, I think, in keeping them motivated."

Of course, developing the knowledge base to understand increasingly complex topics requires more than providing context, for example, in a prereading activity or handout. Similarly, vocabulary and schema are intricately connected but often simplistically addressed in schools. We know that vocabulary knowledge is a marker for conceptual understanding and that both are most influenced by extensive reading. Yet in many schools, content area learning relies on a single text, so students do not have opportunities for repeated encounters with key terms or concepts in a variety of texts, which is one way they build important schema linked to key vocabulary.

A few words about English learners seem useful here. For English learners (ELs), schema development is especially important at various levels: language, discipline, literacy, and learner self-schemas. At the level of language, English learners must contend with words and word meanings. This is particularly true of native speakers of Romance languages for whom words may have similar appearance and meaning, that is, cognates or similar appearance but different meanings, that is, false cognates. For English learners with solid and extensive schooling experiences in their native language, schemas associated with cognates are a valuable resource, assuming that such a strategy is familiar to them. Though in conversation cognates are less apparent, they become relevant in reading and especially in science, a discipline in which much of the vocabulary has Latin roots. In contrast, false cognates may activate incorrect schemas (for example, complexion and *complexión*, assist and *asistir*, or fabric and *fábrica*). For teachers, the implications are both to help English learners recognize the expertise they bring as proficient speakers and readers of their native language and to explain the strategy of testing possible areas of transfer of such expertise across languages. Obviously, teachers who are bilingual in their students' language will be better able to apprentice students into expert biliteracy in specific disciplines.

Schemas for English learners are also important at the discipline level, particularly for organizing knowledge and gaining an understanding of the scope of each discipline. English learners with solid schooling in their native languages often rely on these schemas as a scaffold for learning English. The testing of hypotheses about language involved in the language learning process becomes less uncertain and more engaging when, rather than starting anew, students are able to recognize familiar content in a second language. Imagine, if you will, the difference between watching an unfamiliar movie in a language in which you are not proficient and watching a dubbed version of a familiar movie, especially one for which you have memorized script lines. Thus, an important scaffolding function for teachers of English learners is that of "bridging" (Walqui, 1995) between the students' experiences and background knowledge and the text. When teachers show individual students the ways in which a text may be particularly relevant or meaningful to them, it enhances their comprehension and also can provide a necessary point of engagement for those whose school experiences feel particularly alienating.

Another important aspect of schemas at the discipline level is that of recurrent metaphors used to define and categorize processes or phenomena and that require specific vocabulary or text structures. Examples of these are cycles, taxonomies, systems, processes, definitions, principles, proofs, and rules, to name a few, which may or may not be equivalent across disciplines. Some of these metaphors have evolved to become exclusively associated with specific disciplines, such as the scientific method in science. The ability to recognize these recurring structures as well as key vocabulary and textual arrangements associated with them in each discipline plays a role in the students' ability to understand and organize knowledge. The connections between thought, culture, language, academic disciplines, and text organization are well documented—even though disagreement exists as to the causal direction in this relationship. (See Sharp, 2003, for an excellent discussion on cultural differences in rhetorical preferences and reading comprehension.) Consequently, the ability of teachers to scaffold this process for English learners, particularly by making visible relevant cognitive strategies and through the use of appropriate graphic organizers and similar tools, becomes crucial in helping students achieve. Even when students are familiar with some or all of these discipline-specific schemas, teachers must remain attentive to helping students translate and adjust them across cultures and languages.

Schemas associated with text organization deserve explicit attention in classrooms with English learners. Depending on their native language literacy, students may or may not be aware that most content area textbooks consist of expository prose written to reflect five main functions or relations: (1) general descriptions, (2) descriptions of sequences, (3) comparisons and contrasts, (4) cause-effect relationships, and (5) problem-solution relationships (Vacca and Vacca, 1993). Each one of these structures, in turn, relies on specific words or textual markers to signal these functions or relations—for example, *on the left, on the right, overall, specifically; first, second, third; on the one hand, on the other hand; therefore, consequently; however, yet.* Even though students may understand the meaning of these words, they may not have learned to associate them with schemas about text that they may already possess, particularly because research has shown that transfer between literacy in first and second language as well as across disciplines in either and both languages is far from straightforward (August and Hakuta, 1997).

English learners may rely on schemas for the organization of the content in textbooks that may not be appropriate or useful for current, typical American textbooks. In an effort to make textbooks engaging and appealing to young readers, publishers regularly include many content features that crowd the pages of most middle and high school textbooks. A quick glance at an average page from a science book reveals a colorful arrangement of pictures and other graphic representations of presumably relevant information. In addition to the captions for the illustrations, textbook pages typically contain text boxes or sidebars with biographical information about different science figures, suggested laboratories or activities, and information about related careers in science. Finally, the text on most pages is peppered with headings and subheadings in various fonts and font colors, bold typeface to mark glossary or vocabulary terms (pronunciation in parentheses), and icons marking features such as "checkpoints" and definitions or "factoids." Although, clearly, the intention behind these features is to help readers and provide them with as many ways to access the information as possible, for English learners who are often preoccupied with understanding the meaning of individual words, the plethora of features can be distracting at best or downright daunting and overwhelming. Therefore, some of the most necessary schemas for English learners in reading are those that help them pay attention to the macro features of the text, helping them navigate the frequent distractions and uncertain features of the text. Returning to our example of the science book, in addition to the organization of information at the page level, students need to develop schemas that allow them to understand the organization of most chapters. Given that English learners are likely to need more time to read and understand a given piece of text, they need guidance in focusing their attention and organizing the information they gain efficiently and productively.

A final consideration of schemas with regard to the teaching of reading to English learners pertains to schemas they may have about themselves as readers and learners as well as about teachers and their respective roles and responsibilities. We discussed these issues under the personal and social dimensions. Still, they bear consideration in this section because explicitness on the part of teachers in addressing possible confusion in other aspects of reading and reading instruction ought to be coherent and sensitive to individual student's needs.

Metacognitive Conversation: Creating Classroom Communities of Inquiry into Reading in the Subject Areas

In Reading Apprenticeship, the social, personal, cognitive, and knowledge-building dimensions are woven into subject area teaching through metacognitive conversations—conversations about the thinking processes students and teachers engage in as they read. In metacognitive conversations, the dimensions are integrated as teachers and students work collaboratively to make sense of texts while simultaneously engaging in conversation about what constitutes reading and how they are going about it. This metacognitive conversation is carried on both internally, as teacher and students reflect on their own mental processes, and externally, as they share their reading processes, strategies, knowledge resources, motivations, and interactions with and affective responses to texts.

The social interaction and expert scaffolding that support the external metacognitive conversation gradually lead to internal control and exercise of metacognition in adolescent readers. Over time, adolescent readers become aware of and able to manipulate these metacognitive processes to support comprehension with a variety of texts, and of equal importance, to sustain engagement and comprehension with difficult texts.

In teacher education programs, course readings, class experiences, and assignments can foster these metacognitive conversations among prospective teachers and model them as essential content for middle and high school classrooms. We want preservice teachers to make metacognitive conversation a regular classroom routine linked to and supporting reading to learn in all the disciplines. By analyzing their own reading, preservice teachers learn how to break open the process of learning, sharing what they know and what confusions they have about text, and tapping into one another's ways of reading.

The teachers also engage in highly designed inquiry into middle and high school students' reading, using literacy learning cases developed by SLI. These videotaped interviews of students reading and talking about their efforts to make sense of the text allow preservice teachers to examine their thinking about students as readers and draw implications for their teaching from close observation and inquiry into an incident of student reading. The cases help us scaffold professional conversations and decision making for our preservice teachers, conversations that focus on the literate possibilities, alternative interpretations, and evidence for various hypotheses linked to actual student reading performances. In using these cases, we are opening up a conversation, inviting teachers to dig beneath first impressions of a student's strengths and needs as a reader to surface and examine many possible interpretations of the student's reading performance. Ball and Cohen describe this kind of professional conversation focused on learning as a "narrative of inquiry." They contrast it with the dominant mode of talk among teachers, a "rhetoric of conclusions," often focused on problem identification and solution (Ball and Cohen, 1999, p. 16). Working with the literacy cases allows us to engage prospective teachers in genuine inquiry, even as we help them draw conclusions about ways to build on student strengths for improved academic literacy. Specific classroom engagements that allow preservice teachers to inquire into their own, each other's, and students' reading processes are described in subsequent chapters.

Apprenticeship as a Learning Model

Scaffolding New Teachers' Learning

In our reading in the content area courses, scaffolding occurs on two levels: first in the way we teach about inquiry, literacy, and learning, and then again as an instructional strategy for the secondary content area courses the preservice teachers will ultimately teach. For apprenticeship learning, careful scaffolding—including attention to intentionality among learners, appropriateness of instruction, choice, structure, collaboration, and ultimately, internalization or independence—is essential (Applebee and Langer, 1983; Jay, 2002).

As we scaffold preservice teachers' learning, we help them think about how to do the same, expert to apprentice, with their adolescent students. Through videotapes and written materials, we introduce our "apprentice" teachers to subject area teachers who are incorporating RA in their middle and high school classrooms. We help them see that these teachers focus explicitly on academic literacy throughout the year, emphasizing ways of reading, thinking, and talking that are particular, for example, to science or to mathematics. They see that there is no uniform set of strategies or one way to implement RA, but they do notice and talk about how these teachers concentrate on a handful of reading and discourse routines as appropriate to their discipline, using them over and over again in different ways. The routines stress metacognition—thinking about one's thinking—and collaborative meaning-making.

They learn how RA teachers judiciously incorporate a variety of cognitive strategies, such as visualizing, summarizing, questioning, and connecting to other experiences and texts, to help students develop a repertoire of comprehension problem-solving tools. However, no particular strategy or mix of strategies provides the key leverage point in increasing students' engagement with academic texts. Rather, it is the changed climate of a classroom community in which inquiry into reading in chemistry, or U.S. history, or world literature, or geometry becomes a shared conversation. This emphasis on teaching reading as an essential way of learning in their subject area works against the tendency to view and teach reading as a technical skill, separate from the subject area discourse.

Balancing Knowledge and Tools

Schools of education are often accused of overemphasizing theory and neglecting content knowledge and practical tools for instruction. And although our preservice teachers acknowledge the value of theory, they too are eagerly seeking classroom strategies to support student content learning. We believe that Reading Apprenticeship provides a sound theoretical framework to support coherence in discipline-based reading instruction. More than simply having a well-equipped toolbox of strategies, we want our teachers to have reasons for choosing each tool and an end in view of reading in subject area classes. We work to ensure that new teachers in their understandable desire to develop a repertoire of strategies will not see them as "content" to be learned. Rather, we want them to see strategies as flexible, student-generated processes that serve learning subject area content. We want new teachers to help students choose wisely among an array of reading strategies appropriate to the text, purpose, and reader. With some compendiums of reading strategies, the danger is that new teachers will take a "strategy-of-the-week" approach, piling techniques on students in an attempt to solve problems in understanding academic texts. Too often this results in students superficially applying strategies on the teacher's demand, seeing potentially useful cognitive or knowledge-building strategies as just another way of doing school reading. In a Reading Apprenticeship classroom, students develop a repertoire of strategies and an understanding of when and how to use them to suit their needs in specific literacy situations.

In a Reading Apprenticeship classroom, teachers and students become a community of inquirers into their own and each other's reading processes. Through supported, extensive reading in the content areas, all students expand the repertoire of strategies and knowledge they can employ to construct meaning with challenging academic texts. In this process, they go beyond the functional aspects of reading to explore literacy's connections to power, including individual agency and collective social transformation.

In this context, our goal is for prospective teachers to gain an enriched notion of literacy and to enrich their students' reading and writing experiences, rather than remediate them. Consequently, new teachers are prepared to see themselves and their students as bringing significant resources to the literacy demands of the content areas. Teachers prepared this way do not need to rely on commercially published programs of scripted reading instruction or "skills-in-a-box" approaches to improving student literacy. We believe that new teachers benefit from a deeper knowledge of their own language and literacy processes, the complexity of adolescent literacy, and the varieties of discipline-based reading. And ultimately, students benefit from the new teachers' ability to scaffold literacy learning in the context of challenging academic content (Greenleaf, Schoenbach, Cziko, and Mueller, 2001).

References

Allington, R., and Walmsley, S. (eds.). *No Quick Fix: Rethinking Literacy Programs in America's Elementary Schools*. Newark, Del.: International Reading Association, 1995.

Alvermann, D., and Moore, D. "Secondary School Reading." In R. Barr, M. L. Kamil, P. Mosenthal, and P. D. Pearson (eds.), *Handbook of Reading Research* (vol. 2, pp. 951–983). New York: Longman, 1991.

Anderson, R. "Role of the Reader's Schema in Comprehension, Learning, and Memory." In R. B. Ruddell, M. F. Ruddell, and H. Singer (eds.), *Theoretical Models and Processes of Reading* (4th ed., pp. 469–482). Newark, Del.: International Reading Association, 1994.

Applebee, A. *Curriculum as Conversation: Transforming Traditions of Teaching and Learning*. Chicago: University of Chicago Press, 1996.

Applebee, A., and Langer, J. "Instructional Scaffolding: Reading and Writing as Natural Language Activities." *Language Arts*, 1983, 60(2), 168–175.

August, D., and Hakuta, K. *Improving Schooling for Language-Minority Children: A Research Agenda*. Washington, D.C.: National Academy Press, 1997.

Ball, D. L., and Cohen, D. K. "Developing Practice, Developing Practitioners: Toward a Practice-Based Theory of Professional Education." In L. Darling-

Hammond and G. Sykes (eds.), *Teaching as the Learning Profession* (pp. 3–32). San Francisco: Jossey-Bass, 1999.

Beck, I. L., McKeown, M. G., Hamilton, R. L., and Kucan, L. *Questioning the Author: An Approach for Enhancing Student Engagement with Text.* Newark, Del.: International Reading Association, 1997.

Beers, K., and Samuels, B. *Into Focus: Understanding and Creating Middle School Readers.* Norwood, Mass.: Christopher Gordon, 1998.

Brown, A., Palincsar, A. M., and Armbruster, B. "Instructing Comprehension-Fostering Activities in Interactive Learning Situations." In R. B. Ruddell, M. R. Ruddell, and H. Singer (eds.), *Theoretical Models and Processes of Reading* (4th ed., pp. 757–787). Newark, Del.: International Reading Association, 1994.

Brown, R. *Schools of Thought: How the Politics of Literacy Shape Thinking in the Classroom.* San Francisco: Jossey-Bass, 1991.

Freedman, S. W., Flower, L. Hull, G., and Hayes, J. R. *Ten Years of Research: Achievements of the National Center for the Study of Writing and Literacy.* Technical Report No. 1-C. Berkeley, Calif.: National Center for the Study of Writing, 1995.

Greenleaf, C. L., Jiménez, R. T., and Roller, C. M. "Reclaiming Secondary Reading Interventions: From Limited to Rich Conceptions, from Narrow to Broad Conversations." *Reading Research Quarterly,* 2002, *37*(4), 484–496.

Greenleaf, C., Schoenbach, R., Cziko, C., and Mueller, F. "Apprenticing Adolescent Readers to Academic Literacy." *Harvard Educational Review,* Spring 2001, *71*, 79–129

Grigg, W. S., Daane, M. C., Ying, J, and Campbell, J. R. *The Nation's Report Card: Reading 2003, National Assessment of Educational Progress.* Washington, D.C.: National Center for Education Statistics, U. S. Department of Education, June 2003.

Hudson-Ross, S., and Graham, P. "Going Public: Making Teacher Educators' Learning Explicit as a Model for Preservice Teachers." *Teacher Education Quarterly,* 2000, *27*(4), 5–24.

Hull, G. A., and Rose, M. "Rethinking Remediation: Toward a Social-Cognitive Understanding of Problematic Reading and Writing." *Written Communication,* 1989, 8, 139–154.

Ivey, G. "Reflections on Teaching Struggling Middle School Readers." *Journal of Adolescent and Adult Literacy,* 1999, *42*(5), 372–381.

Jay, J. K. "Meta, Meta, Meta: Modeling in a Methods Course for Teaching English." *Teacher Education Quarterly,* 2002, *29*(1), 83–102.

Keene, E. O., and Zimmerman, S. *Mosaic of Thought: Teaching Comprehension in a Reader's Workshop.* Portsmouth, N.H.: Heinemann, 1997.

Knapp, M. S. *Teaching for Meaning in High Poverty Classrooms.* New York: Teachers College Press, 1995.

Langer, J. A. "Beating the Odds: Teaching Middle and High School Students to Read and Write Well." *American Educational Research Journal*, 2001, *38*(4), 837–880.

Lortie, D. *Schoolteacher: A Sociological Study*. Chicago: University of Chicago Press, 1975.

McKay, S. L. "Toward an Appropriate EIL Pedagogy: Reexamining Common ELT Assumptions." *International Journal of Applied Linguistics*, 2003, *13*(1), 1–22.

Moje, E. B., Dillon, D. R., and O'Brien, D. G. "Reexamining the Roles of the Learner, the Text, and the Context in Secondary Literacy." *Journal of Educational Research*, 2000, *93*, 165–180.

Moje, E. B., Young, J. P., Readence, J. E., and Moore, D. W. "Reinventing Adolescent Literacy for New Times: Perennial and Millennial Issues." *Journal of Adolescent and Adult Literacy*, 2000, *43*, 400–410.

Moore, D. "Adolescent Literacy for All Means Forming Literate Identities." In C. Roller (ed.), *Comprehensive Reading Instruction Across the Grade Levels: A Collection of Papers from the Reading Research 2001 Conference*. Newark, Del.: International Reading Association, 2002.

Moore, D. W., Bean, T. W., Birdyshaw, D., and Rycik, J. A. *Adolescent Literacy: A Position Statement for the Commission on Adolescent Literacy of the International Reading Association*. Newark, Del.: International Reading Association, 1999.

Palincsar, A., and Brown, A. "Reciprocal Teaching of Comprehension-Fostering and Comprehension-Monitoring Activities." *Cognition and Instruction*, 1984, *2*, 117–175.

Pearson, P. D. "Reclaiming the Center." In M. Graves, P. van den Broek, and B. M. Taylor (eds.), *The First R: Every Child's Right to Read*. New York: Teachers College Press, 1996.

Resnick, L. "Literacy in School and Out." *Deadalus*, 1990, ("Literacy in America," special issue), 170–185.

Rogoff, B. *Apprenticeship in Thinking: Cognitive Development in Social Context*. New York: Oxford University Press, 1990.

Schoenbach, R., Greenleaf, C., Cziko, C., and Hurwitz, L. *Reading for Understanding: A Guide to Improving Reading in Middle and High School Classrooms*. San Francisco: Jossey-Bass, 1999.

Sharp, A. *Reading Comprehension and Text Organization*. Lewiston, N.Y.: Edwin Mellen Press, 2003.

Shulman, L. "Those Who Understand: Knowledge Growth in Teaching." *Educational Researcher*, 1986, *15*(2), 4–14.

Smith, F. *Joining the Literacy Club*. Portsmouth, N.H.: Heinemann, 1988.

Stahl, S. A., Duffy-Hester, A., and Stahl, K. "Everything You Wanted to Know About Phonics (But Were Afraid to Ask)." *Reading Research Quarterly*, 1998, *33*, 338–355.

Templeton, S., Beer, D., Invernizzi, M., and Johnston, F. *Words Their Way: Word Study for Phonics, Vocabulary, and Spelling Instruction*. Englewood Cliffs, N.J.: Prentice-Hall, 1996.

Tovani, C. *I Read It, But I Don't Get It: Comprehension Strategies for Adolescent Readers*. Portland, Me.: Stenhouse Publishers, 2000.

Vacca, R. T., and Vacca, J. L. *Content Area Reading*. New York: HarperCollins, 1993.

Walqui, A. *Sheltered Instruction: Doing It Right*. Unpublished manuscript, 1995.

Chapter 3

Apprenticing Teachers to Reading in the Disciplines

Middle and high school students need to become better readers. This is an explicit belief among almost all teachers. Helping them become better readers is someone else's job. This is a tacit belief among those same teachers. Science and math teachers see reading as the province of the humanities. Social studies teachers believe reading instruction more properly belongs in English classes. Secondary English teachers see themselves as responsible for teaching literature and writing, not reading, a skill that more properly belongs to reading "specialists" trained in techniques more connected to cognitive science than to disciplinary content. In fact, content teachers in almost every discipline see teaching content— whether biology or algebra, U.S. literature or world history—as competing with the goal of teaching reading. Many high school teachers also believe that reading instruction belongs in middle school, while many middle school teachers see reading as something that should be learned by the end of third grade.

As teacher educators, we want to challenge the notions that teaching reading is incompatible with teaching content, that reading instruction is specialized beyond the average teacher's capabilities, that improving students' reading is someone else's job. This chapter describes how we work to help preservice teachers see that teaching reading *is* their job and is compatible with teaching their discipline. Toward these ends, we ask the teacher credential candidates with whom we work to read in their discipline, record their reading processes as well as their learning from reading, share their thoughts about reading with a credential candidate from another discipline, and discuss the implications of what they learn for teaching reading in their content areas. The goal of this Reading Apprenticeship portfolio project is to help teachers see that reading in their discipline is learning their discipline, and therefore that teaching reading in their discipline is teaching their discipline. We want teachers of subject area content to see that they are also expert readers in their discipline, that they possess a storehouse of strategies for making meaning from disciplinary texts. When they realize the expertise they bring to reading, they come to see themselves as capable of teaching reading. And when they recognize how much the learning in their field is developed and enriched through reading, they come to value reading even more. Finally, we want teachers to practice apprenticeship in reading, not only to share with others their strategies and ideas about reading in their own discipline but to learn from others outside their discipline about the strategies and ideas they bring and how reading is a discipline-specific activity. In addition to presenting how we implement the Reading Apprenticeship portfolio, this chapter describes what prospective teachers learn when they cross disciplinary boundaries and the potential of projects like the portfolio to demystify reading in various subject areas.

Evolution of the Reading Apprenticeship Portfolio

We work with a diverse group of teachers. All of them are bright, creative, energetic, and committed to the ideal of helping all students learn, but they represent a wide array of disciplines and experiences. All of us work with teachers of English, math, science, and social studies. In addition, some of us work with teachers of physical education, business, art, and music. They represent an equally wide array of experiences with and dispositions toward reading. Some are voracious readers across all disciplines and genres. Others are avid readers in a discipline or genre—fans of mysteries or poetry, for example. Some read the newspaper daily, while others read the journals in their disciplines. Still others admit to reading very little. Some of those who read little are situational nonreaders—full-time intern teachers or student teachers and part-time students who juggle their work and study schedules with the responsibilities of family. A few candidly say they simply do not enjoy reading or think they are poor readers.

We want all teachers to think of themselves as readers and to enjoy reading. We believe this is important for the quality of their own lives, not merely so that they can serve as models for their students. Consequently, we work to create an environment in our content reading classes that speaks to the sheer joy of reading as well as the means for teaching reading as a functional skill or tool for gaining access to power. Several years ago, Dave Donahue began asking the student teachers in his content area reading class to spend about three hours a week reading "because you want to, not because you have to." In addition, he asked them to write about what they read, share their writing with another teacher, and respond to the other teacher's writing. Half of their reading was supposed to connect somehow to the subject matter they were teaching. The assignment, lasting for most of a semester, was designed to help them appreciate the joy of reading by experiencing the three conditions needed to become a good reader: time, ownership, and response (Atwell, 1998). Dave also hoped the teachers would reflect on their own development and learning as readers and come to see reading as an activity of making meaning from texts. Although he believed the project was successful at creating a culture of reading and helping the teachers develop or reconnect to a love of reading, he saw it was less successful at helping them think about how they read and consequently how they would teach adolescents about reading.

When Dave spent a summer poring over the teachers' journals to figure out what they had learned from the project, he discovered that reading and thinking about reading were deepened when the teachers engaged in conversations with colleagues from different discipline areas. Consequently, he modified the assignment to require such dialogue. Rather than allowing teachers to choose col-

leagues with whom to share their reading journals, he assigned partners. Ideally, math and science teachers were partnered with English and social studies teachers.

At the same time Dave was modifying the reading journal
assignment, he began working with other teacher educators in SLI's
TEC to develop content area reading courses based on a Reading
Apprenticeship framework. We realized the reading journals had
the potential not only to foster a new or rediscovered appreciation
of reading but also to help teachers understand the complexity of
making meaning from text, especially when they engaged in conversation about reading with colleagues from other disciplines. As
a consequence, the dialogue journal project evolved into the current Reading Apprenticeship portfolio project.

Logistics of the Reading Apprenticeship Portfolio

Each member of the TEC has modified the project to meet the
needs of his or her students, but the following is a general outline of
the project's structure. (See Exhibit 3.1 for a version of the assignment from Dave's syllabus.) By the second week of class, teachers
from different disciplines have been paired with each other—math
teachers with English teachers, history teachers with science teachers, for example—and each teacher has chosen a text to read for the
project. Ideally, these texts are "disciplinary" in some way, the definition of disciplinary being left to the teachers. For example, in the
past, science teachers have chosen popular science titles such as *The
Whole Shebang* and *The Beak of the Finch* or a series of articles from
journals such as *Nature* or *Scientific American*. Others have chosen
biographies such as *Surely You're Joking, Mr. Feynman*, memoirs such
as *Refuge* by Terry Tempest Williams, and poetry by Mary Oliver.
We have not given out lists of recommended books, instead relying
on the teachers' rationales for why the texts fall into their disciplinary domain. In addition to requiring a disciplinary connection, we
also ask that they choose a text that is new to them but that they

Exhibit 3.1. Apprentice Reading Portfolio

Apprentice Reading Portfolio

Goals

- To reflect on our own development and learning as readers
- To understand reading as an activity of making meaning and to apply that understanding to teaching subject matter
- To practice strategies for making explicit the ability to read in different subject areas

Assignment Rationale

All of you are expert readers in your subject areas. Some of you have read countless poems. Others have probably lost count of how many scientific reports you've read.

All of you are probably also novice readers in some area. For example, a Shakespearean scholar might be lost reading a manual on Web authoring, or a chemical engineer may not appreciate the interpretations made by a Marxist historian examining the growth of industry in the nineteenth century. Unless you have taken a course in accounting, you probably feel this way when you read the instructions for filling out your tax forms!

This assignment is designed to help you think about reading as a complex activity of making meaning from text. You will be making your own strategies for understanding a text in your subject area explicit to someone from a different subject area. You will also be learning strategies to understand texts outside your own area of expertise. Drawing on our experience as readers (and writers), we will be assembling what Schoenbach et al. describe as a mental toolbox (Schoenbach, Greenleaf, Cziko, and Hurwitz, 1999) by describing how we learn from reading and its implications for teaching reading in our classrooms.

**Exhibit 3.1. Apprentice Reading Portfolio
(cont'd.)**

Assignment Overview

I will assign you a partner from another discipline for this project (for example, a history teacher with a science teacher or a math teacher with an English teacher). Each of you should choose a text in your subject area that you've never read before, but that you feel comfortable reading. For example, if you have a background in science, you might read an article in the latest *Science* or *Scientific American* or a chapter in Timothy Ferris's *The Whole Shebang* or Jonathan Weiner's *The Beak of the Finch*. Someone interested in literature might want to read poetry from the Harlem Renaissance, a play by a canonical writer like Anton Chekhov or Arthur Miller, or a short story in a recently published anthology of U.S. writers under age thirty.

Once you and your partner have chosen your texts, you should begin reading.

As you read, use the "think-aloud" process described in *Reading for Understanding* to record your mental activities or strategies for understanding the text. You should write your thoughts on as many of the following prompts as possible:

Types of Think-Alouds

- Predicting

    I predict . . .

    In the next part I think . . .

    I think this is . . .

- Picturing

    I picture . . .

    I can see . . .

- Making connections

    This is like a . . .

    This reminds me of . . .

- Identifying a problem

    I got confused when . . .

    I'm not sure of . . .

    I didn't expect . . .

- Using fix-ups

    I think I'll have to (reread, take action to foster comprehension).

    Maybe I'll need to (read on, persevere in some other way).

During the weeks of September 9, 16, and 23, read your own text, write your thoughts to the think-aloud prompts in a journal, share the journal with your partner, and respond to your partner's journal, at least once a week.

During the week of September 30, exchange texts. You should read your partner's text, continuing to keep a journal of your reading processes, bearing in mind what you learned by reading your partner's journal in the previous weeks.

During the week of October 7, you and your partner should have a metacognitive conversation in which you explore your thinking about reading. In particular, consider:

- How did the personal dimension of reading affect your understanding of the two texts?

- How did the social dimension of reading affect your understanding of the two texts?

- How did the cognitive dimension of reading affect your understanding of the two texts?

**Exhibit 3.1. Apprentice Reading Portfolio
(cont'd.)**

- How did your own knowledge—about the content and about texts—affect your understanding of the two texts?

To receive credit for this assignment, turn in your individual think-aloud protocols as well as a joint summary of your conversation. This summary should answer the questions:

- What have you learned about reading in your own subject area?
- What have you learned about reading outside your subject area?
- How will you use this learning to help your students make meaning from the texts you assign in your class?

Due: Friday, October 10, 2003

---

feel confident about reading. Many teachers have told us this assignment was the impetus to read something that had long been on their to-read list. During this second week, the teachers meet their partners and make plans for exchanging their journal entries about reading.

Starting in the third week of the course and running for approximately three weeks, the teachers read at their own pace (from as little as a page or two in math texts to whole chapters in novels) and record their thinking about reading in their journals. We have no expectation that the teachers will finish a book by the end of the project. Indeed, rushing to finish a book would defeat one purpose of this project: for teachers to pay careful attention to their reading processes. To help teachers understand what kind of thinking goes into their reading processes, we borrowed the think-aloud prompts from *Reading for Understanding* (Schoenbach, Greenleaf, Cziko, and Hurwitz, 1999) to guide their writing about their reading (see Exhibit 3.1 for a list of the prompts).

At the same time the teachers work on this project, we use class time to engage in think-aloud protocols and reading process analysis (described in Chapter Five). We also show videotapes of secondary school students participating in think alouds. These activities help the teachers understand what kind of thinking they should be paying attention to and recording in their journals. Most teachers write from two to three pages a week. Some write considerably more. All report that, at first, the process seems unnatural and slows down their reading. We reassure them that this slowing down is what enables them to unpack the complexity of making meaning from text. We also remind them that reading is not supposed to be this slow. Rather, they are relearning all the processes that have become fast or automatic in their own reading. Understanding these processes allows them to develop an appropriate scaffolding for helping their students read disciplinary texts. In addition, when they help their middle and high school students understand these processes, those students can come to incorporate such thinking with the same degree of automaticity. For a picture of the reading processes these journals capture, see Exhibit 3.2, which gives an example of one English teacher's thinking as she began to read *Their Eyes Were Watching God.*

During each of the three weeks that the teachers record their thoughts about reading in their disciplines, they also share their journals with their partner from another discipline. The partners read the other's insights, offer comments, and ask questions about reading in that discipline. Generally, these responses are short, no more than a few sentences. The responses help the writers of the journals to see whether they are describing their reading in a way that makes sense for someone outside the discipline.

During the fourth week, the partners switch texts—for example, the math teacher reads the English teacher's text, and vice versa.

Exhibit 3.2. A Disciplinary Insider Begins a Novel

The first things I examine when starting a new book are my own preconceptions and knowledge about the book. What do I know about the author? What do I know of the novel, play, or essay? Is it a genre I'm comfortable and familiar with? What is the historical period of the writing and of the story? Sometimes I'll begin something and then decide that I need more background information to make the book resonate with me. I usually have to study the cover for a while and try to figure out the artwork and design that have been chosen, then I read the back cover—actually, I skim the back first to see if I think I'll be interested and who else liked it, and if I'm lucky, there's a little note about the author to help me get an idea of the frame of reference from which that person is writing. . . .

So I finally sit down with the book. I open it and page through to find out what's in it besides the novel itself. In this case, there's the Foreword, the novel itself, the Afterword, the Bibliography, and the Chronology. I go straight for the Chronology. I like to get a reference for when the book came in the author's life in terms of career, personal events, age, and so on, and what else was going on in the world; this way, I can formulate the beginnings of an idea as to how those things shaped each other. Next, I go to the Foreword to find out a little about what I'm going to be reading. I find that I don't pay really close attention, because often, the main discussion is about something that I've not read yet, but I read it regardless to glean as much insight as I can. In this instance, learning about how this novel has come to its current status in the literary canon is very interesting to me and will definitely affect how I read the book, because I'll be looking for more depth and consciously recognizing more of the book's themes than I might if I were reading it for pleasure. I will be more critical and less entertainment-minded.

Having gained an idea of when and where the book was written and how it has resonated, I am ready to begin. I think that this is something I do a lot, but only became conscious of now: as I turned to page one and got ready to start reading, I took a big deep breath, like you do when you're about to jump into a pool or a lake—huge breath, then holding it to test and see how that first line goes. The first line is huge. The first line bears all of the weight of anticipation and all of the promise of the rest of the book. It sets the tone, and in most cases, is the thing that pulls you under into the depths of the work. It's the portal to the new world—sometimes I have to read it four or five times. Sometimes, as was the case here, I read the first line twice (it's a doozy), then read it again with the second line, then read the two together with the third and so on through the first paragraph. After I'd read the first two paragraphs, I went back and started over. I find that this helps me to gather together my thoughts and to ease in to the language of the work. It also helps to catch any missed meanings or descriptions as I accustom myself to the new world of the novel.

They continue to write in their own journals, recording their thinking as they read. The partner with the new text can read that text from the beginning or start where the partner finished reading. In either case, each one uses the other's journal as a guide to reading in a new discipline. The trepidation that some teachers feel about reading in a new discipline is attenuated by knowing they have the guidance of a more expert other in this new endeavor. Other teachers, armed with insights from experts in another discipline, look forward to the adventure of reading outside their specialty.

During the fifth week, the reading partners get together for a face-to-face metacognitive conversation that ties together the conversation begun in the journals. In particular, they consider the following questions about Reading Apprenticeship:

- How did the personal dimension of reading affect your understanding of the two texts?
- How did the social dimension of reading affect your understanding of the two texts?
- How did the cognitive dimension of reading affect your understanding of the two texts?
- How did your own knowledge—about the content and about texts—affect your understanding of the two texts?

They also summarize their learning by discussing these questions and answering them in writing in a paper that they submit at the end of the project:

- What have you learned about reading in your own subject area?
- What have you learned about reading outside your subject area?
- How will you use this learning to help your students make meaning from the texts you assign in your class?

Many teachers choose to record their answers in dialogue format, capturing the flavor of the conversation about these questions.

In these final conversations, teachers explore the four dimensions of reading described by the Reading Apprenticeship framework. They uncover the personal dimension of reading as they identify favorite authors and genres and articulate their motivation for reading in the discipline. Writing to others, they see how their understanding of text is shaped by beliefs and values, past and current experience. Often they are surprised to learn how personal their reading can be when they compare the interpretations or images they developed in response to texts.

The teachers gain an appreciation of the social dimension of reading. Writing to each other, they see that their own understanding is shaped by the ideas and responses of others. They also see how the process of writing and talking with someone else about a text enriches meaning-making. Talking about their reading with someone else leads to a level of engagement with the text that they would not have developed otherwise. Several pairs found the project so engaging that they continued reading with each other after the project's end.

Encouraged by Dave's use of the cross-disciplinary journal assignment, Kate Evans also incorporated it into her content area reading class. But she found that her students tended to have more lively, in-depth discussions about reading and reading processes in small groups rather than in pairs—and incorporating talking with writing about reading began to emerge as more fruitful. In addition, many of her students expressed that they did not identify as readers, that they disliked reading, or that they rarely or never were involved in social interaction around reading. Thus, the focus on the personal and social dimensions seemed most important. So Kate altered the cross-disciplinary assignment in favor of an assignment more akin to a book group or reading circle. This involved having students bring in books—fiction or nonfiction—that they had never read but had found intriguing in some way. Perhaps someone had recommended the book, or perhaps it had been sitting on their shelf gathering dust. Sharing these books in class was a lively experience; students talked about why they might like to read the book, often reading aloud the opening paragraph, sharing information from the book jacket, and displaying the book cover's artwork. They then formed groups of three to six students based on which books most piqued their interest. These groups met weekly to discuss the book; in addition, they wrote about their experiences reading. For instance, a science teacher in a mixed-discipline group reading Barbara Kingsolver's *The Poisonwood Bible* wrote the following during first week of the book group: "I begin to zone out because of the lack of personal connections. . . . When I zone out, I sometimes take a break to avoid not focusing on the story, or I will continue reading because of the pressure to satisfy my reading group. I would hate to be the only person not to complete the reading!"

Three weeks later, she wrote this: "Our first reading, I couldn't really get into the text. I have always had difficulty reading a book from the beginning without losing focus, and the main reason I didn't really understand what was going on [was] because I just tried to get to the final page. But after our discussion I decided to start the book over from scratch and have a fresh new perspective on it, and it worked. . . . I definitely feel our exchange of ideas motivates me to read and become more involved with the text."

The focus on reading in the disciplines was not central to Kate's version of this assignment; she felt that her students would benefit from a more general reading and discussing texts of their choice. And it appeared that this experience enriched their understanding of the social, personal, and metacognitive aspects of Reading Apprenticeship.

Reading with each other, the teachers make explicit to themselves and to their colleagues the strategies they employ and the mental moves they make as readers revealing the cognitive dimension of reading. They notice how they monitor their own comprehension and record the strategies that serve the comprehension. When they read outside their subject areas, they rely on the strategic guidance provided by their partners so they can move through unfamiliar texts and content. They learn that strategies are often discipline-specific—for example, chunking text for comprehension can vary by subject area. Whereas a reader of a novel in an English class may be able to skip whole paragraphs, read ahead, and still develop comprehension, a reader of a math text might find comprehension breaking down after skipping part of a sentence. The teachers also learn that strategies can be genre-specific; for example, directions for administering CPR call for more careful monitoring of understanding than reading a newspaper article about current rates of heart disease in the United States.

Finally, the teachers see the knowledge dimension of reading, particularly as they read with colleagues from other disciplines. They discover that reading develops and demands three different, related kinds of knowledge: knowledge of content, text, and disciplinary ways of thinking. In writing to each other, the teachers share what they are learning as they read and the knowledge they believe would help their cross-disciplinary partner understand the text. They explain how texts in their disciplines work; for example, a history teacher might explain to a science teacher how he reads historical research, studying the biography of the author and reading the foreword and introduction to gain a sense of his or her background and intention, which might influence how that author frames or interprets the past. A physical education teacher may explain to a mathematics teacher how she visualizes the description of a volleyball tournament, viscerally experiences the moves as she reads, and moves back and forth between charts, photos, and text as she reads. The teachers also discuss with each other the differences and similarities in disciplinary modes of thinking that influence interpretation. For example, a science teacher might explain to a colleague in history that truth is a matter of empirical investigation rather than interpretation of data. All these dimensions are part of the metacognitive conversation that is at the center of Reading Apprenticeship. In this case, the conversation is supported and made visible by the journal writing that teachers share with each other.

What Teachers Learn About Reading When They Cross Disciplinary Divides

Issues of Risk, Safety, and Confidence

The preservice teachers wrote often about the risk involved in sharing one's evolving understanding, even confusion, about texts. They also described what contributed to a safe environment for sharing one's understanding and the confidence in their abilities as readers that grew when they saw themselves making meaning from texts—in short, when they saw themselves as readers.

Writing about risk, Sarah, an English teacher, put it this way: "What if, by taking notes on how I came to understand . . . poetry, I revealed a deep-seated ignorance about what poetry is? What if, after all my effort, I just don't get it?" Her partner, Edward, a math teacher, concurred: "I started to worry that my journal would make me appear less than smart, particularly when it was read by an intelligent woman who is planning to be an English teacher."

Thinking about one's own reading poses a risk to one's identity and self-concept, and sharing that evolving thinking with others heightens the risk. Building from her own fears about sharing her understanding of reading poetry, Sarah wrote, "It must scare kids to death to talk and write about literature. How easy it must be for a student to put down a book if reading it makes her grapple with a part of herself she would rather not face. How easy it must be for a student to put down a book if reading it makes him think he is stupid." Thinking about how to create an environment that is safe for Reading Apprenticeship, she continued, "How crucial it is for teachers to deflate the notion that reading should not be a personal experience, and that there is one right, smart way to read."

Although sharing one's emerging thinking can raise the risk, it plays a key role in helping readers develop confidence in their ability to make meaning. Tara, an English teacher, and her partner, Darrel, a math teacher, wrote in their final paper that "she initially didn't have much confidence in her ability to read and understand math." She gained confidence, however, by having a window on Darrel's thinking about the math text. "As she read the text and reflected back on Darrel's notes while writing her own, she found comfort in the fact that she had similar questions to Darrel's." Once she began reading, Tara realized "that she could understand the text, and when she came to confusing parts, she was reassured knowing that Darrel also found the same parts confusing." This insight allowed Tara to see that good readers have questions about texts and are not afraid to raise them, an understanding that she wanted to make explicit for her students, who thought good readers must never have questions about their reading.

Although we make no claims that a project like this will change the lives of our students, it has that potential in some cases. Anton, a math teacher who got out of the habit of reading when he was working seventy to eighty hours a week, wrote, "This is an amazing development about my reading that I have come to understand. . . . I like to read. I do not think that I am going to go and join a book club or anything, but I am no longer afraid to see a few pages of text in front of me."

As teacher educators, we are pleased when new teachers come to see themselves as readers and understand what their students feel as they develop their reader identities. This project allows the new teachers to see that they bring strengths to reading. They also see that when reading some genres or in some disciplines, they are novices and resemble their adolescent students. We believe this can only contribute to a generous view of developing readers—a view based on what they are capable of learning rather than on what they cannot do—consistent with the Reading Apprenticeship framework.

Reading as a Social and Personal Activity

Pam, a physics teacher, described how the social dimension of reading contributed to her ability to understand texts. "Even 'good' readers need others to question and explain to. The concepts in physics are often too subtle to 'pick up' just through self-study. It's easy to think you understand things when you don't. So conversation needs to accompany reading." Writing to Sheila, his science teacher reading partner, Paul, a social studies teacher, commented on how the social aspect of reading added to his motivation to read outside his subject area. "I'm actually interested that this [a book about genetics] is Sheila's favorite subject, so I am more willing to read to get a better sense of who Sheila is as a person. I'm curious about Sheila's work using mtDNA in a lab and would like to know more about that. So I find myself seeing Sheila in the book and how excited she would be if this was what she were working on."

Carmela, a science teacher, and Dena, a social studies teacher, described how the personal dimension of reading shaped their understanding and how their understanding from reading ultimately shaped their conceptions of self: "In doing the reading outside of our subject areas we became more cognizant of how we are constantly making links from the text to things with which we are familiar. We also saw that reading in a different subject area sometimes pushed our comfort zone, yet in finding meaning in the texts, our conceptions of self were expanded."

Although teachers often understand how prior experiences influence what students want to read, how they read, and what they learn from reading, Carmela and Dena's comment is a reminder that reading shapes one's sense of self as well (Ferdman, 1990).

As these journal excerpts illustrate, the Reading Apprenticeship portfolio project allows new teachers to experience dimensions of reading that are too little appreciated when reading is seen as a process understood only by experts with specialized knowledge of cognitive processes. Acknowledging the personal and social dimensions of reading gives teachers an opening to think more carefully about reading—their own and that of others. We see this as an important step in getting content area teachers invested in teaching reading and believing themselves capable of teaching it.

Drawing on Knowledge

Through the Reading Apprenticeship journal project, the teachers we describe here came to see how reading was a discipline-specific activity and how they added to or drew on their knowledge when they read genres associated with their disciplines. Sarah noted: "I became much more cognizant of how I read poetry through doing this project." She found herself resisting a line-by-line analysis, something she initially thought would meet the expectations of this project, and something that reflected how she had been taught to read poetry. She realized instead that she was noticing words and images that connected the poem to her own life. She spent more time thinking about the author's choice of words and the images and associations with each word.

Kurt, a social studies teacher, described the kinds of questions he asked himself and the work he did before entering an academic history text. Before reading *Woodrow Wilson and World War I,* by Robert Ferrell, he said: "I really needed to jog my memory about World War I. Why did people fight? How did the war get started? Was Woodrow Wilson a Republican or a Democrat? What difference might that have made? I looked at the pictures. I went on the Internet and printed up a World War I chronology. I thought about previous books I had read concerning this time period."

Often this knowledge of the discipline and its role in making meaning from texts was invisible to the teachers until pointed out by their partners, who were disciplinary outsiders. Sheila, the science teacher, pointed out to Paul, the social studies teacher, how his disciplinary knowledge contributed to reading a biography of Mother Jones. After reading Paul's journal, she wrote, "I was interested in his first expectations about the book's order: early life, early struggles, . . . call to action. I would never have thought of this." Paul responded, "I didn't even realize I did that."

Pam, a physics teacher, found that she "learned a huge amount about reading physics" through the project. She noted, "First, to read a high school level science text, one needs to already know how to read science and how to read a text." She also appreciated that "to understand physics . . . , one cannot just breeze through a text or article like one might through a novel." She continued: "One must stop, play with objects, solve a few problems (during the chapter, not at the end!). One needs to challenge understanding by trying it out around the house or garage. Therefore, students have to understand something about the nature of science—that unlike math, science is fundamentally experimental. All of science was developed by increasingly sophisticated 'playing around' with things. Scientific knowledge is created, not just learned. So reading is not enough."

Pam's comment illustrates that making meaning from text depends not only on having knowledge about the discipline but thinking in disciplinary ways. In other words, having knowledge about waves and particles is not, by itself, enough for understanding physics readings on those subjects. Rather, one needs to know how knowledge is created, expanded, verified, and reported in a discipline to construct meaning from disciplinary texts.

The Reading Apprenticeship portfolio brings the knowledge dimension of reading to the forefront for new teachers. When our teachers became guides for disciplinary outsiders, they paid greater attention to what they already knew and how that affected their meaning-making. They also gained an appreciation for the knowledge dimension of reading when they read texts outside their own disciplines. In that situation, they raised questions and tried to appropriate a disciplinary insider's way of thinking so they could make meaning from new texts outside their area of expertise. They also realized the importance of supporting the knowledge dimension of reading for their students. Some talked about providing word walls for specialized vocabulary in their discipline. Others talked about creating a classroom rich in images depicting an era in history or the setting of a novel. Others talked about using K-W-L charts—listing what students know, want to know, and learned from reading—or anticipation guides (Chapter Five) to help make explicit and connect what students know to what they might learn from a text.

Employing Strategies to Make Meaning

The teachers we describe in this chapter not only connected reading to their knowledge of the discipline, how texts work, and their knowledge of the world but also became increasingly aware of the strategies they used to make sense of the texts they were reading. As they paid more attention to these strategies, they also saw how some strategies cut across disciplines, how strategies are employed differently depending on the discipline or type of text, and how sometimes one discipline's strategies can hinder understanding when reading in another discipline.

A number of teachers noticed the importance of taking notes or responding to a text with marginal notes. Carmela, the science teacher, observed that her partner, Dena, the social studies teacher, "tends to take notes automatically—especially when reading social theory or work associated with her academic studies." Carmela described why Dena takes notes and how she uses them: "The process of writing notes creates a space where she can pose questions (and add exclamation marks when she strongly agrees or disagrees), and put the text in her own words to make more meaning and significance. . . . The notes help her to process and remember meanings and ideas. It is a tool that she refers back to and finds useful on multiple levels, but particularly when continuing conversations about the issues raised in the readings with other people or texts."

Pam saw that rereading was important, particularly in her own discipline, physics. "Rereading is important. Richard Feynman, probably the most famous twentieth-century physicist, used this strategy: he read until he stopped understanding, then started over with the article or book and read again. He presumed that trouble understanding text pointed to a problem with earlier understanding and read again. One doesn't understand physics perfectly the first time around."

Knowing that a leading figure in physics used rereading as a strategy to make meaning from disciplinary texts helped Pam understand that "good" readers are not necessarily people who understand everything on the first reading.

Ruby, an English teacher, came to appreciate that strategies that help her understand texts in her own discipline do not necessarily help her understand texts in another such as history.

When Kurt and I were first partnered, I was disappointed because I thought (wrongly, as it turned out) that I already knew plenty about reading history. I realize now how much I have to learn. Probably the most important thing is the active role readers of history take when confronted by texts like the World War I book. Rather than sitting back and drawing all my knowledge and enjoyment from the text (as I do with most novels), I needed to be taking notes, checking other sources, and confirming facts.

Many of these teachers described reading outside their subject areas as "more active," implying that automaticity decreased when they left their familiar disciplinary realms. English teachers were most likely to point out the distinction between active and "sitting back" reading, perhaps because the primary genre in their discipline, the novel, can be read two ways—as an academic activity and as a pleasurable pursuit—something that is less often said about reading the primary genres of other disciplines.

Ruby also saw that she drew on other strategies. She commented: "I never realized, for instance, how much forming mental pictures of the action in a story contributes to my enjoyment and understanding." In general, she found reading her partner's history book was "more like 'work.'" She "became a big fan of summarizing, rereading paragraphs, and trying to build a summary in my head of what had just happened. This helped me continue with the text and slowly build my knowledge that way."

Ruby saw the crucial role of Kurt, her partner and a disciplinary insider, in helping her make meaning from texts in a discipline outside her own area of knowledge. She used his journal to see what questions he had about the text and what he did with the information. She wrote that he became "my 'eyes and ears' for this time period."

How Teachers Connect Learning from the Reading Apprenticeship Journals to Practice

The preservice teachers came away from this assignment with a number of specific ideas about how to translate their learning into implications for practice. Most important, many content area teachers came to see that teaching reading is part of their job. Pam, the science teacher, realized that "students need to be taught something about reading the kinds of texts they will be reading," and she saw that as something she could and would do in her physics class.

Tara and Darrel realized the importance of the personal dimension of reading and the need to create a classroom environment that nurtures it. They saw that "asking students to reveal their thought process, to reveal what they don't know, is a huge risk activity. For this reason, it's especially important first to establish a safe environment before proceeding with any kind of Reading Apprenticeship models." They concluded that "students need to know they will not be judged for not understanding what they read, and that it is OK to make mistakes in reading a text, be it English or math." They agreed that they wanted to model the metacognitive conversation involved in reading to give their students the confidence that good readers "struggle." They wrote that "for students, watching their teachers problem-solve or reveal their own struggles could be extremely helpful."

Sheila, the science teacher, learned that she wanted "to help my students make connections between unfamiliar text and their understanding of how the world works. . . . As a teacher, I want to provide the context, the themes into which the facts fit." Her partner, Paul, the social studies teacher, also wanted to help students make such connections after he had the experience of making personal connections to what he thought would be a "boring and nonrelevant" text on genetics and DNA. He was surprised to find that "when I tracked my reactions and had to observe my thoughts, I realized that I do make connections and the reading actually became more fun. In some ways it was more work, but worth it if you want someone to understand what is being read. This is what I want do to with my students." Deborah and Heather, social studies and science teachers, respectively, also discovered the importance of helping students make connections to the text. They said they wanted to create classrooms where they could "find out what knowledge the students already have about the text." They wanted to foster connections to what they saw as their students' "wealth of knowledge. Whatever they know is important and will enhance their reading."

Ruby saw a connection between the social dimension of reading and motivating students to engage with texts. "I can see using a version of this very project in my class to encourage the students to read carefully and pay attention to their comprehension. If they know they will have to discuss what they've read with a peer, they may be more motivated to focus on the assignment." Though the logs are not the only way to encourage students' attention to their mental processes, Ruby planned to build from them in the future.

Dena and Carmela commented on how they would promote the social dimension of reading in their classrooms, saying, "Both of us felt there are many ways we would like to engage students in conversations about their reading." They found "the partnering model is really nice for building relationships and allowing students time to really get into their ideas." They also realized that this would require work on their part: "While we are aware that in the classroom there are many challenges to actually developing new norms and skills, we think the increased engagement and relevance with written work will be worth the extra effort."

The teachers reflected on ways to frame the cognitive dimension of reading. For example, Sarah realized this: "I should be explicit with my students about that, letting them know that even as an English teacher I am often lost when I first read poems. The key is to let yourself get lost in them." Her partner Edward concurred, saying he would let students know that good readers in science treat reading like problem solving. Tara and Darrel also realized the importance of framing what "good" readers do, saying, "We can ask students to reread math texts because of the nature of math, not because of their own lack of knowledge. The implication for students is that rereading math becomes a sign of a good math reader, not a bad one."

Holly and Deborah described a number of strategies, particularly before students start to read, that they believed would be useful for helping students appreciate the knowledge dimension of reading. Their vision of prereading included "helpful vocabulary, a summary of the text, or a frame for it so they know what to expect. If there is a structure or argument in the reading, we would let the students know what it is and how it works. That way they will know to expect it and look for it instead of being tripped up by it."

Finally, the teachers noted how they could scaffold the knowledge-building aspect of reading for students in their classes. Kurt, the history teacher, concluded, "I have learned that providing students with a time line of events and background is very useful in order to get something out of the text. Otherwise it comes across as a series of unrelated facts and people."

Pam saw that learning new knowledge from reading was more than a process of "absorbing" new facts. She saw that she needed to help her students build habits of mind in her discipline and an open attitude toward learning. "It would be helpful for students to know that in science one needs to let the views one brings to the subject be modified. Students already understand concepts like 'energy' and 'force' in a certain way, but it is not the way physicists understand them."

Learning to Demystify Reading

These teachers' conversations across discipline areas served several purposes for learning to teach reading, learning to teach content, and learning to be colleagues in the profession. For each of these purposes, new teachers came to greater understanding because they were involved in a "narrative of inquiry" (Ball and Cohen, 1999, p. 17). In the case of these cross-disciplinary conversations, the inquiry was into their own reading processes as reading experts or novices, depending on the discipline in which they were reading.

As they apprenticed colleagues, these teachers made explicit how knowledge about their discipline and its texts shaped their reading. They uncovered the cognitive strategies that are most appropriate for reading in their discipline. In addition, they shared their motivation for reading in the discipline. In the process, their knowledge and reading strategies were not only apprenticed but their passion for reading in their discipline frequently rubbed off too. As a result, their colleagues found determination to read texts that might otherwise have seemed impenetrable or boring. More important, those same colleagues often enjoyed their reading and challenged assumptions about their literacy in certain disciplines and with various genres of text.

In the process of apprenticing colleagues, these new teachers gained insights into apprenticing students. They realized that by paying attention to their reading processes, they could provide appropriate scaffolding for reading by the students in their classes. For example, one English teacher realized which parts of a play she could skip and which she had to read over and over. She also realized that, when it came to parts of the play that she did not enjoy on first reading, she appreciated them much more on second reading. Knowing this, she advised students on how to overcome reading roadblocks and implement appropriate strategies. Our current goal is to help teachers gain a similar insight into the importance of the social dimension of apprenticeship. In the same way that they find value in learning with each other, we want them to see that such opportunities are equally valuable for the students in their classes.

Our hope is that reading across disciplinary boundaries also gives new teachers greater empathy for the students in their classes who struggle with reading. Although the teachers described here all played the role of expert reader in this project, they also experienced being a novice—and in some cases, struggling—reader. This was particularly true for the novice readers of mathematics. Having had the experience of being apprenticed, we hope these teachers will not blame their students for their challenges with reading. After all, here were colleagues in their profession and teacher credential program, well-educated people who struggled with some kinds of reading. This experience challenged these new teachers' assumptions about what all students should know or be able to do by the time they reach them in middle or high school.

We also believe that cross-disciplinary conversations about texts can help lessen the fragmentation of knowledge that results from organizing teaching and learning by academic departments in secondary schools. We find that, after experiencing this project, fewer English teachers say they can't "do" math, fewer science teachers say they wouldn't enjoy reading history, for example. These teachers gain a greater appreciation for each other's disciplines as well as a sense of their own potential as learners in fields they might have considered beyond them. This has important implications for teachers believing in the capabilities of all their students as learners. When teachers see themselves as incapable of learning a certain discipline, they are more likely to view their students similarly. By contrast, when teachers see that they can learn in any discipline if they have the right support through apprenticeship, they begin to believe that all their students can learn as well if they too provide the proper support. Teachers' vigorous belief in their own ability to learn and read widely as well as their discovered or reinforced belief in their students' ability to learn and read is perhaps the most valuable outcome of this project.

References

Atwell, N. *In the Middle: New Understandings About Writing, Reading, and Learning with Adolescents* (2nd ed.). Portsmouth, N.H.: Heinemann, 1998.

Ball, D., and Cohen, D. "Developing Practice, Developing Practitioners: Towards a Practice-Based Theory of Professional Education." In L. Darling-Hammond and G. Sykes (eds.), *Teaching as the Learning Profession: Handbook for Policy and Practice* (pp. 3–32). San Francisco: Jossey-Bass, 1999.

Ferdman, B. "Literacy and Cultural Identity." *Harvard Educational Review*, 1990, 60(2), 181–202.

Schoenbach, R., Greenleaf, C., Cziko, C., and Hurwitz, L. *Reading for Understanding: A Guide to Improving Reading in Middle and High School Classrooms*. San Francisco: Jossey-Bass, 1999.

Chapter 4

Promoting Inquiry into
Student Reading Practices

Teaching has been called *the learning profession* (Darling-Hammond and Sykes, 1999) because in order for students to learn, teachers must continue learning. Inquiry—by teachers and students—plays a key role in such learning. For too much of the past and too frequently in the present, however, teachers are charged with transmitting knowledge and with implementing experts' theory into practice rather than creating knowledge and developing theory from their own practice (Giroux, 1988). This emphasis on teacher as technician rather than teacher as intellectual has been especially true in preparing secondary content area teachers to develop their students' literacy, particularly reading. Preservice courses and inservice workshops frequently treat reading as a technical activity, one that can only be understood by reading specialists. This approach leaves content area teachers with the impression that reading is a mystery beyond their comprehension, and thus absolves them from responsibility for asking questions about or developing strategies to promote their students' literacy.

As teacher educators responsible for preparing new middle and secondary school content area teachers for their role as teachers of reading, we have used the metacognitive conversations at the center of Reading Apprenticeship to encourage and make explicit students' and teachers' questions about what, why, and how they read. We ask teachers to see this metacognitive conversation as data they can use to think more deeply about their students' strengths and needs as readers. From their analyses, teachers can design an appropriate curriculum for the whole class, make recommendations

about books to hook young people on reading, and create a classroom culture conducive to making students' thinking about reading visible. As often as this inquiry leads to activities, lessons, and
routines, it also leads to new questions about adolescents' reading,
such as these: How do students make meaning from texts? How do
their values, beliefs, and experiences shape their reading? And what
knowledge about the discipline, texts, and the world do they bring
to their reading?

To encourage questioning about adolescent literacy, we ask preservice teachers to conduct a literacy inquiry project. (See Exhibit
4.1 for a version of the assignment as it appears in Donahue's syllabus.) This assignment is inspired by Atwell's (1998) observation
that "my research shows me the wonders of my kids, not my methods. . . . What I learn with these students, collaborating with them
as a writer and reader who wonders about writing and reading,
makes me a better teacher—not great, maybe, but at least grounded
in the logic of learning, and growing" (p. 3). For this assignment,
we ask student teachers to raise questions about their students' literacy. Then they reflect on how to answer those questions, collect
and analyze data, and share findings along with implications for
instruction in a literacy inquiry symposium. Like Atwell, the preservice teachers learn from students, seeing them as resources for
teacher learning.

This chapter describes how we prepare teachers for this kind of
inquiry. We discuss how to support preservice teachers to ask good
questions about their students' reading, collect and analyze data,
and share findings with colleagues. Throughout the chapter, we
make the case that inquiry is central to the work of teaching generally and Reading Apprenticeship specifically.

Asking Questions About Student Literacy

Inquiry starts with meaningful questions. By the fourth week in
their teacher credential program, we ask the preservice teachers in
our reading in the content areas class to think of a question about

Exhibit 4.1. Literacy Inquiry Project

I confess. I started out as a creationist. The first days of every school year I created; for the next thirty-six weeks I maintained my creation. My curriculum. From behind my big desk I set it in motion, managed, and maintained it all year long. I wanted to be a great teacher-systematic, purposeful, in control. I wanted great results from my great practices. And I wanted to convince other teachers that this creation was superior stuff. So I studied my curriculum, conducting research designed to show its wonders. I didn't learn in my classroom. I tended and taught my creation.

These days, I learn in my classroom. What happens there has changed; it continually changes. I've become an evolutionist, and the curriculum unfolds now as my kids and I learn together. My aims stay constant—I want us to go deep inside language, using it to know and shape and play with our worlds, but my practices evolve as eighth-graders and I go deeper. This going deeper is research, and these days my research shows me the wonders of my kids, not my methods. But it has also brought me full circle. What I learn with these students, collaborating with them as a writer and reader who wonders about writing and reading, makes me a better teacher—not great maybe, but at least grounded in the logic of learning, and growing. [Atwell, 1998, p. 3]

Goals

- To view reading and writing as areas for learning by teachers as well as by students

- To use inquiry to connect learning about reading and writing to the content of subject areas in middle and high schools

- To learn from our own and other teachers' questions about reading and writing

Exhibit 4.1. Literacy Inquiry Project
(cont'd.)

Assignment Overview

In the quote shown above, Nancie Atwell describes how her stance toward reading and writing changed over the course of her career as a teacher. This assignment is designed to help you get where she ended up a little more quickly. Based on your observations of students, teachers, and curriculum at your student teaching placement, you will identify a question about learning to read or write. Using the students at your placement as the primary source of data, you will answer that question. At the end of this course, we will share our findings with each other in a literacy inquiry symposium.

Assignment in Depth

What follows is a road map for your work as teacher-inquirers. For each step along the way, I've listed questions and suggestions to think about in order to get the most out of this assignment and do your best possible work. At each step, we will talk in class about the expectations of this assignment and discuss how best to meet them.

1. Identify a Question

What do you want to know about students' ability to read and write? How will answering this question help your students? How will answering this question help you as a teacher? How, if at all, will it help other teachers? A good inquiry is specific, not general. Think about these questions also as you define your inquiry: Who are your students? In what kind of text or writing are you particularly interested and why? Your question may grow out of and be a follow-up to your work with the Reading Apprenticeship portfolio or the reading strategy portfolio.

2. Develop a Method to Your Inquiry

Questions to ask include these: What kind of data would you need to answer your question? Surveys? Interviews? Students' written work? Think-aloud data? Based on your question, from whom do you need data: One student who confounds you? All the girls in the class? Students who don't do reading for homework? Reality check: Can you collect the data you need in a short amount of time? Are students willing to participate in your research?

3. Collect and Analyze Data

Does your method of analysis make sense given the nature of the data and your question? We will talk in class about how to look at quantitative data (for example, survey results) and qualitative data (for example, students' writing or interview responses).

4. Discuss Your Findings and Implications

What do you know now that you didn't know before? What are the implications of your findings for teachers' practice? What, if any, are the implications for continued inquiry by you or others?

5. Write Your Findings in a Research Abstract

Your abstract should include the following information that is standard in most published research:

- Introduction and discussion of the question (why it's important, why you or other teachers care) as well as what others have to say about the question (here you may refer to researchers and authors you have read in this class or other Mills classes)
- Methods (what you did to answer the question, including how you analyzed the data)

Exhibit 4.1. Apprentice Reading Portfolio (cont'd.)

- Findings (what you learned)
- Implications and conclusion (how your research can inform inquiry and practice in reading and writing)

Your abstract will be shared with the rest of the class before the symposium.

6. Share Your Findings with Others at Our Literacy Inquiry Symposium

Based on your interests and the nature of your inquiry, I will group you into panels and roundtables to share your research with the rest of the class. You should meet with the others on your panel some time before you are scheduled to present at the symposium. Discuss with each other your inquiry, findings, and ideas about the implications of your research. When your panel presents to the rest of the class at the symposium, your presentation should focus on what you learned from the discussion. Don't read or rehash the abstract. We will read that in preparation for the symposium. Rather, focus on the similarities and differences in each other's findings. What did you learn as a group about your inquiry topic?

Due: November 24, December 1, 2003

---

their students' literacy, a question that really matters, one for which the answer might make a difference in how they teach. We model questions that allow for understanding student learning and give examples of questions that start useful lines of inquiry and those that do not.

When first asked to come up with a question, many preservice teachers begin by asking *how?* "How do I get students to read? How can I help students to understand a textbook? How can I get students to like books?" These questions not only focus on *doing* something over *learning* something but make the teacher the most important person in reading instruction. These questions are also unanswerable without first asking and getting answers to other questions. Teachers asking these questions are putting implications before findings. Before asking "How do I get students to read?", I need to answer questions about students' beliefs about reading, their prior experiences, their mental processes when they do read. In other words, I need to ask questions that are not about what a teacher should do, but what a student thinks, has done, and can do.

The "How?" questions also imply that one answer exists for all students. Because there is no magic bullet that can get all students to read, understand reading, or even like reading, we ask teachers to think about who they had in mind when they came up with their question: The three students who sit in the back and dare the teacher to get them to read during sustained silent reading (SSR)? The student who says she reads her homework but can never answer a comprehension question the next day in class? The boys who say reading is not cool?

As the teachers reformulate their questions focusing on specific students and their experiences and thinking, they move from a teacher-centered view of the world to a more student-centered one. They see students not as reading problems to be fixed but as sources of valuable information. The following are some of the questions that our preservice teachers asked about students' reading in the last two years:

> Do students usually read directions? What makes a student more or less likely to read directions? What makes directions easier or harder to understand?
>
> Why do the students who say they hate reading hate it?
>
> What do students think of sustained silent reading?

Is there any connection between students' participation in small group discussion and their perception of themselves as readers and writers?

What are the literacy practices of English language learners who succeed in the standard English classroom?

What connections, if any, do students perceive between reading and learning science?

How do math students cope with math problems in everyday texts—such as newspaper articles—and do they have the skills necessary to solve problems embedded in text?

From what sources do students get their information about health and physical fitness?

Do students use different strategies for reading in French than they do for reading in English?

What are the different strategies that students use when reading primary and secondary sources in history?

These questions arise when new teachers move from thinking of reading as an activity that is the same for all students in all disciplines to one that is personal and context-specific. The questions illustrate an interest in the particularities of students' thinking, experiences, and beliefs. Exploring the questions leads new teachers to see that the curriculum starts not with a packaged reading program or solution that fits all, but with deep understanding of students. Henry, a secondary English and social studies teacher, described that evolution in his thinking. "My original question, 'How can I make reading more enjoyable for the students who struggle with it the most?' was the wrong question. One cannot *make* someone else enjoy reading any more than one can make someone enjoy football." He continued, "A more appropriate question would have been, 'How can I tap into the reading that my students *already* do in their lives (of books, magazines, movies, music, neighborhoods, themselves, others) and help them build bridges to classroom texts?'" Though still beginning his question with "how"

Henry inquired into "what" reading his students already do and used that as the basis for then thinking about how to develop reading skills in other contexts.

The questions teachers ask stem from a variety of motivations, but all lead to valuable outcomes. The question about where students get information about physical fitness stemmed from a P.E. teacher's observation that popular magazines, particularly those directed toward teens, promoted many misconceptions about fitness and health. By finding out which magazines the students read, and what they felt they were learning in them, she could use what students were already reading to foster critical thinking about health and fitness. She could also use students' insights into the information in these magazines as a springboard to correcting misconceptions and unhealthy attitudes about body image.

A science teacher's inquiry into reading directions came out of exasperation with students who asked questions that were answered in the directions to a lab assignment. When we encourage teachers to turn frustration into inquiry, however, we are allowing them possibilities for learning and for hope rather than allowing them to remain in despair. Questions about reading in different genres in history resulted from a teacher's impressions that his students reacted differently to primary source documents and oral histories and developed different understandings about the discipline from each kind of text. Asking student teachers to follow up on impressionistic evidence honors their reflection-in-action (Schön, 1983) and brings structured inquiry into their practice. Questions about students who hate reading are often asked by teachers who love reading and struggle to understand why someone would feel differently. Investigating these questions requires new teachers to develop a "double consciousness," an ability to see schools, subject matter, and reading from the perspective of an adolescent and a student as well as an adult and a teacher.

Ralph, an English teacher who investigated the relationship between choice and reading, learned that students who initially appeared to resist all reading actually read materials they chose, often reading these instead of assigned texts. He began to think about the importance of balancing assigned and self-selected texts, especially to support reluctant readers in developing a taste for books and becoming more fluent as readers. His colleague Abby followed a similar inquiry with some reluctant readers in her high school English class. She wondered how these students made choices about what to read and what not to read. Learning that the students actually read a considerable amount outside of school, mostly nonfiction related to their interests, she asked whether by privileging certain texts—for example, literature—over others, we actually reinforce a nonreader identity in students who in fact do a great deal of reading. These teachers sought deeper understanding of choice and reluctance in reading. They learned that reluctance to read assigned texts does not indicate resistance or inability to read in general.

In every case, these teachers' questions stemmed from actual practice and not from an abstract notion of what it means to do research on adolescent literacy, from a real desire to know rather than a formula for doing research. In many cases, the teachers found out more than they anticipated as they confronted unexamined assumptions. To support inquiry as a habit of mind in teachers, we must ensure that they see answering their inquiry questions as significant for their practice and for student learning.

Why Teachers Must Be Inquirers

Although most would agree that these questions raised by teachers are good ones, some might ask this: Why should teachers engage in inquiry to answer such questions when others, including researchers at leading universities, are conducting educational research? Although educational research has its values for indicating overall trends, it cannot answer questions about particular students in a particular context reading particular texts in a particular genre in a particular discipline. A study of a new reading program may show that it raised average test scores by 3 percent in 75 percent of participating schools, but that does not tell a teacher whether his school would be among the 75 percent of schools that improved or the 25 percent that did not. If, on closer examination, it turns out that the 3 percent average improvement includes students whose performance increased greatly as well as students whose performance decreased almost as greatly, the teacher does not know which students' scores would go up and which would go down. The model of educational research described here might be appropriate for studying new agricultural methods where an average increase in per-acre yield is a meaningful statistic. In education, where we care about the progress of every student, such research leaves teachers with less useful information. More useful information comes from looking closely at students, both as individuals and as members of a classroom community. A key value in a Reading Apprenticeship classroom is teachers learning from students, through metacognitive conversation, how to help them improve. As Hopkins (2002) points out, teachers do not value knowledge derived from the perspective of averages. Rather, teachers value knowledge of teaching "from continual participation in situational decision making and the classroom culture in which they and their pupils live out their daily lives" (pp. 35–36).

Aspects of Inquiry as Reflection

As Hopkins (2002) argues, inquiry is not something separate from teaching; it is part of a teacher's work. Stereotypes of research linger, however, and many preservice teachers think this assignment is asking them to experiment with their students. They want to know if they need a control group for their study. They wonder how they'll ever find enough students for their inquiry so they can generalize their findings. They ask whether conducting inquiry with their own students will "taint" their data with "bias."

We allay these fears in a number of ways. First, we consciously and consistently use the term *inquiry* rather than *research* to describe our work. We want to separate the process of inquiry from these teachers' assumptions about scientific research based on the model of crop yields. We also frame inquiry as structured reflection, a stance drawing on Dewey ([1910] 1991), who described reflection as the "active, persistent, and careful consideration of any belief or supposed form of knowledge" (p. 6).

Collecting and Analyzing Data from Students

The questions that teachers usually ask about their students' reading fall into two large categories: "What do students do?" (Or, "What have students done?") and "What do students believe?" Both types of questions get at the unobservable. Both types of questions are important when teachers—and their students—come to see reading as something that happens with one's mind, as students make meaning from text, not with one's mouth, as they read aloud the words on a page. Questions about what students do include questions about their cognitive processes, questions about their reading habits outside of school and in other classes, and questions about their prior experiences. Questions about what students believe include questions about attitudes toward reading and questions about certain types of prior knowledge—for example, ideas about what good readers do when they read. This section of the chapter describes teachers' inquiry into both types of questions.

Deborah, Paula, and Teresa examined their students' self-reported reading processes and came to understand their beliefs about reading and themselves as readers. The inquiries by all these teachers illustrated how to use students as sources of data rather than as the recipients of instruction based on someone else's research. Deborah wanted to know what her high school students believed about how good readers read. Paula wanted to find out why some of her sixth-grade students said they "hate" reading. In a similar vein, Teresa wanted to find out what her most disengaged students thought about books and SSR.

What Deborah learned confounded assumptions she had made about the students. In addition, the process of inquiry itself changed some of her students' beliefs about themselves. For example, one of Deborah's students, Natasha, who considered herself a good reader, believed that good readers "use strategies for understanding." She mentioned looking at headings, pictures, and captions in a text. She also said she "rereads text until she 'gets' it" and noted the connection between her strategies and the purpose of her reading. "What I do depends on the type of reading it is. If there are questions, I read the questions and go back to the documents. If I have to answer something, then I will take notes." By contrast, Deborah found that another of her students, Ben, who does not consider himself a good reader, also uses specific strategies but has a weaker understanding of strategic reading overall. Unlike Natasha, who said good readers use strategies, Ben mentioned two specific strategies—skimming and looking up words in a dictionary—but did not describe the overall importance of thinking about reading strategically. Deborah was able to use this insight to appreciate how strategies are not isolated skills but are embedded in a larger apprenticeship framework.

Like Deborah, Paula gained a valuable window into her students' thinking and strategies. Talking with four middle school girls who professed to hate reading, she learned new information—they had all been in special reading classes in elementary school that they felt stigmatized them, only one had had a positive experience reading in the past six months, and they didn't believe teachers who told them reading was important but did believe older siblings who said the same thing. Paula was fascinated to discover that the girls she interviewed would "skip around in a book, finding easily understood passages." She reflected, "It wouldn't have occurred to me that some students might not understand or care that most books tell a story in a specific chronological order. Of all the concepts I imagined making explicit in my classroom, I never would have thought of that one."

As important as what Paula learned about her students was what the students learned about themselves. Initially, the girls reported reading only fifteen minutes a day during the time devoted to SSR. When they learned that teen magazines, Web sites with text, and song lyrics "count" as reading, they calculated their reading anywhere from forty-five minutes to two hours per day. One of the girls responded, "I can't believe it," as she began to think about herself as a reader for the first time. Paula concluded that the students seemed to believe that if they were having fun, it must not have been reading. She found that one of the "loudest complainers" about reading "keeps a meticulous binder of song lyrics that she reads all the time 'for inspiration.'"

Teresa reported after her inquiry that "the most profound lesson I learned from these boys, through our conversations and through grappling with this data, was that I never authentically knew what these boys' interests were in regards to reading." She described selecting books for Devon without ever asking him what he liked to read. She wrote, "I was projecting what I thought he might be interested in: culturally relevant stories. I cannot assume that a student will like a book solely on a cultural connection, nor can I think I know a student because of my connection to or understanding of my student's culture." She was surprised when Devon, an African-American student, put down the books she suggested on African-American history and culture and picked up books such as *The Wizard of Oz* and other adventure-fantasy stories. Similarly, Kevin, another African-American student, had a strong affinity for books about Asian culture, like *Dragonwings* by Laurence Yep. She concluded, "This shows not only my ignorance but that reading is very personal and individual. These relatively short conversations [with the students] were so valuable that I am now convinced I should allocate time at the beginning of the year to have a conversation with each of my students and include questions about reading to develop a more authentic understanding of who they are individually." Admitting that she had made assumptions about students' preferences in reading based on race and culture, Teresa demonstrated careful inquiry as she listened to students' perspectives.

By investigating their students' reading processes and beliefs about reading, these teachers gained insights they used to rethink instruction. They reconsidered unrehearsed reading aloud in class, a common activity in most classrooms. They sought opportunities for student choice in selecting at least some reading. They were able to incorporate students' already existing strategic thinking into a repertoire of instruction. They created classroom environments where students felt safe sharing what they knew and didn't know. However, not only the teachers gained insights; their students did too. By engaging in inquiry with their teachers, students developed an image of themselves as strategic learners. They saw that part of learning to read is surfacing what they don't know rather than hiding it. They reconceived their notion of teachers, seeing them not as distant and all-knowing fonts of information but as people who admit what they do not know, ask questions, and take action to answer their questions. In this way, students can see their teachers engaging in processes similar to those in which they themselves engage to learn to read better, and the classroom becomes an environment for apprenticeship as students and teachers co-inquire into how and why they read.

Supporting Inquiry, Sharing Findings, and Creating a Culture of Inquiry

Serious inquiry requires support, and our reading in the content areas courses provides explicit and implicit scaffolding for these investigations. Explicit scaffolding includes devoting time to talking about what makes a good question, how questions imply the means for answering them, and why some questions are harder to answer with data than others. As part of the coursework, student teachers share with each other their questions so classmates benefit from others' thinking and can find colleagues with whom to share data collection and analysis. Additional scaffolding consists of discussing how to collect data. We think about how information from surveys, interviews, focus groups, think-aloud protocols, and classroom discussions can be used for this inquiry. This is not a research course in the traditional sense, and we do not spend a great deal of time on methods. Rather, we provide examples of good data collection strategies, share some of our own inquiries, and make time available for students who need additional ideas about how to answer their questions. We help teachers see how routine classroom activities—students' reading journals, for example—can be data for inquiry. We remind our students that they might not answer their questions so much as explore or illuminate the topic.

We stress concretizing and contextualizing questions and using artifacts in the data collection process, particularly when interviewing students. For example, rather than asking students, "What kind of things do you like to read about science?" (and getting the answer, "Nothing," or "I don't know"), we suggest that students look at newspaper clippings, magazine articles from popular and scientific journals, textbooks, fiction, and poetry on the same topic, and that the teacher then ask them how they would read each one, which one they would be most likely to read on their own and why, and what they think they would learn about the topic from the different kinds of text. Instead of asking students "How often do you read outside of school?" we find that asking them to keep a record of everything they read—from a billboard or newspaper headline to a song lyric or Web site—yields better data and is more likely to impress upon students the importance of print. As an alternative to asking students what their favorite book is, we would rather ask them to bring the book to an interview and explain what it is they like about it. Similarly, we find that instead of asking in general what is easy or difficult about reading, we get better data when students look at a particular piece of text and explain what they like or do not like about it, find easy or difficult about it, and what they learn from it or what confuses them. As these examples illustrate, we want teachers to learn how to collect rich data that go beyond students' facile and unreflective answers. We want new teachers to learn how to conduct inquiry, particularly data collection, that helps students learn while the teachers themselves gain information to answer significant questions.

Throughout the semester, we offer opportunities for teachers to check in with us and with each other about the progress of their inquiry, interesting preliminary findings, or unexpected roadblocks. We try to help them see roadblocks as new and unexpected data. For example, student teachers might report that their cooperating teachers will not allow them to implement a certain kind of activity during SSR or incorporate explicit reading instruction into a class because so much content must be covered. These roadblocks become opportunities to explore colleagues' beliefs about the purpose of SSR or the connection, or perceived disconnection, between reading in a subject area and learning in that subject area.

Beyond this explicit scaffolding, the content of our reading in the content areas classes provides implicit scaffolding for the inquiry projects. Rather than teach teachers how to collect think-aloud data, we engage them in think-aloud activities in our classes. Instead of teaching teachers how to ask questions that spark cognitive thinking and metacognitive conversation, we make these questions a part of our teacher credential courses and point out to new teachers what we're doing and why we're asking such questions. We provide opportunities for teachers in our classes to read in all the different disciplines they teach, so that they can appreciate the discipline-specific nature of reading and not confound comprehension strategies in English, for example, with strategies in math. We model for them ways to invite their adolescent students into reading and learning in the disciplines, supported by a metacognitive conversation. We also enlist the support of colleagues teaching other credential courses so that this scaffolding is supported elsewhere, not so much with additional specific ideas for data collection but rather with a general orientation toward the centrality of inquiry in teachers' work.

The Literacy Inquiry Symposium

As noted earlier, the teachers share their findings from these inquiry projects in a symposium held at the end of the semester. The symposium is important for a number of reasons. It provides a forum for the teachers to share their data and analysis with others. Teaching is an isolating profession, providing few opportunities to discuss questions about practice. The symposium counters that norm. More than a time when teachers share the outcomes of their inquiry, it is also a forum for teachers to think together about the implications of specific inquiries for their practice, to discuss alternative interpretations of data, or to extend thinking in one discipline or about a specific genre to possible implications for other disciplines and genres.

The symposium is also important because it prepares teachers to participate in professional circles about teaching and their discipline. Asking teachers to share their findings in a formal setting serves as scaffolding for significant involvement in organizations such as the National Council of Teachers of Mathematics, the National Association of Bilingual Educators, and the National Council of Teachers of English, for example. We want teachers in our credential program to learn how to connect with colleagues across the nation as well as at their school site.

The symposium is not merely one or two class sessions devoted to a series of reports on individual inquiry projects. Such an approach would not only tax the patience of any audience but also fail to build connections across inquiry projects. Instead, we assign students to thematic panels that spend less time reporting individual results and more time discussing crosscutting findings and implications. In a group of approximately thirty teachers, we create seven panels, four reporting one week and three reporting the following week. Typically, each panel has thirty minutes, of which about ten to fifteen minutes are used for reporting and the remaining time used for questions and answers from other teachers. In the past, panels have had titles such as "Student Reading Outside of School," "Students' Attitudes Toward Reading," "Students' Use of Strategies," and "Reading Different Genres in the Disciplines." The last panel might include the following:

- A tenth-grade health education teacher learning how genre affects learning by asking students to read textbook selections, popular magazine articles, and literary nonfiction about HIV and to describe how they read each and what they learned.

- A middle school English–social studies core teacher exploring whether students employ different strategies when they have a choice in reading by asking students to describe how they read a selection from their literature anthology compared with how they read a book for sustained silent reading.

- A high school business teacher examining how students feel about reading from the computer manual to solve a software problem versus reading the help Web site online.

- An eleventh-grade U.S. history teacher seeking to know what kinds of dialogues students have with primary source documents—for example, early twentieth-century immigrants' letters to their families in Europe and Asia—by asking students to "talk to the text" (that is, annotate in the margins).

Teachers meet before their panel's presentation, share their findings with each other, and discuss common themes. This meeting is a valuable part of the process. The teachers spend time talking through the importance of their findings, making connections, and exploring even further the pedagogical implications of their inquiries. Across grade levels and disciplines, they may find that students misapply the reading strategies of one genre or discipline to another. They may learn that students think all reading is "just reading" no matter what the discipline. They may even realize that they themselves have been giving students advice about reading in general that is appropriate only to their discipline. These common crosscutting themes form the heart of the panel's presentations to the rest of the class.

To avoid the need for extensive reporting on individual projects, we ask the teachers to share a one-page abstract of their inquiry. This abstract reports the question, its significance—to the field, the teacher, or both—the methods used to answer the question, findings, and implications for practice. Students bring enough copies for the class so that everyone can read the abstracts prior to the symposium and come with questions and comments. Like the presentations themselves, the abstracts serve as scaffolding for teachers' participation in subject area conferences and professional organizations. Abstracts also serve as a more succinct means than full-length papers to share findings with colleagues who are learning about thirty other inquiry projects.

Reading Apprenticeship for Apprenticing Teachers and Students in Inquiry

Through Reading Apprenticeship, teachers learn that their students are at the center of reading instruction. They see that although there is great value in learning strategies to improve students' ability to read, they cannot "overlay" these strategies on a class of students and hope that the reading comprehension of all of them will improve. Strategies do not work like fertilizer on a field because students are not crops, and reading improvement is not the same as a larger harvest. Reading Apprenticeship requires that teachers learn about their students—their beliefs, prior experiences, and thinking, particularly how they make meaning from text. No teacher education textbook can tell teachers who their students are and how their minds work. This must be an area for inquiry.

When teachers inquire into their students' lives and learning, they change the relationship between teacher and student from the expert-novice metaphor that describes most classrooms into a relationship among reciprocal learners. For some, apprenticeship conjures images of medieval guilds with expert, master craftsmen passing skills to those learning the trade. For many, this is also the model of preparing teachers. Many speak of master teachers and student teachers, implying that teaching and learning in the profession are one-way phenomena based on status. Rethinking apprenticeship, we want to shift the focus from status and passing on knowledge to focusing on how those with skills make them explicit and provide an environment where others can appropriate those skills.

When teachers inquire into student learning, expertise becomes more evenly distributed. Although teachers have more expertise at reading in their disciplines, they may not have much expertise at making explicit the metacognitive conversation in their minds that enables them to comprehend subject area texts. Students may not initially possess this expertise either, but when they learn how to pay attention to their thinking and understand how they read, they become the experts on their own thinking. In a Reading Apprenticeship classroom, this expertise is shared, creating a climate of inquiry as teachers and students pose questions not only about texts but about how they are making meaning from them. This project is designed to nurture this climate of inquiry.

Our goal is to prepare teachers to ask useful questions. New teachers ask lots of questions. Most often, those questions focus on their own performance—for example, "How can I teach students to find the main idea?" This project shifts inquiry from teacher performance to student thinking. We want teachers to gain access to student thinking and to think about data from students and the implications for instruction. We believe this assignment serves those ends. Most important, perhaps, we want teachers to have a sense of hope about their future in the profession and their students' learning. We know that the work of teaching is hard and that new teacher turnover is high. We have found, though, that when teachers are confident about their ability to answer questions about student learning, they gain confidence in their ability to meet the challenges of teaching. When they inquire into student learning, they gain information that often gives them hope—not necessarily because their methods are foolproof or their curriculum is flawless, but because with a deeper understanding of student thinking they have a direction for their own work as teachers. This may be one of the most important reasons for supporting an inquiry orientation toward teaching.

References

Atwell, N. *In the Middle: New Understandings About Writing, Reading, and Learning with Adolescents.* (2nd ed.). Portsmouth, N.H.: Heinemann, 1998.

Darling-Hammond, L., and Sykes, G. *Teaching as the Learning Profession: Handbook of Policy and Practice.* San Francisco: Jossey-Bass, 1999.

Dewey, J. *How We Think.* Buffalo, N.Y.: Prometheus Books, 1991. (Originally published 1910)

Giroux, H. *Teachers as Intellectuals: Toward a Critical Pedagogy of Learning.* New York: Bergin & Garvey, 1988.

Hopkins, D. *A Teacher's Guide to Classroom Research.* Buckingham, England: Open University Press, 2002.

Schön, D. *The Reflective Practitioner: How Professionals Think in Action.* New York: Basic Books, 1983.

Chapter 5

Linking Reading Strategies to Content Instruction

There is no shortage of books of instructional strategies for content reading instruction in secondary classrooms. And therein lies both a benefit and a problem. Preservice teachers need support to guide students in reading to learn from content area texts, so strategies that build background knowledge, help students grapple with difficult text, and distinguish main ideas from supporting details are all relevant. But instructional strategies in the cognitive and knowledge-building dimensions are neither freestanding, appropriate across all subject areas, nor sufficient to the task of apprenticing students as readers in the discipline. In RA classrooms, we have found that successful strategy instruction, often based in the cognitive and knowledge-building dimensions of the framework, builds on supported learning about reading and readers in the social and personal dimensions. Strategies to support comprehension become powerful learning tools when they occur as part of a broader metacognitive conversation that links all four of the classroom dimensions in the framework. The strategies themselves require a collaborative context of inquiry into how and why we read in different disciplines and the increased agency that students develop as readers in academic texts. In an RA classroom, this shift in stance toward reading and toward students as apprentice readers is key.

To help our preservice teachers think about cognitive and knowledge-building strategies in the broader framework of RA, we ask them to consider parallels and contrasts between the main course text, *Reading for Understanding* (Schoenbach, Greenleaf, Cziko, and Hurwitz, 1999), and a supplementary reference with classroom strategies. Jane Braunger invited her students to consider the ways in which *Reading for Understanding* and *Strategic Teaching and Learning* (California Department of Education, 2000) "talked to each other" as well as the ways in which they "disagreed or talked past each other." The teachers prepared for a classroom conversation by noting parallels and contrasts they saw in:

- The model of reading in each text (either explicit or implicit)
- The model of learning in each text (either explicit or implicit)
- The teacher's role in content area reading
- The student's role in content area reading
- The role of strategies in content area reading

The preservice teachers saw a number of parallels, specifically the focus on increasing students' ability and responsibility to learn from academic text and the need for explicit modeling and scaffolding of learning with strategies such as question-answer relationship and reciprocal teaching. At the same time, they noticed an important difference, which one student described with a culinary metaphor. The collection of instructional strategies, she said, was like a cookbook—a good one, with a varied collection of recipes. In the hands of a seasoned cook, it could be an excellent source for constructing and delivering to the table excellent menus for a variety of occasions and guests. The problem with a good cookbook, though, is that it isn't sufficient for the decisions a cook needs to make. The student noted that, in the absence of big-picture understandings about nutrition, everyday cooking, and entertaining, a beginning cook might feel overwhelmed and simply start at the beginning, mastering the cookbook by moving through it. She compared this situation with hers as a new teacher. With RA as a framework for content area reading instruction, she could more confidently choose instructional strategies that fit the demands of her subject area, the needs of her students, and her style as a teacher. As she engaged students in the metacognitive conversation in her classroom, she could learn from and with them how to support them as readers in the discipline. Instructional strategies would emerge from this highly interactive and inquiry-based context, rather than appearing as the teacher-chef's strategy du jour.

Instructional Strategies in Reading Apprenticeship

The key here is knowing powerful strategies and being able to call them up and adapt them to the text and task at hand. In *Reading for Understanding*, the authors describe how they presented this idea to their high school students as assembling a "mental toolbelt" (Schoenbach, Greenleaf, Cziko, and Hurwitz, 1999, p. 75). Students learn strategies to help them make sense of challenging subject area texts and are given extended opportunities to practice these strategies in class and learn from each other how to use them selectively and effectively. Gradually they become able to use the strategies automatically, as needed. They have equipped their mental toolbelt for subject area reading.

In the same way, we want our preservice teachers to understand and know how to teach their students high-leverage strategies for reading texts in their disciplines. In this chapter, we describe some key instructional strategies that we offer our students, modeling their use and engaging students in using them to comprehend texts in our courses. We explicitly model how to scaffold instruction in various strategies, and we implicitly model our values for teaching reading as a part of teaching the disciplines and for developing students' agency as readers of academic texts.

Lesson Plans

Lesson plans are the workhorse assignment of any teacher education course, and for good reason. Writing a formal lesson plan requires the kind of thinking that new teachers must master to succeed in the profession: the ability to articulate goals and objectives, to conceptualize essential questions that bring coherence to instruction, to design engaging and thoughtful activities, and to plan assessment for student learning. Such thinking is a valued part of numerous courses in teacher preparation programs.

When we began using a Reading Apprenticeship framework in our content area reading courses, we continued to require new teachers to write one formal lesson plan incorporating reading strategies that developed their students' reading abilities as well as their content area knowledge. Because we did not want our students to think that reading could be taught in a one-shot lesson, we reminded them that these lessons should not be reading lessons, where the teacher takes time out from examining content knowledge to deliver discrete reading strategies disconnected from the content. As teacher educators, we were familiar with the trap of putting reading into a curricular ghetto apart from subject matter; it is a trap because such an approach can leave middle and high school students thinking that reading is a skill that can be learned in a lesson or two. It can also leave them thinking that reading is a skill without any specific connection to the subject matter or genre of what they are reading.

The teachers in our classes understand the limitations of reading lessons and generally are committed to embedding reading instruction in their curriculum. But they also feel tremendous pressure to "fix" their students' "problems" with reading, such as limited background knowledge in the subject of texts and difficulty in finding main ideas. Consequently, resource guides, published curricula, and their cooperating teachers' handouts on reading seem to hold out the attractive possibility that if they only teach enough lessons on reading skills, their students' problems will be fixed and they will be able to continue with content instruction, assured that their students now understand how to access knowledge from assigned texts.

Over the last several years, we became concerned that our lesson plan assignments, despite our intentions otherwise, fed this notion that reading is a problem that can be fixed in a few lessons or that what students need is an all-purpose collection of reading strategies that will make learning from subject area texts easy. Although we asked the teachers in our courses to develop plans that embedded reading strategies in the context of lessons developing students' subject matter knowledge, we also heard teachers referring to these as their "reading lessons," implying that reading had been cordoned off from the rest of the curriculum. We saw lesson plans on how to understand the structure of a textbook. Although such knowledge is valuable for middle and high school students and worthy of a lesson, those plans did not demonstrate how understanding text structure would be incorporated into the structure of a course beyond one block or period. More worrisome, we also saw a few teachers' lesson plans that incorporated reading without any explicit instruction in how to read at all. These teachers believed that by asking students to read on a regular basis, they would improve their ability to read. Assigning reading is necessary but not sufficient for developing adolescents' reading skills. Without modeling and guided instruction, students continue to see reading as mysterious. In contrast, with explicit instruction and multiple opportunities to practice a skill such as drawing an inference or generating a summary, making meaning from texts is demystified.

As a consequence of these concerns, we moved away from a freestanding lesson plan assignment and instead now ask preservice teachers to identify at least one strategy that will improve their students' ability to read and understand content area texts. We ask that they weave this strategy as a thread throughout their student teaching by incorporating it in more than one or two lessons. For examples of strategies, we ask the teachers to consider ideas from resources such as *Reading for Understanding* (Schoenbach, Greenleaf, Cziko, and Hurwitz, 1999), *When Kids Can't Read* (Beers, 2003), and *Strategic Teaching and Learning* (California Department of Education, 2000). Depending on the strengths and needs of their students and the kinds of texts and purposes for reading in their classes, the student teachers then choose to thread strategies like talking to the text, question-answer relationship, reciprocal teaching, or anticipation guides through their courses. By thinking of strategies as threads rather than discrete lessons, teachers can help students gradually gain control over the strategies, providing appropriate scaffolding and using it less and less as students gain greater independence with more challenging texts and reading tasks.

Lessons threaded with explicit attention to embedding one reading strategy can then serve as a template for making this thread an automatic routine implemented by teachers in their class. As teachers gain experience integrating one thread they can add additional threads as appropriate. This approach is in keeping with notions of apprenticeship and how they might apply to learning to teach. Rather than overwhelming new teachers with dozens of ideas for strategies (of which most resource books contain many examples), all seemingly equally worthy of "trying out," or worse, "covering," we would rather they make decisions about choosing the strategies that will have the greatest leverage in improving their students' reading and practicing these strategies so that they truly become routines instead of the focus of one lesson.

We admit this shift was not accomplished without mixed feelings. We worried that requiring teachers to write fewer lessons as part of their preservice program would diminish their ability to do so. We also considered the estimation of our courses by colleagues at our own and other institutions who may feel that we are sacrificing a degree of rigor in teacher education. We believe that such concerns are overridden by the benefits of practicing ways to embed a few appropriate and powerful reading strategies in the context of subject matter lessons.

Reading Process Analysis

To help new teachers understand reading as a complex problem of making meaning from texts rather than simply a technical process of decoding, we ask them to engage in reading process analyses, where they examine their own reading of various subject area texts. This activity becomes the basis for preservice teachers to uncover all the thinking and strategies that they see as a "natural" or "instinctual" part of reading but that are in fact learned and have become "automatic" for skilled readers like themselves. The reading process analysis also becomes the basis for inquiry into the literacy learning cases introduced in Chapter Two. After showing videotapes of middle and high school students reading the same texts used in the reading process analysis, we ask the preservice teachers to analyze the demands of the texts, pay attention to the reading processes of an adolescent reader, and examine the strengths and needs of this reader. We do this not so that the preservice teachers will diagnose the students but so that they can think about how paying attention to the reading processes of students can yield valuable information with implications for planning reading instruction in content area classes. We believe that engaging with these cases will allow new teachers to see adolescents' reading as a site for inquiry. We encourage these teachers to question their initial assumptions about students as readers, to learn from students, and to remain open to multiple interpretations of what students' reading processes imply for instruction.

We initiate the reading process analysis by asking the teachers to read a one- or two-page excerpt from a disciplinary text. We have used selections from history books examining totalitarianism, algebra books explaining linear and direct functions, and short stories and primary source documents. To prompt teachers to uncover their reading processes, we ask them to "talk to the text"—that is, write down their thoughts, ideas, questions, images, and confusions, all the things running through their minds—as they read. We then ask them to discuss what they noticed about their reading with a partner in the class to gain additional perspectives on how someone else read the exact same text. Finally, we collect all the mental processes of the teachers as they read, using four interacting areas of reading as categories—fluency, motivation, cognition, and knowledge—to chart their thinking. Usually when first engaging in this process with new students, we chart their responses by category but without naming the category. We then ask the teachers to notice patterns in the categories and to name them by what the items in that category have in common. During subsequent reading process analyses, we also chart by category but ask the teachers to tell us under which category they would place the various mental processes they are uncovering in their reading. (See Chapter Nine of *Reading for Understanding* [Schoenbach, Greenleaf, Cziko, and Hurwitz, 1999] for a full description and examples of this reading process analysis, which is called the Four Interactive Areas of Reading.)

In the fluency category, we include all their thinking related to disruptions in their ability to make meaning from the text. One powerful realization by teachers here is that fluency is not always tied to oral reading. In other words, fluency is about a mental process, not only about how well one reads out loud.

Under motivation, we include all their thinking, positive and negative, connected to the affective side of reading. With negative responses, we probe for what the teachers did to continue reading so they can see the processes in which they engage to continue with difficult and sometimes disagreeable texts. This becomes the first step for them in thinking about how they can help their students make similar moves through texts.

The cognition category is where we list all their strategies for reading. Not surprisingly, this is the largest category and the breadth and scope of strategies illustrates for teachers the distributed nature of skills in a classroom community.

And finally, in the category labeled knowledge, we collect their ideas about how reading contributed to and drew on their knowledge in three realms: knowledge of the world, the text, and the discipline. As teachers examine the information in this category, they begin to see how reading might be different for someone without their background knowledge.

This is the exact same process we encourage teachers to implement with their own students so adolescents can make visible their reading processes for themselves and others. Not surprisingly, however, when teachers engage in this activity, their processes differ from those of adolescents reading the same text. Their discoveries about their own reading processes lead to areas for thoughtful consideration of adolescent readers' processes and design of appropriate curriculum.

For example, related to motivation, many teachers comment on how excerpts from middle and high school textbooks make them angry or depressed for a variety of reasons. They comment on boring and unclear writing, the "authorless" voice of texts, the failure to capture the contested nature of knowledge in their discipline, and the biased or limited perspective on content. Invariably this leads to some teachers saying that textbooks are just bad and should be abandoned. Although few might argue that reading a textbook is an enjoyable experience or even the best way to gain disciplinary knowledge or perspectives, comments about abandoning textbooks provide an opportunity to discuss why adolescents should be able to read such texts, apart from the value of those texts or the amount of attention they should be given in a classroom. For example, many gatekeeper exams, from placement tests to SATs, ask students to read and interpret text selections similar to those found in textbooks. And although many teachers have their critiques of textbook knowledge, they also realize that they are able to put their own ideas in dialogue with and debate textbooks, a skill they want their students to master as well.

Examining the role of knowledge, many teachers are surprised by how much they have to draw on their existing knowledge to make meaning from the text selections, raising questions about how students with less content area knowledge make meaning from the same texts or develop knowledge using such texts as a starting point. This leads to opportunities for examining how to build a classroom environment and incorporate other texts and artifacts to build students' content knowledge as they read rather than as only a "front-loaded" precondition for reading.

Many teachers also notice that the reading strategies that have made them strong readers in their area of disciplinary expertise do not always work when reading texts in other disciplines. For example, teachers with expertise reading literature know that when they are confused they can often read ahead and their confusion will be cleared up. Such a strategy rarely serves those same readers when their comprehension breaks down reading a mathematics text. As a result, teachers come to understand the importance of helping students understand the discipline-specific nature of reading.

Reading process analysis leads to important understanding by each teacher of the personal dimension of reading as they surface their own affective responses to texts. The cognitive dimension of reading stands out when they pay attention to all the strategies they use to understand what they read. And as they pay attention to the subject matter content of what they are reading, the knowledge dimension of reading becomes obvious through reading process analysis. As they focus on their own reading and how they make meaning from texts, it can become easy for teachers to lose sight of the social dimension of reading, of how much they learn about reading when they learn what others do to construct meaning. As teacher educators, it becomes especially important to give time for teachers to share the results of their reading process analyses and to point out the reasons for doing so. As we discuss in Chapter Ten, new teachers want their students to understand their reading processes and make opportunities available to them to do so. What they are less likely to do is provide opportunities for students to share those processes. By providing those opportunities for our preservice candidates and being explicit about why we do so, we can perhaps help them to see the necessity and the possibilities of providing such opportunities for their students.

Text and Task Analysis

The preservice teachers develop a keen awareness of the complexity of reading as they engage in multiple reading process analyses. In a text and task analysis, they build on those insights as they examine a particular text and the reading-learning task associated with it. They do so from the perspective of the students who will be assigned the text, focusing on what knowledge and strategies are needed to complete the reading task successfully. The assignment asks them to study the text and identify several types of knowledge as well as reading strategies to consider in planning for its use with students. It also asks them to consider teaching-learning opportunities the text offers in each of these categories. This activity serves as a scaffold for building prospective teachers' pedagogical content knowledge, seeing what a text assumes about student knowledge, and exploring what makes particular concepts difficult to learn. A text and task analysis helps prospective teachers link schema building or cognitive strategies to authentic reading and learning in the curriculum.

This analysis provides a direct experience of apprenticing students to subject area reading by anticipating the knowledge and strategies they will need to apply in order to learn from the text. It leads to class conversations on making good instructional decisions about what to teach directly, what to facilitate through small group or whole class topic-centered conversation, and how to help students apply particular strategies in reading to understand the text. Text and task analysis also engages prospective teachers in extended work with subject area texts, prompting such questions as "What will my students bring to this text that will help them understand it?" "What does the text assume they already know?" "Are those assumptions valid?" "What difficulties might students have with this text?" "How might I plan for activating what they know and helping them past the difficulties?" "How can students collaborate on making meaning with this text?"

During a class meeting, prospective teachers work in subject area groups, conducting the text and task analysis on materials they are using with middle or high school students. Figure 5.1 contains sample responses from a group who examined a page and a half segment introducing patterns of evolution in a high school biology text (Feldkamp, 2002). The full text excerpt is shown in Exhibit 5.1.

As the science teachers worked with the biology text excerpt, they expressed concern about the conceptual density in a selection that purported to be an introduction. Subject area teachers and literacy specialists have decried the textbook habit of "mentioning"—layering abstract concepts one on top of another in a presentational style that presumes students either already have necessary conceptual understandings for the topic under discussion, in this case, evolution—or equally dangerous, supplying definitions for key vocabulary

Exhibit 5.1. Text Excerpt on Patterns of Evolution

exaggeration. For example, during no stage of development does a gorilla look like an adult fish. In the early stages of development, all vertebrate embryos are similar, but those similarities fade as development proceeds. Nevertheless, the similarities in early embryonic stages of vertebrates can be taken as yet another indication that vertebrates share a common ancestry.

Similarities in Macromolecules

Darwin hypothesized that more-similar forms of organisms have a more recent common ancestor than do less-similar forms. He arrived at this hypothesis by observing anatomical features only. He could not have known how true this rule would prove at the molecular level—for homologous proteins, as well as RNA and DNA molecules. For example, many species have the red-blood-cell protein, hemoglobin. The amino acid sequences in the hemoglobin molecules of different species are similar, but not identical. The amino acid sequences in human hemoglobin and gorilla hemoglobin differ by one amino acid, while the hemoglobin molecules of humans and frogs differ by 67 amino acids. The number of amino acid differences in homologous proteins of two species is proportional to the length of time that has passed since the two species shared a common ancestor. Thus, the more-similar the homologous proteins are in different species, the more closely related the species are thought to be. Information provided by molecular biology can confirm the evolutionary histories suggested by fossils and anatomy.

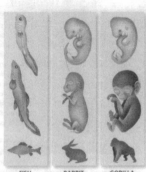

FISH   RABBIT   GORILLA

FIGURE 15-9
This is a modernized version of Haeckel's drawings of embryological stages in different species. Although modern embryologists have discovered that Haeckel exaggerated some features in his drawings, it is true that early embryos of many different vertebrate species look remarkably similar.

PATTERNS OF EVOLUTION

There are several ways that species can change to adapt to their habitats. The pattern and speed of evolutionary change result from the changing requirements of the environment.

Coevolution

The change of two or more species in close association with each other is called **coevolution.** Predators and their prey sometimes coevolve, parasites and their hosts often coevolve, and plant-eating animals and the plants they feed on also coevolve. One example of coevolution is plants and the animals that pollinate them.

In tropical regions, some species of bats feed on the nectar of flowers, as shown in Figure 15-10. These bats have a slender muzzle and a long tongue with a brushlike tip, which aid them in feeding. The fur on the bat's face and neck picks up pollen, which the bat takes to the next flower. Flowers that have coevolved with these bats are light in color, enabling the bats, which are active at night, to easily locate them. The flowers also have a fruity odor that is attractive to bats.

FIGURE 15-10
Some species of bats, such as this long-nosed fruit bat, have coevolved with the flowers they feed on.

Convergent Evolution

Sometimes organisms that appear to be very similar, such as a shark and a porpoise, are not closely related at all. This kind of similarity is the result of **convergent evolution.** Convergent evolution occurs when the environment selects similar phenotypes, even though the ancestral types were quite different from each other. Sharks and porpoises have very different origins. Sharks are fishes, and porpoises are mammals. Many features of these animals are similar, however, and have been selected by the environment they share. Their large, streamlined bodies and even their fins resemble each other. Analogous structures, such as similar fins in very different animals, are associated with convergent evolution.

Divergent Evolution

In **divergent evolution,** two or more related populations or species become more and more dissimilar. Divergence is nearly always a response to differing habitats, and it can ultimately result in new species.

One important type of divergent evolution is adaptive radiation. In **adaptive radiation,** many related species evolve from a single ancestral species. The Galápagos finches are an example of adaptive radiation. They diverged in response to the availability of different types of food in their different habitats.

Sometimes the process of divergence can be sped up artificially, through **artificial selection.** All domestic dogs are the same species, *Canis familiaris.* Dogs have been bred by humans for certain phenotypic characteristics, resulting in different breeds with different traits, as you can see in Figure 15-11. Thus, the process of divergent evolution in this species has sped up many times beyond what could have occurred in nature. Divergent evolution operating over very long periods of time has produced the seemingly endless variety of species alive today.

FIGURE 15-11
The rate of divergent evolution among dogs has been increased by artificial selection by humans.

SECTION 15-3 REVIEW

1. The mouthparts of an adult horsefly are modified for biting. The mouthparts of a mosquito are modified for piercing skin and sucking blood. Are the mouthparts of the two species homologous or analogous? Explain your answer.

2. Birds and bees have wings. Are their wings homologous features or analogous features? Explain your answer.

3. The hemoglobin of humans is nearly identical to that of a gorilla. What does this suggest about the length of time that has passed since the last common ancestor of humans and gorillas lived?

4. Fruit fly embryos and frog embryos differ from each other more than frog embryos and human embryos do. What does this tell us about how the three species are related?

5. Are vestigial structures acted on by natural selection?

6. **CRITICAL THINKING** Some monarch butterflies contain chemicals that are toxic to birds. Another species of butterfly, the viceroy, has some protection from predation because it closely resembles the monarch. What pattern of evolution is illustrated by this example?

 CHAPTER 15

Figure 5.1. Text and Task Analysis on Patterns of Evolution Text Excerpt from *Modern Biology*

Directions: With a partner, read the text excerpt that students will be assigned as well as any lesson materials or handouts. Use this sheet to note what's involved in successfully completing this task. What knowledge or skills does a reader need in each of these areas? What teaching or learning opportunities does this text offer?

Topic or Discipline Knowledge	Textbook Knowledge	Vocabulary and Conceptual Knowledge	Reading Strategies (Affective and Cognitive)
Evolution as an accepted scientific theory	Organization signaled by text features: levels of headings, boldface for key words.	Terms with specific scientific meanings: patterns, requirements, selection, radiation.	Gain awareness of own attitude toward evolution.
Theory as evidence-based (not an opinion or a guess)	Pictures add to the print info (though here, the picture of two dogs, that is, of divergent evolution, is placed next to the paragraph on convergent evolution).	Large concepts in phrases, such as "changing requirements of the environment" and features of animals that "have been selected by the environment they share."	Read to find definition and example of each type of evolution.
Knowledge about species and phenotype (from previous course reading and classwork)	Examples provided to illustrate a concept, for example, bats and particular flowers that have coevolved.	Important prefixes: **coevolution, convergent, divergent.**	Synthesize and summarize regularly, relating examples to the concept they illustrate.
Teaching-learning opportunities:	In-depth information on evolution not here; this is an intro with illustrative examples, no analysis of the evidence.	**Teaching-learning opportunities:**	Compare and contrast the types of evolution.
Specific science meaning of theory	**Teaching-learning opportunities:**	Review key vocab learned or used to date with specialized meanings in science, for example, trait, habitat, dominant. Bridge from current understandings of terms in this selection (patterns, requirements, selection, radiation) to their meanings in this scientific context.	Reread.
	Textbook as a distillation, not an in-depth explanation		**Teaching-learning opportunities:**
	Concept density		Use the section's organization to guide reading, that is, three types, definition, examples.
	Caveat re: "reading" pictures and diagrams (may confuse)		

and presuming that this will suffice to build the concepts. Faced with the reality of textbooks that don't go deep enough or provide enough support to build conceptual understandings, we have already noted how prospective teachers are likely to decide that textbooks aren't useful. And they would be in good company with many experienced teachers with lengthy critiques of textbooks honed over years of teaching.

In preparing teachers to apprentice students to reading in their disciplines, however, we ask them to use their expertise as readers in the discipline to bring students into the conversation about how textbooks work, how to identify and use their organization, and how to interact with the text to construct a reasonable understanding. This is part of making the invisible processes of reading—by an expert—visible and accessible to students. Rather than abandon the textbook, the RA teacher scaffolds the reading task for students, with a goal of increasing their ability to read a textbook as one of many texts in the subject. For example, for the biology excerpt used in the preceding text and task analysis, prospective science teachers see that by focusing on concepts, and having students engage in question-answer-relationship in small groups as they read, they can help students move beyond vocabulary definitions to see the connections among concepts critical to an understanding of evolution. Other strategies, such as reciprocal teaching or think-aloud, would work well here too. The point for the teachers to understand is that with appropriate support, students can read and learn from concept-dense and otherwise "inconsiderate" text—that is, text that provides insufficiently elaborated information for the reader to construct a meaningful understanding (Armbruster and Anderson, 1981).

Question-Answer Relationship

To demonstrate how teachers can scaffold questioning as a means for students to improve their understanding of texts, we engage students in a question-answer-relationship (QAR) strategy based on the work of Taffy Raphael. This activity requires students to think of questions at four different levels: *right there, pulling it together, author and me,* and *on my own.* Right-there questions can be answered using information directly from the text. Pulling-it-together questions can also be answered by the text, but they require students to synthesize information from various parts of the text. Author-and-me questions rely in part on information from the text but also require students to draw on their own knowledge. On-my-own questions ask students to develop an answer or an opinion on their own, based on knowledge they have gained from the text. Framing these different types of questions helps students see the relationship between asking questions of a text, how one reads a text, and ultimately how one makes meaning from that text. It also helps students see how some questions are more appropriate than others for unlocking the meaning of texts. Whereas right-there questions might be useful with a science textbook, for example, that is full of specific, technical information, author-and-me questions are more useful for helping readers make inferences about a character's actions in a novel. Asking questions that go beyond right-there allows students to see that reading texts requires critical thinking, getting at the big picture, imagining—all skills that illustrate the complexity of reading.

After the students have developed their questions, one student chooses another and asks a question. The chosen student then answers the question and explains how she or he did it—by finding the information right there, pulling information together, and so on. That chosen student then picks another student and the process continues until everyone has had a chance to ask and answer a question.

For example, Dave has used a short article on cell structure and HIV transmission to illustrate the potential of QAR to help readers develop understanding of a text. The article contains highly technical scientific information as well as rich imagery comparing a cell with a boatload of treasure and HIV to a pirate ship. Some students struggle with the technical information while others work hard to understand the article's metaphors. Consequently, students' questions reflect their difficulties. A right-there question such as "What is protease?" contrasts with another right-there question, "How is a cell like a treasure boat?" What new teachers learn from this process is that even right-there questions are not as easy as they may seem. The article defines *protease* but uses terms that can be as technical for some students as the term *protease* itself. And although the article includes a sentence that makes clear some of the ways that a cell is like a ship, if the metaphor does not make sense for students, they are left without a picture of what a cell is like.

Preservice teachers sometimes find themselves struggling to categorize their questions. Even when they have what they know is a good question, they will ask, "Is this OK for a pulling-it-together question?" From the number of differing opinions in class about the categorization of a question, they soon see that it would be easy to lose sight of the forest for the trees, to become bogged down in trying to find the right label for a question rather than considering how that question illustrates an effort to understand a text. As a result of this question-asking process, the preservice teachers see that the value of questions is not merely in making sure that students get the right answer or in labeling a question correctly, but in surfacing each reader's difficulties and the varied interpretations and readings of a text.

Anticipation Guides

While the bell is ringing and the students are scrambling to stuff their books and papers into their backpacks, the teacher yells out: "Read Chapter Four for tomorrow!" When Kate asks her preservice teachers if they have seen or experienced this scenario, most of them say they have. Some admit to doing this very thing as teachers, while others say this is how teachers are often depicted on film and TV. We talk about the problems with the read-X-for-tomorrow approach to teaching reading—namely, that it's assigning, not teaching, students to read. In addition to the fact that many students won't do the reading, those who do have no sense of purpose

for reading and no suggestions for which approaches to this particular text might be helpful to them. What, then, can teachers do
before students read to pique their interest? To help them establish
purpose? To build on personal and text knowledge? Once these
questions are raised, preservice teachers generate ideas based on
teaching strategies they have performed or observed—such as skimming the text and raising questions, discussing the title and making
predictions, looking at the photos and diagrams, and drawing on
the students' prior experiences that relate to the text. In fact, over
the course of the semester, the preservice teachers experience many
of these instructional strategies because Kate devotes the last few
minutes of each class session to an "into." And discussion of the
readings the next week also involves a metacognitive discussion of
how the "into" affected their reading experience.

One "into" teaching strategy that Kate presents at the beginning of the semester is the anticipation guide (see Exhibit 5.2).
Designed for use with *Reading for Understanding*, the anticipation
guide fosters thinking about some of the book's central tenets before
and after reading. It is written in a provocative way to stimulate discussion. After the class discussion described earlier, Kate distributes
the guide and the preservice teachers respond to it alone. They
then discuss in small groups and are free to change their answers if
their ideas change as they hear the ideas of others. Finally, a whole
class discussion ensues. Kate makes sure she does not answer her
students' questions; instead, she probes the assumptions and values
behind their questions and poses alternatives. For instance, someone might say, "Students are always saying the reading is boring. We
really need to teach them to deal with boredom." In response,
another might say, "But the reading really *is* boring! How often do
you sit down to read a textbook for fun?" At this point, Kate might
say, "It sounds like we have several possible issues here: Should
reading be fun in school? Is reading that's fun the way to foster reading? Is it the way to help them read academic texts?" This type of
questioning is likely to prompt more discussion—discussion, it's
important to note, that addresses some of the fundamental issues in

Exhibit 5.2. Anticipation Guide for *Reading for Understanding*

Indicate your thoughts about the following statements before we read *Reading for Understanding* on line B (before). Keep this in your book. We will revisit it after you read to see if any of your thoughts have been changed or been enriched and indicate your thoughts on line A (after).

	Agree				Disagree	
1. The role of the middle school or	5	4	3	2	1	(B)
high school teacher is to teach content,	5	4	3	2	1	(A)
not reading and writing.						
2. Reading and writing should be	5	4	3	2	1	(B)
included in all classes.	5	4	3	2	1	(A)
3. If adolescents are struggling to	5	4	3	2	1	(B)
read, it's usually because they are	5	4	3	2	1	(A)
having trouble decoding words.						
4. If adolescents are struggling to read	5	4	3	2	1	(B)
and write, it's usually too late to improve	5	4	3	2	1	(A)
significantly.						
5. If adolescents are struggling to read,	5	4	3	2	1	(B)
it's often because the kinds of reading	5	4	3	2	1	(A)
in secondary school differ from elementary.						
6. It's a good idea to teach adolescents	5	4	3	2	1	(B)
to persist in reading if they are bored.	5	4	3	2	1	(A)

Thoughts or questions about any of the above *before* reading:

Exhibit 5.2. Anticipation Guide for *Reading for Understanding* (*cont'd.*)

Thoughts or questions about any of the above *after* reading:

Check the following if you think they might be qualities of a proficient reader:

_____ Reads fast.

_____ Can read most anything with deep understanding.

_____ Often talks to others about what she or he is reading.

_____ Rarely gets confused while reading.

_____ Persists in reading even when bored.

_____ Never skims over parts.

_____ Clarifies ambiguity while reading.

_____ Creates a mental picture while reading.

_____ Asks questions while reading.

Check the following if you think they might be qualities of a proficient writer:

_____ Writes most things without revising.

_____ Rarely misspells words.

_____ Often asks someone else to read her/his work and make suggestions.

_____ Uses writing to "think."

_____ Writes letters more often than e-mails.

_____ Rarely gets frustrated while writing.

Thoughts or questions about any of the above *before* you read:

Thoughts or questions about any of the above *after* you read:

Reading for Understanding. In fact, Kate will say throughout the discussion or at the end: "OK, so when you read *Reading for Understanding*, see if you can get at what the authors are saying about this."

Throughout the reading of the book, the class revisits the anticipation guide, discussing how Schoenbach, Greenleaf, Cziko, and Hurwitz (1999) might answer the questions on the guide. This encourages a close look at the text. After the preservice teachers have finished the book, they examine the guide to see if any of their ideas have changed. They also talk about the use of an anticipation guide as a tool for guiding student reading and discussion. Eventually they create their own anticipation guides for use with a particular text, and they write about how they will use it not as a static "worksheet" but as a way to enrich students' interaction with reading.

Analysis of Diversity, Language, and Language Learning

One of Tomás Galguera's goals in preparing teachers to apprentice adolescent English learners into academic literacy is for them to become aware of the features of language in general, and specifically, academic English. Subtle differences in these features often define the status of those who use either oral or written or both forms of, in our case, academic English. Another of his goals is for preservice teachers to realize that, despite prevailing deficit views of English learners, all students come to classrooms with linguistic and cultural experiences and abilities. Reading Apprenticeship builds on these experiences and abilities. In addition, many preservice teachers have experiences in foreign language classrooms that influence how they conceive of teaching English learners. Therefore, it is important that they realize that a foreign language student experience differs dramatically from that of a second language student (Valdés, 2001).

With these goals in mind, Tomás relies on a number of assignments that require preservice teachers to notice and examine their

assumptions about student diversity, language, and language proficiency, and the relations between these assumptions and their
teaching in general but especially with students from multiple cultures and languages. Therefore the assignments we describe in this
section are different from the strategies we have discussed thus far.
Rather than examples of RA strategies intended to enhance preservice teachers' understanding of reading process and reading
instruction, which they can in turn use in their own classrooms,
Tomás's assignments included here are examples of pedagogy for
preservice and in-service teacher education and professional development.

Student Diversity Dimensions

In an effort to problematize conceptions of linguistic diversity
that most beginning teachers bring with them, Tomás uses a student diversity dimensions inquiry project to focus their attention
on students and on language as categories of teacher knowledge
(Exhibit 5.3 describes the assignment). In this project, credential
teacher candidates obtain demographic and background student
information from their student teacher placements at four concentric levels: a focal student and the student's classroom, school,
and school district. The information the assignment requires represents three variables that have been found to be powerful pre-
dictors of academic achievement among English learners:
academic English proficiency level, cultural and linguistic background, and schooling experience and academic proficiency
(August and Hakuta, 1997).

A cognitive apprenticeship approach in teaching assumes that
the "master" practitioners know their novices well enough to build
on the strengths and abilities they bring with them to the learning
situation. As such, teachers must balance their knowledge of students as members of cultural, linguistic, and other relevant demographic groups and as individuals. Specific to RA, Bernhardt (as
cited in Urquhart and Weir, 1998) identifies several variables that

Exhibit 5.3. Student Diversity Dimensions Assignment

For this assignment, you're to choose a student from whom you can learn something useful about teaching English learners. Keep in mind that, as I've mentioned in class, I want you to think of "English learners" in a broader sense than the categorical definition provided by the U.S. government for "Limited English Proficient" (LEP) students.[1] So, thinking about academic English as the language we are all learning, is there a student from whom you are likely to learn something about language learning that might inform your teaching?

After you decide on your focal student, use the following questions to guide your inquiry:

- What do you know about this student's schooling experience? How would you describe her or his academic strengths? What assets does she or he bring to class? Also, what aspect of academic development would she or he benefit most from realizing?

- What do you know about this student's oral (listening and speaking) and written (reading and writing) proficiency? Is she or he literate in a second language? Focus on the student's abilities rather than on her or his deficiencies.

---

1. Section 9101 of Title IX of *No Child Left Behind* defines "Limited English Proficient" as "an individual (A) who is aged 3 through 21; (B) who is enrolled or preparing to enroll in an elementary school or secondary school; (C)(i) who was not born in the United States or whose native language is a language other than English; (ii)(I) who is a Native American or Alaska Native, or a native resident of the outlying areas; and (II) who comes from an environment where a language other than English has had a significant impact on the individual's level of English language proficiency; or (iii) who is migratory, whose native language is a language other than English, and who comes from an environment where a language other than English is dominant; and (D) whose difficulties in speaking, reading, writing, or understanding the English language may be sufficient to deny the individual (i) the ability to meet the State's proficient level of achievement on State assessments described in section 1111(b)(3); (ii) the ability to successfully achieve in classrooms where the language of instruction is English; or (iii) the opportunity to participate fully in society."

Exhibit 5.3. Student Diversity Dimensions Assignment (cont'd.)

- How would you describe this student's home language and culture? If a native English speaker, how would you characterize the English variety she or he grew up speaking?
- What else would you like to learn about this student that would help you become a better teacher?

Compile this information in a brief narrative to share in class next time (print four copies). On the syllabus, I say that this report is to be one page long. Though this is by no means a strict requirement, *I do expect you to be succinct in describing your focal student based on the questions above.*

In addition to this narrative, I want you to share with your colleagues the following information about (a) your classroom, (b) your school, and (c) your district:

- Overall academic level
- Apparent and reported percentage of English learners
- Apparent and reported ethnic-racial and linguistic diversity

You'll have to think of ways to assess and describe your classroom composition along these three dimensions of diversity—consult with your cooperating teacher. The information for the school and district is perhaps more readily available at the following Web sites:

> http://www.cde.ca.gov/ (click on Ed-Data or Data Quest under "Student & School Data")
>
> http://www.greatschools.net/modperl/go

You don't have to write a report on these data. However, be prepared to share it in small groups as well as including it in your final Language Proficiency Assessment report due March 4.

Finally, in deciding how to obtain the information for this

portion of the assignment, consider gathering data or samples of your focal student's work to analyze in class on the assigned date. Specifically, you'll need to bring data that will allow you to assess an aspect of oral (listening or speaking) *and* written (reading or writing) proficiency in academic English. Therefore, you may consider making a recording of your conversations with your focal student. (Make sure that she or he is OK with this first.)

are particularly relevant. These are (a) literacy level in first language (L1), (b) language and literacy acquisition experience, (c) relationship between L1 and L2 (second language), (d) relationship between L1 and L2 cultures, and (e) L1 and L2 scripts or writing systems. The focal student minicase that the preservice teachers write as part of this assignment includes these variables as well as additional information pertinent to the personal dimension in the RA framework. Clearly, teachers need to understand their students' past schooling experience to guide their development as literate individuals, especially when apprenticing English learners whose understanding of literacy and being literate may not agree with discipline-specific norms or be the same as those of beginning teachers.

This assignment also builds on the understanding that cognitive apprenticeship is based on and contributes to productive relationships between teachers and students. In developing such relationships, teachers of English learners must take into consideration cultural as well as linguistic factors. Students' oral proficiency in English limits their ability to communicate with native English-speaking peers and teachers, which further restricts their development in English (Valdés, 2001). It is for this reason that this assignment asks preservice teachers to pay attention to establishing a relationship with their focal students, rather than simply interviewing them. Reading Apprenticeship depends on teachers knowing their students well and cultivating productive relationships with them, *especially* students who, because of their culture or limited English proficiency, are likely to avoid them.

Through conversations—not interviews—Tomás's students learn about their focal students' linguistic (including English varieties) and cultural backgrounds, their oral and written academic English proficiency, and their literacy development, prior schooling experience, and current academic abilities. The credential teacher candidates must also obtain similar summary information about their focal students' classrooms, schools, and school districts. The sources of information for this second part of the student diversity dimensions assignment include the California Department of Education Web site (http://www.cde.ca.gov/), cooperating teachers, and their own students. In small groups, Tomás's preservice teachers share the information they gather and contrast their experiences gathering data for the project. At this time, they also complete an individual reflection in which they summarize their project findings and the implications these have for their future as (likely) teachers of English learners (see Exhibit 5.4).

Exhibit 5.4. English Learner Minicase and Concentric Layers of Information: Group Sharing and Discussion

---

30 minutes (10 minutes each, 4-person groups)

1. *In designated groups,* take turns (round-robin style) sharing the information that you collected about your focal student and your classroom, school, and school district according to the three dimensions of diversity we've discussed:

   English proficiency

   Schooling background and academic proficiency

   Language-ethnicity-cultural background

2. Comment on your focal student's literacy level in English and, if applicable, native language. What do you know about her or his past schooling experience? What do you know about her or his culture in relation to your classroom's culture?

---

3. Provide a context for your focal student and your classroom by describing demographic school and district data that you obtained online.

30 minutes

4. *After everyone shares the above, as a group* discuss the following questions:

> What did you learn from completing this assignment not only in terms of your focal student and other students in your classroom but also your school and school district?

> How does the information that you gathered in this assignment inform your approach to teaching language (oral and written) in your subject?

> What does this all mean for you as a future teacher?

15 minutes

5. In writing, summarize your findings for this project and the implications of these findings for your future as a teacher. Specifically, comment on what you learned about diverse students and yourself as their teacher.

After a few years of assigning the student diversity dimensions project, Tomás has noticed a tendency among his students to resist or even reject the categories that schools and districts use to classify students, arguing that this information reflects societal biases that are the very root of many education problems. Their commitment to equity and social justice is both inspiring and encouraging. Still, all teachers must come to understand that the categories exist and that there are real patterns of achievement, literacy level, and overall quality of educational experience associated with these categories. Tomás's students often express discomfort and rejection of racial, ethnic, and cultural labels. Some see this assignment as perpetrating the problem (prejudice and institutionalized racism) from which a great number of education-related problems arise. Realizing that much discomfort originates in uncertain feelings and beliefs about their own ethnicity and race, Tomás, Dave, and their Mills College colleagues now include multiple opportunities throughout their teacher education program for consideration, sharing, and discussion of their students' own ethnicity and race and possible connections between this and their decision to become teachers. As a frame for this discussion, Tomás relies on Fishman's (1989) conceptualization of ethnicity as made up of a sense of a genealogy and geographical and historical origin; associated beliefs, behaviors, and customs; and an awareness of and participation in one's ethnic ways.

In analyzing their findings and thoughts, Tomás's students frequently describe a tension between the need to know students while resisting potential stereotypes and prejudices or self-fulfilling prophesies that may be triggered by this information. The importance of achieving this balance was made clear by the contrast between the publicly available demographic school data and test scores on the CDE Web site and what students learned about their focal student. Despite their relative accessibility, district and school data lacked usefulness for most of our students and had little influence on their teaching. Consequently, they mistrusted it. In contrast, information they gathered about their classrooms and especially their focal students had greater significance and influence on their practice, despite the difficulties they experienced in assessing the literacy level in both. They noted differences between institutional, standardized measures and the likely subjectivity of their own assessments. In the following quote, recorded by Tomás, one of his students eloquently articulates her thoughts on this subject:

> The process of gathering information for this project reinforced the manner in which rhetoric proclaims the wonders and successes of multicultural, linguistic, racial, and other diversities, while reality and my own perceptions continue to reproduce great inequities in terms

of expectations and levels of performance. I think it is extremely valuable for teachers to collect and critically study information relating to the cultural and linguistic backgrounds of our students. However, I would not want to consider this information too closely until I have had a chance to assess and become familiar with my diverse learners' schooling and literacy on my own. Perhaps in this way I will merely continue to reproduce the inequalities I see, but I feel strongly that official school data and information tend to have at least as much bias and misleading connotations as does my own subjectivity.

Students also wrote about the difficulties they had in determining their own students' academic proficiency, and specifically, their reading ability. Tomás's preservice teachers typically resisted relying on test scores for this only to discover a dearth of assessment tools and means for English learners at most schools. They also found the tests and test scores used by the state and their schools focused almost exclusively on oral English proficiency (Valdés, 2001), which made literacy assessment particularly difficult. Despite Tomás's students' efforts to assess the literacy level of English learners on their own, with running records, miscue analysis, and similar means, most faced logistical obstacles and time constraints.

Preservice teachers who were able to gain access to their students' school records often expressed surprise about their students' classification as "limited English proficient." They often mentioned having noticed that these students had difficulties with written English, despite appearing to be fluent in English. Finally, Tomás's students often mentioned the enormity of the challenges associated with teaching such diverse students and their doubts about their ability to do so well. A few of them observed that, to succeed, they needed to examine their own assessment process, as in the following quote: "Examining students' linguistic, academic, and ethnic backgrounds requires an examination of oneself as a teacher to better support one's students. Without reflection on my own process of determining academic ability, setting expectations, supporting students' linguistic development, and understanding the diversity in my classroom, I am likely to reinforce inequity rather than work against it."

Academic Oral English Specimen

To foster a deeper understanding of language, and specifically, the academic variety of English they are expected to teach, Tomás asks his students to carry out an inquiry project in which they focus on the characteristics of academic oral English (AOE). For this, his preservice teachers record and transcribe, or at least write down, as close to verbatim, a student's utterance that exemplifies some aspects of AOE (Exhibit 5.5 describes the assignment). Language processing, in contrast with most other cognitive functions, has a modular quality akin to that of a "language organ" (Chomsky, 1959). Such modularity allows us to focus our attention on the content of the language rather than its surface features or even grammar. Yet this very modularity becomes an obstacle for teachers as they think about what aspects of language they ought to teach English learners. This is particularly true of oral language. Thus, in preparation for this project, preservice teachers read assigned materials to help them recognize, and subsequently, analyze their AOE samples at the sound, word, utterance, intonation, kinesics, cognitive, interactional, and sociocultural levels. This structured analysis is necessary for them first to recognize and begin to describe the characteristics of AOE, and eventually, incorporate language development into their teaching.

Tomás also uses video recordings of classroom interactions during class time to help his students practice recognizing and recording AOE specimens. At a designated date, the preservice teachers bring in their AOE samples to share and analyze in small groups. For this, they use a graphic organizer on which they describe the characteristics of their transcriptions according to accepted linguistic categories (see Exhibit 5.6). After this structured analysis, Tomás's students turn in a copy of their transcription and a written report with their analysis and reflections on the implications that this assignment has for their future as teachers.

Exhibit 5.5. Academic Oral Language Specimen

In preparation for our discussion about the characteristics of academic English, I want you to record and analyze sample student utterances that you believe are representative of this language variety. So, during the following days, keep your ears and eyes open and record (either in writing or with a tape recorder) at least one such sample of student speech. In two weeks, you'll share and analyze transcripts of your oral academic English samples during the first hour of class. Therefore, you'll need to bring to class the following:

1. Your transcription of student utterances that, in your opinion, are examples of discipline-specific academic oral English. Do your best to accurately and completely capture what the student said, including additional related utterances and gestures. I leave it up to you to choose the context. However, for the purpose of this exercise, it may be particularly useful to choose an instance of a student addressing either the teacher (you) or the entire class. Include in your transcript the words and utterances of the teacher (you) and/or other participants. This, by the way, doesn't have to be too long. You'll notice that there are natural breaks in normal classroom activities that often punctuate interactions, particularly between teachers and students. Use these to select what to transcribe—most classroom interactions aren't longer than three or four turns per participant. Please bring enough copies of your transcript to share in groups of three.

2. Additional notes about contextual information such as the student's and possible participants' tone of voice, cadence, volume, gestures, and body posture. Also, make sure to explain the events leading up to the situation in which you heard the utterances included in your transcription. You

**Exhibit 5.5. Academic Oral Language Specimen
(cont'd.)**

should also note any outcomes of the student's words that may help your colleagues to better understand the incident you are sharing.

In class, you will first share your transcripts and notes with two other people, then individually and later as a group you will analyze all three samples guided by a framework that I will give you, and finally you will have a discussion on the relevance of this work in the context of educating English language learners. At the end, I'll ask you to write a summative reflection on your group discussion in contrast with your own position, which will help you write your final report.

Your final report due the following week should include the following:

- A copy of your transcription and notes describing the interaction, the context, and other pertinent information.

- Your analysis of the transcript.

- A summary of your group discussion, contrasting it with your own views on oral academic English. I also want you to reflect on the implications that the outcomes from this assignment have on your future as a teacher.

In reading their work, it is evident that Tomás's students generally are aware that, as teachers, they are responsible for teaching academic English to students. They have a sense that part of their job will be to make sure that, if nothing else, they model language that is grammatical and correct. They believe that the use of slang in their classrooms should not be banned, but discouraged and corrected. Through this inquiry project and other awareness-building exercises, credential teacher candidates begin to realize the com-

Exhibit 5.6. Analysis of Transcriptions

Categories	Characteristics of Academic Oral English
Choices of words and utterances	
Volume, intonation, cadence	
Kinesics (body language)	
Turn-taking and interaction patterns	

plexities of language and its political dimensions. Ironically, their very proficiency in academic English is their main obstacle to becoming aware of the discourse that is valued in schools and society. As in the proverb, "Fish will be the last to discover water" (Bruner, 1996, p. 45), it takes time and effort for teachers to notice, describe, and label the language associated with the "culture of power" (Delpit, 1988, p. 282) in its various facets. Though few teachers would disagree that students ought to learn to use academic English, it is not clear for them what this entails. Thus, it is crucial for beginning teachers of English learners to understand the features and functions of academic English (Wong-Fillmore and Snow, 2002).

Most credential teacher candidates such as the ones Tomás and all of us work with are not sure to what extent teaching academic English, and particularly oral academic English, ought to be their responsibility. It is far easier for English teachers to see how they should be concerned with their students learning to use academic English, particularly in its written forms. However, teachers in other subject areas are often surprised and slightly bothered by the expectation to teach language skills to their students. Tomás's students find themselves caught in the dilemma of wanting to validate and value their students in all of their linguistic diversity, while also realizing that their students' futures depend greatly on their ability to learn concepts and skills valued by society, especially academic English. The following is an example of one of his student's writing that reflects some of these tensions:

> Teaching and assessment of academic English are tricky. Teachers should encourage multiple forms of communication in their classrooms. No language style should be deemed "incorrect." Confidence is vital to learning. Nothing is as essential to identity as language. When a teacher tells students that their native language is wrong, confidence can be shattered and learning can disappear. That said, to attain vast opportunities in American society such as it is, one must be able to communicate in academic English. So, teachers must walk an unclear line of celebrating all languages while ensuring their students become proficient in the language of power. . . . Teachers must convey to students that the language they speak at home is not deficient. However, if students want to be able to access the power structure of this society, and thereby exact change, they need to be able to speak this language to attain the respect of those in power.

Choosing Strategies Wisely

In the same sense that we caution preservice teachers to be thoughtful about using strategies, we encourage teacher educators to do the same. Preservice teachers are often looking for something to use tomorrow to help the students in their classes who struggle with subject area texts. Learning about a particular strategy, they are often anxious to try it out the next day before they have had a chance to think about how it connects to a theory of reading or whether it is appropriate to the genre of texts they use or the discipline they teach. Also important is the appropriateness of a strategy for students who are English learners.

Similarly, faculty who teach reading in the content areas courses can feel pressure to satisfy the demands of preservice teachers in their courses for strategies to fix adolescents' reading problems. It would be easy to build a preservice course around two or three strategies per session: introduce the teachers to the strategy, give them time to practice with each other in class, and turn them loose on their students the next day. We fear such an approach would leave new teachers thinking that nothing works to improve young people's reading. By encouraging our students to try new strategies each week without thought to the connection to subject matter content, consistency across time in a course, or reference to the demands of a text and the needs of particular readers, we would only be perpetuating a way of teaching that divorces learning to read from learning content and that assumes reading is a basic skill that can be transmitted with a single inoculation of some best practices.

We take a different approach in preparing middle and high school teachers. We appreciate the importance of equipping new teachers with a toolbelt of strategies for teaching reading. We see our responsibility extending beyond furnishing the strategies that make up the toolbelt, however. We believe these tools, including those presented in this chapter, need to be connected to a conceptual framework, in this case, Reading Apprenticeship, for them to make sense. Without theoretical understanding of the nature of reading, how can teachers, novice or veteran, make choices about which strategies to implement with their students? And teachers preparing to work with English learners need a conceptual framework that can support reading as language and offer appropriate strategies. We believe strategies need to be chosen carefully and embedded consistently in daily instruction. One-shot approaches to "fixing" the reading problems of students only lead to frustration among teachers and students alike. We see teachers as more than technicians who deliver various unconnected strategies from a workbook or binder of resources. Instead, we see them as thoughtful decision makers who need apprenticeship in choosing strategies that meet the needs of their students and the demands of texts.

References

Armbruster, B., and Anderson, T. *Content Area Textbooks*. Reading Education Report No. 23. Urbana: University of Illinois Center for the Study of Reading, 1981.

August, D., and Hakuta, K. *Improving Schooling for Language-Minority Children: A Research Agenda*. Washington, D.C.: National Academy Press, 1997.

Beers, K. *When Kids Can't Read: What Teachers Can Do*. Portsmouth, N.H.: Heinemann, 2003.

Bruner, J. *The Culture of Education*. Cambridge, Mass.: Harvard University Press, 1996.

California Department of Education. *Strategic Teaching and Learning: Standards-Based Instruction to Promote Content Literacy in Grades Four Through Twelve*. Sacramento: California Department of Education, 2000.

Chomsky, N. "Review of *Verbal Behavior* by B. F. Skinner." *Language*, 1959, 35(1), 26–58.

Delpit, L. D. "The Silenced Dialogue: Power and Pedagogy in Educating Other People's Children." *Harvard Educational Review*, 1988, 58(3), 280–298.

Feldkamp, S. (ed.). *Modern Biology*. Austin, Tex.: Holt, Rinehart and Winston, 2002.

Fishman, J. A. *Language and Ethnicity in Minority Sociolinguistic Perspective*. Philadelphia: Multilingual Matters, 1989.

Schoenbach, R., Greenleaf, C., Cziko, C., and Hurwitz, L. *Reading for Understanding: A Guide to Improving Reading in Middle and High School Classrooms*. San Francisco: Jossey-Bass, 1999.

Urquhart, A. H., and Weir, C. J. *Reading in a Second Language: Process, Product, and Practice*. Essex, U.K.: Addison Wesley Longman, 1998.

Valdés, G. *Learning and Not Learning English: Latino Students in American Schools*. New York: Teachers College Press, 2001.

Wong-Fillmore, L., and Snow, C. "What Teachers Need to Know About Language." In C. Temple Adger, C. E. Snow, and D. Christian (eds.), *What Teachers Need to Know About Language* (pp. 7–53). McHenry, Ill.: Delta Systems & Center for Applied Linguistics, 2002.

Chapter 6

Broadening the Curriculum with Alternative Texts

A Reading Apprenticeship approach to adolescent literacy focuses attention on *how* and *why* we read. Another aspect of academic literacy is *what* students read. Clearly, approaches to reading traditional academic works such as textbooks successfully can support students' academic success. Yet providing students with other types of texts is important too. The content area alternative text collections assignment asks preservice teachers to collect and explore the use of readings other than the textbook. As stated in *Reading for Understanding*, "Teachers should provide students with well-written, interesting, and varied texts in the academic disciplines so that students will be more able and likely to actually read and understand them" (Schoenbach, Greenleaf, Cziko, and Hurwitz, 1999, p. 10). With this assignment, then, preservice teachers begin to collect an array of readings that might spark student interest and foster fluent reading. These texts are also likely to help students see how classroom topics are relevant. In addition, they may provide alternative views to the positions espoused in the textbook. These and other purposes for using a variety of texts in a secondary classroom are discussed throughout the semester in an RA content area reading classroom. Exhibit 6.1 provides specific information on the assignment. Exhibit 6.2 provides the scoring rubric for the assignment.

Exhibit 6.1. Content Area Group Alternative Texts Collection

Goals

- To provide your students with multiple perspectives (particularly non-mainstream and English language learner perspectives) in their subject area reading

- To incorporate more connections to current events and the larger world into your content area teaching

- To develop an appreciation for, and to explore various reasons for, supplementing or replacing poorly written, outdated, or non-engaging texts to provide students with a livelier, more engaging reading experience

Procedures

Collect the following reading pieces that are (1) related to your teaching discipline, and (2) likely to be of high interest to adolescents. Listed are the minimums—if, in your search, you find other pieces you'd like include, you are welcome to include them. You must include:

- At least one reading from the perspective of a person from a non-white-European background

- At least one reading from the perspective of an English language learner or nonstandard English speaker

- At least one reading from the perspective of a woman

- At least one reading from the perspective of a person from an underrepresented cultural group (gay-lesbian-transgendered, physical or learning disability, and so on)

- Two magazine articles (from popular magazines for adults or teens) that relate to your discipline that might be interesting for students

- Two newspaper articles related to your discipline

- One nonfiction book related to your discipline

- One novel (preferably young adult fiction) related to your discipline
- One poem related to your discipline and/or music lyrics related to your discipline
- One comic book, cartoon, or visual related to your discipline
- One children's book
- One Web site

Note that the following are likely to be of high interest to students: main character is teen or young adult; action; humor; fantasy or sci-fi; social justice; someone "fighting the system"; non-mainstream ideas; controversy; text related to current events.

Product for Alternative Texts Collection

Reflection and analysis: Write a short (3-4 page) paper describing:

- What you collected and why you think the pieces will appeal to adolescents, including a description about which non-mainstream perspectives are included in your collection
- The ideas you have for engaging students with these works, as opposed to merely assigning them (think about strategies discussed in this class!!)
- What you learned putting together this collection

At the end of the paper, include a bibliography fully citing your texts.

- Content area group text collection: Make copies of the texts (or if book length, include a photocopy of the back cover or part of the book that includes a bit of a summary— such as on the inside cover flaps) for your content area group classmates by Session #12.

Exhibit 6.2. Alternative Texts Collection Paper Scoring Rubric

Name_____

1. Paper explains what you collected, why you think the pieces will appeal to adolescents, including a description about which non-mainstream perspectives are included in your collection.   /4

2. Paper explains the ideas you have for *engaging* students with these works, as opposed to merely assigning them (think about strategies discussed in this class).   /4

3. Paper describes what you learned putting together this collection.   /4

4. Bibliography is included, fully citing your texts.   /1

5. Paper is well-written and edited for errors.   /2

   /15

Our students draw from many genres and sources for the alternative text assignment. Here is a sampling of those that have been used:

- Articles from contemporary magazines (such as *Time*, *The Economist*, *Ms.*, *Scientific American*), as well as a variety of teen magazines
- Newspapers
- Primary source documents
- Web sites
- Coloring books (for example, *Zoology Coloring Book*)
- Children's books
- Young adult novels (that is, novels aimed at adolescents)
- Films

- TV shows
- Comic books
- Novels
- Short stories
- Biographies
- Autobiographies and memoirs
- Essays
- Poetry
- Song lyrics
- Speeches
- Cartoons
- Creative nonfiction
- Case studies

These readings connect to the discipline that the preservice teachers teach (or will teach) and may center around a particular unit, theme, or skill. Although some preservice teachers in Kate's classes choose a specific focus for the assignment (such as Mexican art for an art class, teenage historical figures for a history class, or team sports for a physical education class), most decide to collect an array of alternative texts that they might be able to use throughout a year of teaching. While collecting these texts, the preservice teachers are asked to consider what is likely to be of high interest to their students, such as a piece that focuses on a teenager or young adult. Other possible high-interest topics include action, humor, fantasy, controversy, and issues related to social justice and fairness. In addition, those who are currently teaching discuss the particular students they work with. Based on their discussions with and observations of the students—often enriched by the data they are collecting for their inquiry project—they gather texts with students' interests in mind. Of course, teachers cannot assume that any given text—no matter the subject and style—will appeal to all students. Therefore, part of this assignment is for the preservice teachers to reflect on how they might encourage active engagement with these texts, as opposed to merely assigning them.

A Central Tension:
Textbooks Versus Alternative Texts

This assignment sparks discussion of a central tension in the content area classroom: Should teachers teach students how to read disciplinary texts they are likely to find dry and boring? Or should teachers foster interest in their subject by providing students with texts that are more exciting to read? Often this discussion is infused with issues of equity. Some teachers point out that their students do not know how to "play the game of school"—how to persevere through dry academic texts, how to take notes during a "boring" lecture, how to take exams most effectively. Other preservice teachers say that what's most important is sparking student interest in the topic—that this excitement must come first, fueling a desire to learn. We view this dialogue as productive. And although we do not try to resolve it, we do try to highlight moments in the discussion when students propose both-and thinking versus either-or thinking: alternative texts can augment academic texts. In other words, reading multiple texts on one subject can help students see how various points of view enrich and counter one another. For instance, what may seem to be "objective" information in one text might be challenged in another. What's also important to note here is that how teachers will balance the use of textbooks with other texts is likely to be an issue they will explore throughout their professional lives.

This textbook versus alternative text tension can lead to taking a close look at textbooks. What's included? In what order? What's given the most attention? What's left out? As preservice teachers come to see that the textbook provides one perspective, we talk about how their students are more likely to gain a deeper understanding of a subject when reading about it from other perspectives. We also discuss how textbooks are written and how that can affect the content. Committee-written textbooks often adopt a middle-of-the-road stance, which can mean an absence of non-mainstream voices. Alternative texts can introduce these different voices to the classroom, providing a forum for an enriched view and for critical literacy. In addition, because of the lengthy writing and adoption process, textbooks can never be as timely as, say, a newspaper article or a Web site. Alternative texts can help students see the applicability and relevance of a subject. And as previously mentioned, the unique voices, timely topics, and varying genres of alternative texts are more likely to mean a pleasurable reading experience.

Alternative Texts: What and Why

An important part of this assignment is ongoing discussion: What are they finding as they collect? Why do they think a particular text is important? To whom do they think it might appeal, and why? Do they have a particular student or group of students in mind? Discussion of such questions helps us explore what alternative texts might include. This ongoing investigation is important because teachers of different disciplines and backgrounds may hit different roadblocks, or have varying resistances. These points of tension can be fruitful to explore. For example, in Kate's class, Ha, a P.E. teacher, said that she couldn't imagine having her students take time out from activity to read, even if the reading was "fun." During a class discussion she said, "Students love P.E. I don't want to turn them off by making them read." Ha's comment led to a series of students agreeing with her—that so much of school was about reading, writing, and sitting in a seat, and that physical education should be just about movement. Then Phil, a history teacher, said, "I have to disagree. I hated P.E. in school. I hated what was expected—competition, physical aggression. The gym was one of the most frightening places in school. I think it gave me a psychological block against sports. But now as an adult I love to mountain bike and hike. If there would have been some idea that 'physical education' was more than team sports and competition when I was in high school, I might have had a different feeling about P.E." A few students concurred. Then Aden, a science teacher, said she liked P.E. in high school, especially volleyball and weight lifting, but was a reluctant reader. She wondered if having access to texts that explored her interest in these sports might have turned her on to reading.

Phil's and Aden's comments led the class to discussing how P.E. teachers might consider posting articles in the locker room about sports, and health and fitness issues, that might appeal to students. Josephine, another P.E. teacher in the class, mentioned how she brought books to her students—such as one about American bicyclist Lance Armstrong and another about the formation of the Women's National Basketball Association. She talked about how she herself enjoyed these books and shared them with students, making them available for students to borrow. Eventually, she asked students to choose one sports or health topic, or one athlete, to read about and to share their interests with the class.

Brian, a science teacher, said he understood Ha's dilemma but had come to believe that reading was important in science. "I wanted science to be totally hands-on," he said, "but I will not have enough class time to cover the wealth and breadth of the subject without having my students read." Although some students in the class, representing a variety of disciplines, continued to insist that reading should not be part of P.E., it became clear that for others in class, their conceptions of literacy in the classroom were broadening. In addition, such a discussion capitalizes on the multiple disciplines and personalities in the room: several assumptions were challenged, such as "Everyone loves P.E." (all classrooms will have students with negative dispositions on the subject); "No one would ever want to read for P.E." (some students might enjoy access to readings on P.E. topics, and—based on the teacher's objectives and students' needs—reading is likely to enrich learning); and "Reading always means sitting down with a book" (a print-rich environment—such as articles and posters on the walls, or short book talks from a growing classroom lending library—can contribute to literacy).

Although the class will sometimes develop a consensus on this topic, the discussion is rarely finished in class. As the students continue to work on this assignment—weighing it against their personal experiences and those in their student teaching placements—they continue to raise new concerns. And teachers in traditionally nonreading classrooms are not the only ones to voice such concerns. English and history teachers tend to feel overwhelmed because, as one preservice teacher said, "I could use everything in print for an English class!" It may be helpful to prompt these students to collect alternative texts related to one unit. For example, Georgia was preparing to teach *To Kill a Mockingbird* in her tenth-grade English class, so she decided to collect alternative texts that would enhance the reading of that novel. She collected primary source documents, such as newspaper articles, from the novel's historical era. She also collected poems, songs, and short stories that addressed themes the novel addresses.

Transforming Curriculum, Transforming Conceptions of the Discipline

Other students who were currently teaching decided to look at their curriculum to examine what it needed. Lilith realized that much of her art curriculum focused on white male artists. As she began to explore art magazines for alternatives, she said, "I was surprised to see that in [these] magazines, most demonstrated artworks were created predominantly by men. It took me several of these magazine issues to find a couple of articles written by women artists." She included one of these articles about watercolor landscape paintings in her collection. "I browsed through at least five or six art magazines to find one black artist's article," she noted. "I was surprised that it was not easy. I am about to write to these magazine editors, suggesting they include more artists from diverse backgrounds." Tom, a business teacher, realized that his curriculum mostly portrayed business owners and entrepreneurs as older white males. Perusing the newspaper, he found an article about an immigrant from Jamaica who, at age twenty-one, started her own film production company. In a magazine, he located an article about three college-age women and a man who started a retail clothing store. And online he found an article about Napster's youthful cofounder Sean

Parker. "I think it's important for my students to see that business can include them, that it's not just about corporations run by guys in suits," he said.

Similarly, Caroline, a French teacher, was concerned that her curriculum enforced certain images of French speakers: that they all live in France and are white. She collected readings depicting French-speaking people from all over the world, as well as nonwhite populations in France. One of her pieces was lyrics to a song by the famous black French rap artist MC Solaar, which she felt "promises to pique the interest of teens since the rap genre has a . . . hip image. Additionally, the subject of the song . . . is a girl dealing with body-image issues. . . . [My] students often have a very stereotypical view of French culture as being almost completely white, yet there are many people of African descent who live there and contribute their non-European cultural heritage to French society."

As reflected in her use of French song lyrics, another issue Caroline wanted to tackle was her reliance on the textbook. She wanted students to have more interaction with authentic French texts, or realia, so she included in her collection bus schedules, recipes, menus, and newspaper articles in French. "My hope," she wrote, "is that these alternative texts will bring French alive for students and motivate them to be active and engaged learners in my class."

At times, the searching itself sparked teachers' ideas for curriculum development. Leticia, a social science teacher, came across an article in the magazine *Marie Claire* about leg lengthening, a surgical procedure some women in China are undergoing to gain height. This led her to think about her unit on dynastic China, and how she could tie in the *Marie Claire* article to readings about foot binding. She didn't stop there, though. She realized that there were connections to be made under the broader question: "Why do people or societies think certain things are 'beautiful?'" She decided that a good way to start to explore this question would be to have students examine images from contemporary American magazines for current images of beauty and compare them to images from previous eras.

In addition to discovering new curricular paths, some students use the assignment to analyze some of their own teaching practices, or the practices of other teachers they know. Trish, who had no teaching experience but had done some classroom observations, wrote about a middle school math teacher who places a math "quote of the day" on the board each Monday. Students copy it into their math journals along with the homework assignments for the week, and then engage in a brief discussion about what the author meant by the quotation. Trish wrote, "An example might be Aristotle's quote: 'The mathematical sciences particularly exhibit order, symmetry, and limitation, and these are the greatest forms of the beautiful.' The discussion usually brings up the meanings of difficult words from mathematics and other areas, such as 'symmetry' and 'exhibit.'" Building on this teacher's idea, Trish also thought she might like to share a math poem every week or two with her students. She found numerous examples online that, as she put it, blended "knowledge with humor." For example:

> A mathematician
> Confided
> That a Mobius band
> Is one-sided.
> And you'll get quite
> A laugh
> If you cut it in half,
> For it stays in one
> Piece when divided.

Trish liked the idea of using humor to present math ideas. One book she found, *Fractals, Googols, and Other Mathematical Tales*, by Theoni Pappas, highlights mathematical concepts through the use of stories told from the perspective of Pappas's cat. In addition, Trish thought that newspaper articles that require mathematical knowledge in order to be read accurately were excellent resources for the math classroom. For instance, she found an array of articles in one issue of the newspaper that used statistics, graphs, and means versus medians. "This is such an easy way for students to see that they need math in their everyday lives," she said. She thought that after she brought some articles in for the class to discuss, she would like to invite students to bring some in, too. "Can you imagine a student reading the newspaper as part of her math homework?" wrote Trish.

Unlike Trish, Juana had a lot of teaching experience and drew directly on her knowledge of her high school art students in this assignment: "My students respond strongly to stories of hardship, injustice, good overcoming bad, and stories of other cultures. I chose books with art content that include various perspectives. One is about a Down's syndrome child, another is an anthology of gay and lesbian youth experiences. I've also included readings that deal with the slavery experience and Latino culture. These books are very different, but they have the common thread of showing how art can be used to express important and emotional events in our lives."

She felt that themes of "oppression and hope" would "help students understand that art is not just an activity to wile away the hours, but that art can also be used as a tool to . . . express one's views and opinions, and to [work toward] actively creating change." In addition, Juana received new information about her art students from her literacy inquiry project that she tied in to this assignment. In a survey of students at her school, she found that "24 percent of the students responded that they had never read a book about art, and 48 percent had never done Internet research [about art]. The response to writing about art, however, showed that only 8 percent had not written about art. It appears, then, that journal writing is a common practice among art teachers, while providing opportunities for students to read is not." Juana felt that this information gave her even more impetus to use reading in her art classroom.

Anthony, an economics teacher, also drew on his experiences with his students when compiling his collection. He shared that the Public Information Department of the Federal Reserve Bank of New York publishes eight separate comic books on economics, such as the story of inflation, banks, and monetary policy. "My students tell me that the illustrations and simple dialogue presentation of the information provides them with an understanding of the material. It speaks to them in a voice they are more accustomed to hearing." He said that he and his students discussed the different approaches to information about economics provided by the comics, the text-book, and a television news program.

Sharing the Experience and the Product

For some preservice teachers, collecting alternative texts opened up their sense of what their classroom could look like. In fact, the very collecting itself felt rather subversive for Greg, an English teacher, who said this:

> For weeks I prowled the local newspapers and national magazines that we subscribe to at our house, hunting down stories that would interest teenagers. It was fun for me because I found it liberating. In my English classes, the department gives us a bit of leeway in what we assign kids to read, but the major texts—*Lord of the Flies*, *To Kill a Mockingbird*, *A Separate Peace*—are prescribed. . . . These are the same books I read in high school twenty-five years ago. So, I found it somewhat thrilling—and maybe even a little rebellious—to pick texts that might serve a different function.

Other teachers talked about how they now see possible teaching material everywhere. "It's hard for me to read the newspaper now without cutting out something I think my students might like," said Stacy, a history teacher.

The culmination of this assignment is for the preservice teachers to photocopy all the materials they can for their content area peers in the classroom. That means grouping together the students by discipline. If someone in the class is the only one from her or his discipline (for instance, Kate sometimes has just one teacher in business, art, or music), that person can decide which group she or he might like to join. In their groups, the students pass out copies of articles, song lyrics, book chapters, and so on. If there is something they could not make a copy of—such as a poster or a whole book—they bring it to share, along with the citation. During the sharing, students explore new ideas for other materials and their uses, often drawing on ideas developed throughout the course. For example, they are likely to address how they might have students look at the title of a piece and generate ideas about what they expect the piece will be about—and how they will foster prediction throughout the reading. They might draw students' attention to the format of a piece to build text knowledge—for example, how does a newspaper article's introduction help prepare the reader for the rest of the article? Any teaching strategy (such as an anticipation guide or reading circles) or cognitive strategy (such as encouraging visualization or questioning) that seems appropriate for a given reading might be addressed in this session. As a result, students leave the session with a binder full of ideas and materials they may be able to use in their own classrooms. Students sometimes say they wish there was even more time to talk about these materials. Many recognize the wealth of ideas and information they have received from their colleagues. "Everybody seemed to tap different resources," said Reika, a math teacher, "which made the sharing even more fulfilling."

A Wide Range of Possibilities

A key component of Reading Apprenticeship is extensive reading, which helps to build content knowledge, foster reader identity, and strengthen reading fluency and stamina. This assignment helps new teachers to see that reading in the classroom can have a wide range of possibilities. Sometimes, though, the idea of possibilities can be overwhelming for new teachers, whose lives are pressed for time. This assignment sends them out with a starter binder of concrete examples of what to use, and suggestions for how to use them. This way, they won't have to reinvent the wheel in order to introduce more varied texts into their classrooms.

Reference

Schoenbach, R., Greenleaf, C., Cziko, C., and Hurwitz, L. *Reading for Understanding: A Guide to Improving Reading in Middle and High School Classrooms*. San Francisco: Jossey-Bass, 1999.

Chapter 7

Supporting English Learners with Reading Apprenticeship

But we all figure out at some point what to pay attention to when reading, no? I remember that when I was like in fifth grade, I realized that if I remembered the headings in textbooks, I could pretty much remember everything I read. It's like when I took French in college. At first I was having a hard time reading the textbook, but then my teacher gave me these kids' books in French, and those I could read because they didn't have hard words. I can see how we need to help kids with some vocabulary words before they read a chapter, so that they can understand what they read—as long as they speak enough English and have some reading skills. In any case, that's just good teaching, isn't it?

This quotation from a preservice teacher, a teacher credential candidate in one of our courses, raises important questions for us as we prepare teachers to teach reading to increasing numbers of English learners. First, what are teachers' beliefs and biases about English learners, language acquisition, and the teaching of reading in a second language? And how do these beliefs and biases relate to their teaching practice? Second, are teachers aware of processes and functions related to language use and acquisition? Do they understand the social and political implications associated with these processes? Third, do teachers understand the process of reading and learning to read in a second language and how this relates to reading and learning to read in one's native language? Finally, what beliefs, dispositions, and biases inform teachers' vision of teaching practice and to what extent is this vision inclusive of and sensitive to students' linguistic and cultural diversity? Our task as teacher educators is further complicated by policies and structures that, at best, seem unresponsive to the rich linguistic and cultural student diversity, and at worst, define such diversity as deficits. In this chapter, we describe approaches we have used to prepare beginning secondary teachers of English learners to teach reading.

If teachers believe that teaching reading is someone else's job, they believe that they are even less responsible for teaching English learners. This belief does not reflect reality. The most current figures cite 1.6 million limited English proficient (LEP) students in California (California Department of Education [CDE], 2003) classrooms and an estimated 4.4 million nationwide in 1999–2000 (National Center for Education Statistics [NCES], 2001), numbers that are likely to increase. Schools with English learners are not exclusive to California. For instance, between 1997 and 2000, Guam (162 percent), South Carolina (82 percent), and Minnesota (67 percent) reported the greatest increases in LEP student enrollment (Kindler, 2002), yet only 68 percent of LEP students nationwide were reported as receiving language development services (NCES, 2001). Clearly, the teaching of reading to English learners can no longer be the exclusive concern of a sector of teachers and teacher educators. This is especially true if, as we argue, we move away from outdated and inadequate categorical definitions of English learners to include native speakers of marginalized varieties of English.

Using a Reading Apprenticeship framework, we have striven to help beginning teachers of English learners gain awareness of the multiple forms and functions of language and the relationship of these to teaching reading. Thus, we expect beginning teachers to teach in a variety of situations, including mainstream courses with

English learners whose test scores and overall academic performance have allowed them to be "redesignated" as "fluent English proficient" (FEP)[1] students. In the same classrooms, they must also be ready to teach native speakers of English varieties who are not sufficiently proficient in academic English. At the other extreme, our students must also be able to teach beginning to intermediate English to recent immigrant students with low English proficiency levels in English as a Second Language (ESL) or English Language Development (ELD) courses. Most likely, however, and a much more challenging scenario facing the preservice teachers we teach is that of teaching in content ESL-ELD courses in which the teacher's task is to teach English through subject-specific content (for example, math-ESL). Similarly, they are expected to be able to teach in Specially Designed Academic Instruction in English (SDAIE) or "sheltered" courses, for which they are to make content accessible while simultaneously maximizing language development opportunities. In almost all cases, however, the levels of English and academic proficiency as well as the linguistic and cultural backgrounds of the students in these classrooms are highly diverse, a fact that would complicate the task of any teacher, but especially a beginning teacher.

A parallel goal of ours is for credential teacher candidates to appreciate the diverse experiences and expertise that language minority students bring with them to the classroom and understand the complexities that learning to read in a second language entails. In this chapter, we begin by questioning the nature and implications of categorical views of English learners and their teachers.

---

1.   The label "fluent English proficient" (FEP) is often used to redesignate students who came into the school system as LEP and have demonstrated "native-like fluency" on an English language test. However, the term *fluent* is not an appropriate description of language proficiency. Fluency implies relative ease in comprehension and production. As with reading, fluency is necessary but not sufficient to become a proficient language user.

Building on the Reading Apprenticeship framework, we argue that the preparation of teachers for English learners must include abundant, purposeful, and structured opportunities to develop critical language and cultural awareness. We then describe what we have learned from Tomás's use of the student diversity dimensions and academic oral English specimen exercises described in Chapter Five, as evident from analyzing his students' language development plans. We close by reminding readers of the importance of inquiry as a driving force in teacher preparation for English learners and arguing for a focus on language and culture through the lens of Reading Apprenticeship.

Categorical Definitions of English Learners

Thus far we have used the labels *LEP* and *English learners* to describe students whose language background is other than English. However, the definition of *limited English proficient* is problematic for us in at least two ways. First, rather than focusing attention on linguistic diversity as a national resource well worth preserving and enhancing, the term emphasizes the students' linguistic limitations. We are not alone in criticizing this term, and other authors have written eloquently on this subject (Nieto, 1999). A deficit definition of diversity has also been used to support remedial reading programs, which often are used with English learners. A second problem in using LEP to designate linguistically diverse students arises from its implicit dichotomous or categorical view of language diversity. If we were to adopt this classification scheme, you would think that students either are or are not LEP. The truth is that English learners are highly diverse not only in English proficiency levels but also in student characteristics such as particular linguistic and cultural background, national origin, schooling experience, and individual traits, among others. It is not at all unusual for teachers, especially those teaching in school districts in which the presence of English learners is recent, to teach students whose English proficiency ranges from early-beginning to advanced, whose schooling experiences are widely different, and whose linguistic, cultural, and socioeconomic status and nationality represent multiple groups, including a majority of U.S.-born students.

Another way in which categorical labels and designations of language minority students are problematic is the tendency among educators and policymakers to assume that the differences between LEP and non-LEP students are greater than differences among students inside each category. We know from research that important similarities exist in the achievement patterns of nonnative and native English learners, especially when the latter are speakers of varieties of English that are not deemed standard. This is especially true when one focuses on reading and relies on narrow assessments of literacy. We also know from research that a Reading Apprenticeship approach is effective in classrooms with students who are native speakers of either an English dialect (Ebonics, for example) or a language other than English (Greenleaf, Schoenbach, Cziko, and Mueller, 2001).

There are both political and conceptual reasons for categorical definitions of language minority students. Yet in order to begin to understand what it means to teach linguistically and culturally diverse students as well as prepare teachers for them, we must analyze and question the assumptions behind the categories, and ultimately, deconstruct them. Furthermore, in the spirit of cognitive apprenticeship, we must also guide preservice teachers in a similar exploration not only of the ways in which students are defined and classified but also of the ways, values, and norms associated with academic behavior, and specifically, reading in the various subject disciplines. In short, preparing teachers of English learners to teach using a cognitive apprenticeship model requires that we help them appreciate and balance individual student characteristics with patterns associated with culture, language, ethnicity, gender, and class, among other variables. For this, we rely primarily on inquiry projects that ask credential teacher candidates to look at individual students and district and school records as well as at general language features and specific language features associated with various disciplines.

Most of our students come to teaching from diverse professional and personal contexts, having been successful academically, professionally, or both. They also share a concern for social justice and equity, which often led them to choose teaching as a profession in the first place. Though their interest in becoming teachers who will make a difference is inspirational and energizing, it can also work as an obstacle to their learning about their own students in all their complexity. Our students often comment on their commitment not to allow labels and prejudices to affect how they perceive their current and future students. Perhaps naïvely, many of them insist that they do not want to think of students in terms of race or ethnicity, language group or English proficiency, and academic ability; they want to see them only as individuals. Although an unbiased stance is precisely what is necessary to apprentice students into the academic realm of schools, teachers' perceptions of students are in fact influenced by the very constructs and categories they claim to reject. At the very least, beginning teachers must contend with policies, policymakers, schools, and researchers who use these constructs and categories to discuss public education and especially the achievement and attainment levels of English learners.

Recent developments in federal and state educational policies for English learners seem to stem from a similar concern not to discriminate against students based on linguistic diversity. The passage of the 2001 No Child Left Behind Act (NCLB) marked a clear departure from categorical approaches to meeting the needs of students at the federal level. Rather than devoting separate sections for foreign language instruction, migrant education, and programs for language minority students as in previous versions of the federal law, NCLB now combines all these programs into a single section: Title III. The rationale behind such a move, as well as the emphasis of English-only instruction over native-language instruction, suggest a concern for the integration of language minority students into mainstream classrooms. Title III also requires states to establish language content and student performance standards; this could result in much-needed coherence and continuity in the schooling experience of English learners. Yet Title III includes no provisions for the preparation of teachers of English learners, a feature of past ESEA authorizations.

In California, similar policy trends have emerged, most notably with the passage of Proposition 227, the popular voters' initiative that effectively ended most bilingual education programs. Among the "findings and declarations" under Article 1 of the initiative, one finds "high dropout rates and low English literacy levels" as evidence of the failure of "costly experimental language programs" (that is, bilingual education) for English learners (Unz and Tuchman, 1998). More recently, California passed legislation that eliminates what was once known as the Cross-cultural, Language, and Academic Development (CLAD) emphasis for both single and multiple subjects teaching credentials. The CLAD emphasis, which was considered by many to be visionary in its efforts to define the competencies required to teach content in English to language minority students, and which almost every preservice teacher education program in the state offered, created a category for content and instruction in preservice (and in-service) teacher preparation and professional development. Although, as we have argued, categorical views of teaching and students do not reflect reality, they can be helpful as a first step, especially with issues related to culture and language. These, by their very nature, require a concerted effort and attention for which artificial designations and categories, such as "CLAD" and "English learner" can be useful. Time will tell whether legislative efforts to mainstream English learners and teaching approaches associated with them will in fact normalize the inclusion of language and culture concerns in teacher preparation or whether this will result in less attention devoted to the preparation of teachers for English learners.

Language and Cultural Awareness in Learning to Teach

The very nature of language and language use works against our efforts to foster critical language awareness among beginning teachers. The English language, far from monolithic, is in fact made up of several "Englishes" (Byalistok and Hakuta, 1994) or a conglomerate of related varieties, including those most closely compatible with current language arts and reading standards. "Academic English" and "standard English" are terms typically used to describe the language most teachers hope their students become proficient in. However sensible this may seem, the task confronting teachers is quite daunting in its magnitude and complexity. First, the English Language Development standards for California public schools (California Department of Education, 2002) are but performance indicators that fail to capture both surface features and deep grammar rules of academic English. Furthermore, proficiency in academic English does not automatically translate into an ability to describe it, much less teach it. In fact, being able to understand the particular characteristics of the variety of English they want their students to become proficient in requires a deliberate effort on the part of teachers (and teacher educators). Much like fish in water, most teachers "swim" in academic English, often noticing the nonacademic language students produce, but not their own language.

Most teachers believe they model correct English usage for their students and a few go so far as to correct their students for using "wrong" or inappropriate language. However, few teachers are capable of describing the pragmatic, semantic, morphological, phonological, kinesthetic, and discourse features of academic English, let alone teach it explicitly. At best, teachers are familiar with grammar rules they learned as students and may teach these to their students, although research has shown that increasing numbers of teachers are reluctant to do so. (See Hudson, 1999, for a summary and discussion of possible reasons.) In addition to its features, most teachers lack an understanding of the functions of academic English (for example, arguing, analyzing, describing, requesting, and so on) despite their likely ability to perform such functions.

Wong-Fillmore and Snow (2002) have issued a list of recommendations for ways to address this serious problem in teachers, especially teachers of English learners. These recommendations include several linguistics courses, which, ideally, ought to be part of the preparation of every teacher. The goal is to enhance teachers' understanding of language and language learning as content knowledge, which in turn influences pedagogical content knowledge (Shulman, 1987). In other words, in order for teachers to teach English learners as well as possible, they must not only understand language and how one learns it but also learn to teach in ways that are informed by this knowledge. However, the reality we face as teacher educators is one of increasing credentialing requirements, which make it even less likely to follow Wong-Fillmore and Snow's recommendations. Our challenge in preparing teachers of English learners in general, but especially those apprenticing their students as readers in the various subject disciplines, consists of finding ways to develop language awareness (van Lier, 1995) that will allow them to become better teachers of English learners—all in the equivalent of one semester-long course.

Teaching Process Awareness

The Reading Apprenticeship framework provides us with ways to think about teachers as expert readers who apprentice students into discipline-specific literate communities. However, when we think about preparing teachers to apprentice English learners, we must take into consideration that most of them lack experience as expert readers in a second language. In keeping with cognitive apprenticeship principles, Tomás has developed a number of second language learner process awareness exercises. In Chapter Five we described the student diversity dimensions and academic oral English specimen exercises as examples. In addition to providing students with necessary experiences and points of departure for discussion of practical and theoretical aspects of teaching English learners, these exercises also provide us with valuable data to inform our practice as teacher educators.

Tomás uses a language instruction heuristic derived from a chapter in which Prator (1991) discusses the essential components of language instruction methods and the various philosophies and trends that have influenced language instruction over time. Prator stresses the importance of three interrelated components of teaching: knowledge of the students, knowledge of language as a subject, and instructional goals and objectives. This heuristic provides Tomás's students with categories of inquiry for the course projects and for their own teaching (see Figure 7.1).

Prator uses the metaphor of a tripod to describe the influence of all three components on one another as teachers plan and make decisions about curriculum and pedagogy. What language teachers know about their students as individuals and as language learners has a bearing on what they see as relevant in language and language learning. Conversely, teachers' understanding of and expertise in the target language play a role in their perception of students as language learners. An appreciation of students and an assessment of their linguistic proficiency in turn influences teachers' decisions about goals and objectives they strive to teach in any given lesson. Their goals and objectives similarly influence their perception and assessment of students—if in no other way, then as relative proximity to student outcomes defined by such goals and objectives. Finally, a reciprocal relationship also exists between goals and objectives and teachers' understanding of language as a subject. The ability of teachers to define clear language learning goals and objectives depends greatly on their understanding of the target language (that is, academic English) both generally and specifically. Having to define clear goals and objectives furthers their understanding of the target language.

Tomás organizes his course to reflect Prator's three categories of teacher knowledge. In addition, he emphasizes an experiential approach in order to foster the critical awareness toward language and culture necessary in teachers of English learners. This experiential approach constitutes an extension of the reading process awareness required for reading apprenticeship into learning and teaching processes. Korthagen and Kessels (1999), in their analysis of preservice teacher education, recommend such an approach

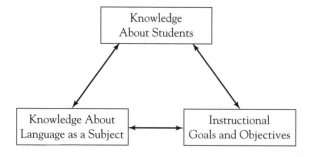

Figure 7.1. Language Instruction Heuristic

as a way to integrate theoretical and practical knowledge with teaching practice in beginning teachers. Rather than teaching preservice teachers theory and models intended to inform and shape their practice, Korthagen and Kessels stress the importance of their becoming aware of and analyzing their feelings and reactions toward specific teaching situations, considering possible practical conclusions from these, and making connections with pertinent theories, in this order. Tomás also relies on this model of teacher knowledge and practice for data collection and analysis, as the prompts on the task analysis handout demonstrate (see Figure 7.2).

Reading Apprenticeship Dimensions and English Learners

The dimensions of classroom life that support a reading apprenticeship constitute the overarching conceptual framework that guides the Reading Apprenticeship approach in preparing future teachers of English learners. The social, personal, cognitive, and knowledge-building dimensions as well as the metacognitive conversation behind adolescent reading development gain new meaning when examined from the perspective of a teacher of English learners. Thus, the ability to engage in a metacognitive conversation in the classroom presupposes not only a minimum oral proficiency level among

Figure 7.2. Task Analysis

Task name and description	"Gut feelings," reactions, first impressions	Advantages, useful practical tools	Potential problems, things to watch out for	Related concepts, pertinent theories, models	Specific and concrete possible future uses

students but also a classroom culture in which such a conversation is possible. Apprentice readers need to feel safe that the form and content of their contributions to such conversation will be valued and not simply marked off for their errors. Furthermore, classroom conversations are usually governed by rules and norms that are not necessarily apparent to students whose culture and language are different from those favored in most public school classrooms. Therefore, teachers must be able to understand and appreciate these differences and create inclusive norms and practices so that metacognitive conversations can take place. It is for this reason that we want credential teacher candidates to learn about their students' culture and language as well as the characteristics of academic English.

The need to pay attention to cultural and linguistic norms of interaction overlaps the social dimension, particularly regarding the connections between oral and written language and classroom status. We all learn language through interactions, which is why this dimension gains significance for English learners. Although safely learning about literacy practices in and out of the classroom, their relationship to power, and how and what one reads ought to occupy teachers' minds, teachers of English learners must also think about the linguistic and cultural implications behind all this.

Similarly, teachers must consider subtle yet crucial cultural and linguistic factors when thinking of the personal dimension. The very notion of a reader identity may pose difficult challenges to students who originate in communities with high illiteracy rates and lack culturally congruent role models. Similarly, students from backgrounds in which texts are predominantly religious may have a difficult time developing a reader identity that on the one hand agrees with our bias in favor of a reader as someone who "talks to the text," and on the other hand respects their sacred association with text.

As far as the cognitive dimension is concerned, the cultural and linguistic biases of English learners are also likely to influence the strategies and skills they bring to texts. These biases tend to be influenced by the structure of the text, vocabulary, and textual markers, as well as differences in the role of texts in various cultures, which we already mentioned.

Finally, culture and language also influence the manner in which knowledge is built and organized. This is particularly true for English learners with schooling experiences outside of the United States. For them, the textbooks not only are organized in subtly different ways from those they grew accustomed to in their native countries' schools but also convey different practice and values associated with reading in the content areas, as well as different word meanings and connotations. English learners with a strong academic foundation may recognize familiar content. This simplifies the learning process for these students, but it makes it even more imperative for teachers to assess and appreciate the background of all their students.

The issues we raise regarding the conceptual framework behind Reading Apprenticeship should not be taken as insuperable obstacles to literacy development among adolescent English learners. Quite the contrary, in considering the metacognitive conversation and the four dimensions of classroom life we have adopted to guide our work in preparing credential teacher candidates, we have gained an awareness of important aspects of our task in relation to the preparation of teachers for English learners. What follows is a summary of what we have learned from our efforts to help beginning teachers think about teaching reading with English learners in mind.

Findings from Language Development Plan Analysis

Most credential teacher candidates have had varying levels of experience in curriculum development and teaching. Few, however, have had much experience preparing and teaching language development curricula. Furthermore, to the extent that they might have been students in a foreign language course (a requirement for

CLAD credential emphasis), their "apprenticeship of observation" (Lortie, 1975) is likely to suggest approaches to teaching that are not necessarily appropriate for English learners in most public school classrooms. Examples include asking students to repeat aloud conversational utterances or decontextualized sentences, reading aloud scripted dialogues, memorizing grammar rules and vocabulary lists, and filling out grammar worksheets.

As we discuss in Chapter Five, one of the functions of the curriculum or lesson plan for credential teacher candidates is to provide us with information to assess their understanding of teaching and learning and how this relates to their practice. Another function is to provide a link between their university courses and their student teaching practice. For beginning teachers of English learners, curriculum plans allow us to focus their attention on the linguistic requirements of lessons and the opportunities for language development in them. Therefore, Tomás asks credential teacher candidates to evaluate the oral and written academic English proficiency levels required to complete the plans' tasks successfully. He then asks students to modify their plans to incorporate oral and written language use strategies that are appropriate for academic settings.

Although Tomás's students are familiar with the idea of weaving through their lessons opportunities to develop a strategy explicitly, they often lack the language awareness necessary to notice the strategies they use in school as native English users. This is particularly true of listening and speaking strategies. To help them think of oral and written language strategies needed to succeed in middle and high school classrooms, Tomás relies on three sources: *Reading for Understanding* (Schoenbach, Greenleaf, Cziko, and Hurwitz, 1999), "What Teachers Need to Know About Language" (Wong-Fillmore and Snow, 2002), and the California Department of Education's English Language Development (ELD) standards (http://www.cde.ca.gov/standards/).

To help his students rethink their lessons with language development in mind, Tomás asks them to bring to class examples of curriculum that they have taught. One requirement is for the curriculum to have at least the potential for developing language in one or more of its skill areas (listening, speaking, reading, and writing). Also, to provide them with specific images of the skills associated with academic use in the classroom, Tomás asks his students to familiarize themselves with the ELD standards. In groups of three, they work together to locate the curricula they taught within the language abilities the standards describe, identifying language strategies that these represent. The groups are designed to include at least one student who is currently a student teacher in a classroom with English learners and at least one student from each subject group (English–social studies and math-science). The contrast of curricula from different subject areas helps credential teacher candidates notice particular language strategies associated with each subject. A discussion of the strategies that their lessons assumed in students helps Tomás's students to insights such as that when "talking math" one often resorts to formulas, diagrams, and other graphic representations. Another example is a discussion that science and social studies teacher candidates had about hypotheses and language conventions associated with them.

Together, the credential teacher candidates in Tomás's courses help each other come up with appropriate language strategies to teach explicitly, including them in their otherwise "regular" plans. These strategies must reflect preferred language uses for each subject as well as having a logical relation with the activities and content of the curriculum being taught. Their final write-ups must include a narrative of the credential teacher candidates' evolving understanding of planning for language development on an ongoing component of teaching. They must also evaluate their plans and reflect on possible future modifications and their own areas of future growth.

After analyzing their past curriculum plans and modifying them to include the development of academic language strategies, Tomás's students consider ways to weave these strategies into their future teaching. Because not all students teach in classrooms with

English learners, only a number of credential teacher candidates believe they are able to practice teaching with attention to language development. This is one of the greatest challenges that Tomás faces: helping his students understand the importance of language in school when their student teaching placements have no visible English learners. In an attempt to dissolve credential candidates' categorical understanding of teaching and language development as something one does only in classrooms with LEP students, it is essential that we reconceptualize teaching from a treatment to be applied to particular student populations to one that considers the multilayered and complex linguistic, cognitive, affective, and social dimensions in the classroom. Thus, Tomás challenges his students to consider the oral and written academic English demands of every lesson they teach and appropriate ways to teach language-use strategies that will enhance middle and high school students' reading abilities.

The analysis and planning of curricula for language development represent the third component in the language instruction heuristic Tomás uses, and as such, this assignment provides him with an opportunity to discuss the relationship between content and language-related instructional goals and objectives. One of his goals in this discussion is for credential teacher candidates to be able to distinguish between language and content as variables influencing students' academic performance. This assignment also provides him with an opportunity for inquiry into the learning-to-teach process for beginning teachers of English learners. He is especially interested in gaining insights about how his students understand the relationship between reading and listening and speaking strategies.

After analyzing their curriculum plans and reading their narratives describing the manner in which they created them, it became apparent that a significant proportion of our students had difficulties writing lesson plan objectives that explicitly and specifically addressed academic English language development. The objectives they listed in their plans often included procedural steps necessary for a particular lesson. For example: "Students will use a story map." Also, they often wrote objectives that focused on subject matter content, but they did not mention language development. In a seventh-grade math lesson, one of Tomás's students had students solving written word problems but did not actually *teach* anything related to literacy in the context of math at this grade level. For one of the three lesson objectives, this student wrote, "Students will practice reading and solve problems." In the narrative describing the development of her understanding of what it means to include language development in her plans, the student commented on the importance of teaching students reading skills to be able to solve word problems, a conclusion she reached after assessing and interviewing her focus student for the student diversity dimensions project. She chose to focus on an English learner who, according to her, "was clearly smarter and knew more than the test scores showed." In her narrative, the lesson's author acknowledged having difficulties coming up with language development objectives because, according to her, there was relatively "little reading" to be done in math and "most of the text is pretty straightforward."

Although most curriculum plans included objectives that pertained to aspects of reading instruction, in approximately one-third of all plans the instruction did not match the objective, even after analyzing them in small groups. In these papers, there was no description of how the students would learn the reading skills that the objectives assumed, although the skills were indeed necessary to complete the specific tasks and activities. An example was a tenth-grade history lesson that was part of a larger unit on the industrial revolution. This particular teacher credential candidate envisioned having his students research various sources (predominantly books and Internet sites) focusing on the impact of the industrial revolution on a particular country, city, or community. Afterward, his students would present their research findings to the whole class in small groups. One of the objectives he listed was for "students to be able to summarize important information." However, he did not include any explicit instruction on how to do this.

His plan did include a worksheet on which he asked students specific information, such as, "How did society change because of the industrial revolution?" This student's narrative for this lesson mentioned having successfully taught this unit at his current placement, where the only two English learners among his students were "quite proficient in English." In assessing his lesson plan, the class teacher wondered whether the lesson included sufficient scaffolding for English learners at lower levels of proficiency.

Urquhart and Weir (1998), in their comprehensive and thorough book on second language reading, point to de facto similarities that exist between testing and widespread approaches to teaching reading, particularly reading comprehension. The practice they describe consists of handing out a text to students with little or no preparation. After the students read it (often individually), they answer a list of questions either aloud or in writing, and the teacher tells them whether the answers are right or wrong. Though there may be differences in the stakes associated with either situation, a reading "lesson" such as this requires students to demonstrate, and at best, practice reading. It does not teach reading. Most of the assignments Tomás received included either explicit instruction or meaningful opportunities for guided practice of reading strategies and development in one or more of the Reading Apprenticeship dimensions. They also offered opportunities for metacognitive conversations about reading, language use, or the nature of language and language learning. Thus, these plans demonstrated clear links between our students' knowledge of their students, the nature of academic English, and their goals and objectives.

An example was a science lesson for a seventh-grade classroom with a majority of English learners that was developed by Max (not his real name), a science teacher credential candidate in one of our courses. The lesson was part of a unit on watersheds and hydrology that had included the construction of models as well as a field trip to the town's main creek. In this lesson, students in groups of four were to spend time summarizing and discussing what they had learned thus far and generate questions they had about the history of the creek and its current features. (A segment ran underground encased in a large concrete pipe.) After recording this on the appropriate sections of a K-W-L chart, each group was asked to share one of their bits of knowledge and one question with the rest of the class. Max used this as the starting point for a whole class discussion about possible reading strategies to obtain the necessary information from a brochure detailing a history of the town's creek. In addition, students were to consult two topographic maps, one depicting the current creek and another depicting the creek as it was a hundred years prior. Each group of students also received a set of descriptions of fictional characters that represented different ethnicities, genders, backgrounds, and occupations. Students chose the character with whom they identified most or in whom they were most interested. Their final task was to write a letter to the character of their choice describing the ways in which the creek had changed over the years. In the letter, students were also required to discuss the strategies they had used to read the maps and the historical account, mentioning at least one strategy they had used and possible difficulties they had experienced. Finally, Max asked his students to come up with and present to the class one conclusion and one question related to this assignment. Max actually taught this lesson, which provided him (and Tomás) with valuable information.

In his narrative, Max mentioned being aware that a majority of his students were Hispanic, which led him to modify the texts used to include several such words. While teaching the lesson, he also made sure to discuss cognates and their usefulness to Hispanic readers of English science texts. Furthermore, his decision to include this lesson in the unit came about because of a conversation he had had with his focus student from the student diversity dimensions assignment. His focus student told him about playing in this creek with friends, which caused Max to wonder about the quality of the water and the creek's history. Max's decision to have students choose a conclusion and a question to report to the large group was in turn influenced by his academic oral English project. He noticed that students often understood various aspects of the content, yet were too intimidated to contribute to in-class discussions. Consequently, he decided to make the task attainable even for students with limited proficiency by having them choose only one conclusion and one question that no other group had yet reported. As can be expected, not all of our students turned in work as exemplary as Max's. In what may be yet another likely illustration of the lasting influence of the apprenticeship of observation (Lortie, 1975), a small but disturbingly significant proportion of Tomás's students' lessons were variations on reading comprehension tests.

In their narratives, several of our students referred to the Reading Apprenticeship portfolio and other related exercises, particularly from Dave's reading methods course. They mentioned thinking about the Reading Apprenticeship dimensions and related concepts while planning and analyzing their lessons and realizing that the conceptual framework was still useful to teach reading to English learners, though it adds a layer of complexity to their task.

A Cautionary Note

In this chapter we sound a cautionary note for teacher educators interested in preparing teachers to teach literacy to English learners using a Reading Apprenticeship approach. The task of gaining awareness of how one reads as an expert reader of discipline-specific texts in order to apprentice novice readers expands in complexity when one considers gaining a critical awareness of the roles of language and culture in teaching and learning. Clearly, gaining such awareness while gaining the corresponding pedagogical skills and dispositions requires much greater time than the duration of most preservice teacher preparation programs. Two semesters is barely enough for beginning teachers to become aware of what learning to read in a second language entails, let alone develop curriculum that reflects such awareness.

In our experience, "good" teaching of English learners is not necessarily synonymous with "good" teaching in general (at least in the context of Reading Apprenticeship). This is yet another variation of

Reyes's (1992) admonition against "one-size-fits-all" approaches to teaching English learners. The awareness required by a Reading Apprenticeship approach to teaching literacy is necessary but not sufficient when teaching English learners. First, teachers must be able to recognize and overcome pervasive deficit views of English learners and work with and see the potential in cultural and language differences in order to develop meaningful relationships with students. A mentor-apprentice relationship is built on mutual trust and respect and requires a safe environment to thrive. This requires that teachers empathize with and understand the experience of English learners to help them navigate the territory that spans their prior literacy-related experiences and subject-specific literacy. The obstacles, such as readers bringing up ineffective schemas for particular text structures or their orientation to the text, have linguistic and cultural elements that are normally invisible to most teachers. Furthermore, teachers often believe that the strategies and dispositions required to become literate develop naturally in all students, as evidenced by the quotation with which we opened this chapter. The metacognitive conversation at the center of the Reading Apprenticeship model informing our practice has a place not only in our classrooms but also inside us if we are to develop the critical awareness necessary to prepare teachers who can lead students from all linguistic and cultural backgrounds to become literate. The Reading Apprenticeship framework thus becomes not a recipe or a packaged method but a lens for inquiry and thought. The goal of inquiry-driven preservice teacher preparation is not just to help students construct knowledge about literacy but rather to develop a set of strategies and dispositions that teachers of reading can use to understand literacy better in the larger context of language and culture.

References

Byalistok, H., and Hakuta, K. *In Other Words: The Science and Psychology of Second-Language Acquisition*. New York: Basic Books, 1994.

California Department of Education. *English Language Development Standards for California Public Schools*. Sacramento: Author, 2003.

Greenleaf, C. L., Schoenbach, R., Cziko, C., and Mueller, F. "Apprenticing Adolescent Readers to Academic Literacy." *Harvard Education Review*, 2001, 71(1), 79–129.

Hudson, R. "Grammar Instruction Is Dead—NOT!" In R. S. Wheeler (ed.), *Language Alive in the Classroom* (pp. 101–112). New York: Praeger, 1999.

Kindler, A. L. *Survey of States' Limited English Proficient Students and Available Educational Programs and Services: 1999–2000 Summary Report*. Washington, D.C.: National Clearinghouse for English Language Acquisition and Language Instruction Educational Programs, 2002.

Korthagen, F.A.J., and Kessels, J.P.A.M. "Linking Theory and Practice: Changing the Pedagogy of Teacher Education." *Educational Researcher*, 1999, 28(4) 18–26.

Lortie, D. C. *Schoolteacher: A Sociological Study*. Chicago: University of Chicago Press, 1975.

National Center for Education Statistics. *Overview of Public Elementary and Secondary Schools and Districts: School Year 1999–2000*. Washington, D.C.: Author, 2001.

Nieto, S. *Affirming Diversity: The Sociopolitical Context of Multicultural Education* (3rd ed.). Needham Heights, Mass.: Pearson/Allyn & Bacon, 1999.

Prator, C. H. "Cornerstones of Method and Names for the Profession." In M. Celce-Murcia (ed.), *Teaching English as a Second or Foreign Language* (2nd ed.). Boston: Heinle & Heinle, 1991.

Reyes, M. de la Luz. "Challenging Venerable Assumptions: Literacy Instruction for Linguistically Different Students." *Harvard Educational Review*, 1992, 62, 427–446.

Schoenbach, R., Greenleaf, C., Cziko, C., and Hurwitz, L. *Reading for Understanding: A Guide to Improving Reading in Middle and High School Classrooms*. San Francisco: Jossey-Bass, 1999.

Shulman, L. "Knowledge and Teaching: Foundations of the New Reform." *Harvard Educational Review*, 1987, 57, 1–22.

Unz, R. K., and Tuchman, G. M. English Language Education for Children in Public Schools. (Proposition 227). 1998.

Urquhart, A. H., and Weir, C. J. *Reading in a Second Language: Process, Product, and Practice*. Essex, U.K.: Addison Wesley Longman, 1998.

Van Lier, L. *Introducing Language Awareness*. Harmondsworth, England: Penguin Books, 1995.

Wong-Fillmore, L., and Snow, C. "What Teachers Need to Know About Language." In C. Temple Adger, C. E. Snow, and D. Christian (eds.), *What Teachers Need to Know About Language* (pp. 7–53). McHenry, Ill.: Delta Systems & Center for Applied Linguistics, 2002.

Chapter 8

Evaluating Reading Intervention Programs

The classroom experiences and assignments described in this book illustrate how our reading in the content area courses consistently represent teaching as a decision-making enterprise. Whether moment-to-moment decisions about student instruction or larger choices about curriculum and assessment, teachers' decisions are informed by a variety of factors, such as their understanding of the discipline, their insights into student learning, and their knowledge of local and state standards for achievement. However, our teachers are entering the profession at a time when growing numbers of schools are turning to published programs to serve the needs of students identified as underperforming or struggling readers. Increasingly, middle and high schools are adopting remedial reading programs and assigning students to them on the basis of standardized test scores. In such a context, a teacher's decisions are often replaced by the program's sequence, or even its script.

In Chapter One we noted how the growing number of underprepared teachers, especially in urban schools, has been the justification for adopting scripted, sequenced programs of reading instruction (at elementary grades) and remediation (at middle and high schools). Proponents assert that such programs make it possible for underprepared teachers to provide needy students with carefully planned instruction and appropriate materials, allowing students, in effect, to learn despite their teachers' inadequacies. School administrators worried about low achievement scores in reading, and faced with growing numbers of inexperienced or underprepared teachers on their staff, look to such programs to provide instruction that will raise test scores.

Critics of scripted programs respond that the problem of teacher preparedness will not be solved by adopting scripted programs that further distance teachers from the knowledge they need about literacy and learning. They cite a wealth of research stretching back to the first grade studies (Bond and Dykstra, 1967) and amplified by current studies that emphasize the central importance of a well-prepared, capable teacher to student learning at all levels and in all content areas (Allington and Cunningham, 1996; Darling-Hammond, 1996, 2000; Snow, Barnes, Chandler, Hemphill, and Goodman, 1991; Wilson, Floden, and Ferrini-Mundy, 2001). Furthermore, underprepared teachers leave the profession in larger proportion than do well-qualified teachers; in California, for example, a study by the state standards board found that 40 percent of emergency-permit teachers left the profession within a year, and two-thirds of them never received a credential (Darling-Hammond, 2002). So substituting scripted programs for the professional development in literacy learning that underprepared teachers need works against both the short-term goal of effective classroom instruction and the long-term goal of a stable, knowledgeable teacher force.

As our well-prepared graduates enter schools that have scripted reading instruction in place, they face not only the apparent disregard for their knowledge and expertise as instructional decision makers but also the school's apparent disregard for factors affecting reading achievement. A student for whom English is a new language may score poorly because of language issues, not because of reading ability. Recent changes in Title I funding have removed the categorical definition of English learners (ELs), with its requirement that these children receive appropriate language-based learning experiences. Instead, more and more, ELs are being assigned to skills-based reading intervention classes on the basis of achievement test scores. So instead of the rich, engaging language experiences that help a new English speaker develop facility and fluency in the language, the child may receive basic skill instruction that ill serves his needs for language and conceptual development. Similarly, students who are native English speakers but have resisted or struggled with reading in school will not find in such basic skills programs the motivation to bond with books.

Inquiry into Published Reading Intervention Programs

Jane designed the reading program inquiry to engage new teachers in an exploration of published reading programs developed as interventions for low-performing middle and high school readers. The reading program inquiry invites teachers to develop a critical stance toward such programs, essentially weighing the benefits and burdens they carry. (See Exhibit 8.1 for full directions for the inquiry.)

Working in four- to five-person teams, the teachers examine a published reading program targeted at adolescent readers seen as needing intervention. In Jane's class, each team looked at one of three programs then in use in the Bay Area: *Corrective Reading* (Englemann and others, 1999), *Language!* (Greene, 2000), or *Caught Reading* (Hawkes, 2000). In studying the programs' goals, components, and teaching-learning activities, the teachers are invited to draw conclusions about the model or definition of reading that informs the program, its assumptions about how students develop as readers, its assumptions about the sources of student difficulties in reading, and the knowledge a teacher would need to use the program. The teachers also decide how, if at all, they might use any of the programs based on the needs of their students and the demands of the disciplines they teach.

Program Contrasts with Reading Apprenticeship

The inquiry allows teachers a hands-on experience of the program—its statement of rationale, teacher resources, student materials, and assessments. In their presentations of findings, the teams in Jane's class noted some crosscutting themes in these three programs. Particularly striking were the theories of literacy and learning they saw

Exhibit 8.1. Reading Program Inquiry

Program: _____

Review Team: _____

Concerned about standardized test scores that show unacceptable numbers of students reading significantly below grade level, many middle and high schools are adopting compensatory reading programs. Student placement in these programs may be determined through cutoff scores on standardized achievement tests in reading, and assignment at particular levels in the program may be decided by tests that accompany the program.

Your task in this inquiry activity is to learn about one of these programs (*Corrective Reading, Caught Reading,* or *Language!*). Spend time becoming familiar with the goals, components, and teaching-learning activities of the program. In your group, discuss and draw some conclusions about the following, providing evidence to support your thinking.

1. Who is the target audience for the program? How do the materials appeal to this audience?

2. According to this program, what is reading? Is the model implicit or explicit? How does this compare to other models we have read about and discussed? Consider specific readings for this class that set forth models of reading or describe attributes of reading. What parallels or contrasts do you see? Find specific examples.

3. What does the program assume about how reading is learned? What is the teacher's role? What is the student's role? What kinds of materials, interactions, and experiences are involved?

4. What does it assume about the kinds of difficulties students have with reading? What are the sources of students' difficulties?

5. How does the program address these difficulties? What's needed for students to improve as readers?

6. What do teachers need to know and be able to do to teach with this program?

7. What do students need to know and be able to do to learn with this program?

8. How does this program relate to middle or secondary school content area learning? Consider stated or implied reasons for reading, content contained, and types of texts—for example, in science, literature, social studies, and mathematics.

As a group, decide if you would recommend this program for use with students in middle or high school. If you recommend it, specify how and with whom you would support its use. If you do not recommend it, what would you offer instead to improve the reading of students who struggle? Consider your experience to date with students in these settings, your understandings of academic literacy, and your knowledge of your content area.

as underpinning the programs' content and processes. The teachers saw in these a stark contrast to principles and theories central to Reading Apprenticeship as an instructional framework. Critical differences are explained in the following sections.

A Model of Reading as Accurate Decoding and Word Recognition. Reading Apprenticeship draws on a model of reading as a strategic process in which readers construct meaning by interacting with text. In this process, they use what is in the text—words and their meanings—but also bring their own knowledge and experiences to construct meaning. In the metacognitive conversation, readers learn from each other how to apply reading processes to understand texts in different disciplines and appropriate new strategies to add to their repertoire. In contrast to this socially interactive and constructive model of reading, the published intervention programs proceed from a model of reading as a technical skill, basically a matter of learning to correctly decode or pronounce words in print and to identify words and get their meaning. It follows then that adolescents with reading difficulties need remediation to learn or relearn basic skills at the word level.

Considering their own students in light of these programs, the teachers in Jane's class were struck by a frequent admonition in our course, borne out by their own classroom experience: don't confuse inexperience with inability (Allington, 2001). From their perspective, their "struggling" readers had basic decoding and comprehension skills but lacked experience reading the types of texts they needed to learn from in middle and high school subject area classes. The teachers were learning how to engage and sustain students in reading challenging texts, so the low-level model of reading presented in these programs appeared to be a huge step backward. At most they could describe the programs as offering a functional model of reading: to read and follow directions, find the main idea, and draw the right (approved) conclusion or interpretation. Given the pressure on schools to prepare students for high-stakes tests, though, these programs were filling a niche: for test prep on reading. None of these programs provided support for critical reading or multiple interpretations of a text. None presumed, much less provided instruction in, discipline-specific ways of reading.

A Deficit Model of Students as Readers. From the functional model of reading described in the preceding section flowed the programs' assumption that students did not bring useful resources to reading to learn. From the diagnostic assessments included in most of the programs to the instruction provided in the student materials, the clear assumption was that the students were blank slates on which particular letter-sound patterns and word meanings could be imprinted.

Given the wide range of interests and experiences among their middle and high school students, the teachers criticized the programs for failing to tap the resources students brought from the literacies they utilized outside of school as a bridge to academic literacy. The multiple literacies of adolescents required by multiple texts and an expanded notion of text forms—for example, film, CD-ROM, the Internet, popular music, television, magazines, and newspapers—have been well documented (Moje, Dillon, and O'Brien, 2000). The teachers had firsthand experience of their students' engagement in these multiple literacies, so they faulted the programs for failing to acknowledge and build on students' various background knowledge or experiences with texts of different kinds. Such an omission not only misrepresented the literate capabilities of students but incorrectly located the problem with academic literacy as the students' failure to learn rather than the institution's failure to teach reading as the complex mental activity it is (Greenleaf, Schoenbach, Cziko, and Mueller, 2001). The teachers felt that one of their most important goals—developing students' agency for their own academic literacy—would be frustrated if they had to teach with these programs.

Uniform, Sequenced, Skill-Based Instruction.   In all of the programs, teacher decisions about instruction were limited to deciding the student's placement in the program. Usually a pretest designed specifically for that purpose determined this level. An implicit assumption was that students identified as poor readers needed all or part of the sequence of instruction, and that the sequence was a logical and useful one for adolescent literacy. Such an assumption runs counter to current understanding that learning to read is not a linear process of acquiring discrete skills, nor does development as a reader past elementary school proceed in a linear, sequenced process.

In one of the programs, *Language!*, teachers noted that the publisher's description of "teacher-friendly" guidelines could just as easily be seen as "teacher-proof," given the highly scripted instructions they contained. Indeed, teachers noticed that all the programs offered their instructional sequence and materials as a support for busy teachers. Another take on this, though, was a disdain for the teachers' ability to make informed decisions about their students' literacy instruction. In all the programs the emphasis on mastery of isolated skills in decontextualized text excerpts had a flip side as well: the low-level understandings about reading that such a goal produces.

A particular concern teachers had with the scripted, sequenced instruction was the role of the teacher—as direction giver, monitor, and evaluator. With Reading Apprenticeship as the framework for developing academic literacy, these teachers saw themselves as more experienced readers who could model appropriate ways of reading, thinking, and talking in that discipline. Metacognitive conversations take place as the teachers join with the students in grappling with difficult texts, helping them learn ways to monitor and repair comprehension. Reading in an RA classroom is a collaborative enterprise. In contrast, reading with these intervention programs seemed more a series of practice drills on isolated skills, capped by periodic assessments to measure skill mastery. And the programs presented the skills as sufficient in themselves; the preservice teachers noted that the programs were silent on how to help students develop both a repertoire of strategies and the knowledge about when and how to use any of them for effective reading to learn. Probably most disturbing to the teachers was the lack of opportunity to embed such skill and strategy instruction in the subject area course, helping students see the relevance of any of these tools to actual texts and tasks. The teachers' concern here mirrors recent research on effective literacy instruction in middle and high school that shows the importance of teaching students strategies not only for accomplishing literacy tasks but also for thinking through the process and becoming metacognitive about when and how to use particular strategies (Langer, 2000).

Poorly Written Text Selections with Little Relevance to Adolescents. In one of the programs, glossy covers of student books showed diverse, attractive teens in various activities: skateboarding, playing soccer, riding bicycles, playing rollerblade hockey. Once they opened the books, though, the teachers wondered how the texts inside could possibly speak to the lively teens depicted and presumed to benefit from this program. An example follows from Lesson Thirty-Eight of *Corrective Reading* (Engleman and others, 1999). It is a story to be read aloud by students taking turns.

Sink That Ship

Kit made a boat.
She made the boat of tin.
The nose of the boat was very thin.
Kit said, "I think that this boat is ready for me to take
on the lake." So Kit went to the lake with her boat.

The teacher's guide explains that the reading selections in the decoding strand are designed to provide practice in sequentially taught decoding skills; in other words, the content of the selections is not of concern. However, in the next selection, "The Goat and Kit's Boat," the treatment of a problem with the leaky boat made the science teachers' hair stand on end. Kit's pointy-prowed boat has punched a hole in a large ship, sinking it. She's rescued the people and animals on that boat and transferred them to her tin boat. Water begins to come over the sides of the boat, so Kit uses a hammer and nails to punch holes in the boat to drain the water.

And the water did begin to drain, but not
very fast. Kit said, "These holes are not letting
water out faster than the water is coming in the
boat. We need a bigger hole in the bottom."

They turn to a goat (rescued from the ship) to help:

The goat made a little hole and kept on
eating until that hole was bigger than a melon.

The water rushed out of the boat and
everybody cheered. "Let's hear it for the goat,"
somebody yelled. And everybody cheered again.

The "story" ends with the cheerful boatload of people and animals sailing safely to shore.

The scientific misinformation here is egregious, and especially destructive to one important goal for struggling readers—that they find personally meaningful uses for print, one of which is to obtain accurate information. The preceding selection was obviously written only to provide practice in particular letter-sound combinations, a questionable practice if the goal is to help students find reasons and ways to engage with literacy. Compounding the problem of text written solely for decoding practice, though, is the lack of attention to anything other than skill instruction to help adolescents develop a reader identity, a sense of why and how reading might add to their lives. By stark contrast, in a Reading Apprenticeship classroom students and teachers investigate relationships between literacy and power, share reading processes and solve reading problems collaboratively, notice and appropriate others' ways of reading, share book talk, and build a sense of agency as readers.

Dealing with Published Programs

One inquiry group summed up their assessment of the intervention program this way, "If this is your program, run fast and take the kids with you!" Scripted intervention programs are often monitored for consistent implementation, so flexible use by teachers is often not possible. But even if the option of selective use of program components were available, these new teachers felt the program's emphasis on isolated reading skills and the consequent message of reading as a technical skill would be more of a hindrance than a help for their struggling readers. These teachers felt the urgency of bringing such students to meaningful engagement with texts, building their confidence and their stamina as readers. They felt this program would be a setback.

Another group decided that their program contained some potentially useful features, particularly some of the subject area readings for practicing comprehension strategies and the use of small group work to support students' comprehension. Still, the emphasis on teacher-directed instruction prompted this group to say that the program's motto could be, "Do as you're told, and you'll be able to read." Again, this message stands in stark contrast to the RA goal of student knowledge of when and why to use any reading strategies.

Teachers commented that this inquiry into published reading intervention programs was both eye-opening and troubling. Some took the stance that "forewarned is forearmed," especially as they approached their first teaching jobs in districts where these programs were in use. For English teachers, who might be required to teach from one of these programs, the challenge would be keeping big-picture ideas about reading and learning at the center of their work with students: providing many opportunities to read connected, authentic texts, talk about reading processes and problems, and develop stamina and engagement as readers. For teachers in other subject areas, the reading program inquiry reinforced their desire to model reading as a problem-solving process using texts in their disciplines. The general feeling was that students receiving instruction in one of these programs deserved every chance they could get to experience reading as an accessible process that leads to successful academic learning. The antidote to these programs' limited view of both students and literacy is subject area teaching that allows students to experience reading as a critical learning tool and supports them in becoming competent, confident readers.

Kohl's advice to teachers on working with published programs is worth repeating here, especially in light of our goal in our Reading Apprenticeship classrooms to engage teachers and students in collaborative inquiries about reading to build student agency: "It helps to take the most expensive, slickly produced material that is forced on you and, with students, find ways of using it that fit your needs rather than the manual's instructions. Sometimes it is interesting to use the teacher's manual as a text with the students so you can examine together what the experts expect of teachers as well as students" (Kohl, [1973] 1989, p. 189).

Text Comprehensibility and Accessibility for English Learners

As noted earlier, English learners are increasingly being assigned to skill-based intervention programs of the type just described. The concerns raised in this chapter about these programs apply to their use with English learners as well—the impoverished model of reading as a technical skill, the low level of engagement possible with the texts, and the lack of attention to individuals' strengths and interests. However, the task of learning subject area content from reading in a second language adds complexity to the situation. Meeting the needs of English learners in subject area literacy is thus more challenging.

Walqui's (2003) professional development module, "Teaching Reading to Adolescent English Learners," describes various supports that enable English learners to assess academic texts and the textual features that can make text difficult for English learners. In an article included in the module, Walqui and DeFazio (2003) recommend that teachers focus on making text comprehensible, and advise against substituting passages with short, simple sentences as the route to this. Instead, their advice is to "amplify, don't simply" (p. 8). To help teachers make critical decisions about texts to use and adapt for English learners, they conclude their article with the following guidelines (Walqui and DeFazio, 2003, pp. 8–10):

> When evaluating whether or not particular text is appropriate for English learners, consider the following:
>
> 1. Do appropriate scaffolds allow the students to derive meaning from the text?

2. Does the text under consideration focus on essential components of the subject matter, or is there tangential material?

3. How useful are the subtitles and other markers for English learners? Are they descriptive? Do they provide framing questions?

4. Is the text overloaded with complex paragraphs and sentences or is linguistic complexity avoided except as necessary? Are there appropriate referents and connections to help English learners access the material?

5. Is the use of technical language and material limited to what is essential, with appropriate redundancy and elaboration built in?

6. Does the text offer typographical enhancements, which would aid English learners in their comprehension of the text?

When particular text is deemed essential to the curriculum, but the text as written provides obstacles for English learners, what options are available?

Of course, adapting the text is one possibility, but this option requires writing expertise and time. Offering a variety of scaffolding devices in these situations may provide students a suitable way to access otherwise incomprehensible texts. What are some of these possible scaffolds?

1. Provide several different versions of the material that the students are studying, including material in the students' first languages. This will allow students to draw from their own fund of knowledge and apply those schemas to the more difficult text.

2. Meet with colleagues in the same discipline to adapt the most crucial elements of a text. For example, decide together which are the key components of the text, photocopy these, cut them into the predecided chunks, and add headings and

framing questions between the chunks as you reassemble (paste) them onto new pages. This technique helps students read the text in manageable chunks and practice skills that good readers have appropriated.

3. Offer students the opportunity to adapt the texts. Rather than assigning the entire chapter to a student, assign different portions of the chapter to different students or groups of students who will rework the material to make it more accessible to English learners. Students can then use the material as an aid to reading the original text. This may diminish the amount of material covered, but it will help to ensure that what is covered is understood.

What Makes Text Difficult?

The inquiry into published intervention programs described earlier in this chapter showed the preservice teachers that a hierarchy-of-skills model—decoding words, then understanding vocabulary, then comprehending text—was the basis of these programs for students seen to be struggling readers. The teachers saw this model as inappropriate for their students, and in fact worried that it spent critical time reteaching basic skills, such as phonics, that were not so much lacking among their students as underutilized by them because they rarely engaged in sustained reading of academic texts. These teachers were committed to bringing more text into their subject area classrooms and apprenticing students at all confidence and achievement levels to learn from a variety of texts. The next logical area for investigation was what makes text difficult and how to address these factors to support student learning from text. For this purpose, we used an in-class assignment called a text-leveling exercise (see Exhibit 8.2).

As a start, the inquiry invites prospective teachers to consider first-hand what makes text difficult, going beyond text levels determined

Exhibit 8.2. Text-Leveling Exercise: A Group Inquiry
on Factors Involved in Text Difficulty

Introduction and Directions (5 minutes)

Introduction: The *purpose* of this activity is *to identify various factors that affect text readability.* Teachers are aware of readability formulas that are often used in assigning grade levels to novels and textbooks. What they may not know, however, is that the approach used in most readability formulas is quantitative for the text in question:

Average number of syllables in the words

Average number of words in a sentence

Average number of sentences in a paragraph

We know that more than word and sentence length is involved in text difficulty. After all, a seven-year-old who's into dinosaurs rolls right along with "triceratops" and "tyrannosaurus," but a one-syllable word like "angst" or a simple sentence like "April is the cruelest month" can be a puzzle for an adult reader.

In this activity teachers will take a *qualitative approach* to readability, considering *factors other than word and sentence length* that contribute to it. The selections used are taken from scales developed by Jeanne Chall and colleagues as part of a *qualitative method for leveling texts* (Chall, Bissex, Conard, and Harris-Sharples, 1996). We will use the text selections *to prompt discussion about what makes text easy or hard.* With insights from this experience, teachers can support students' extensive reading, helping them consider factors beyond numerical readability level when they choose a book.

Source: Chall, Bissex, Conard, and Harris-Sharples, 1996.

**Exhibit 8.2. Text-Leveling Exercise: A Group Inquiry
on Factors Involved in Text Difficulty
(cont'd.)**

Directions:

- Ask the teachers to work in groups of three, within content areas.
- Distribute one set (envelope) of the text selections to each trio.
- Explain that the envelopes contain a set of short text excerpts that cover a range of difficulty, actually from early elementary through college. (The expository social studies excerpts are all about the American Revolutionary period and the life sciences excerpts are all about amphibians.)

Activity (25 minutes)

For the next 15 minutes, teachers should lay out the selections, then read and talk about them as they arrange them from easiest to most difficult. Tell them not to worry about terms or language, such as passive voice, dependent clause, internal definition. *Just describe what came up.*

- The goal here is not an exact order, but a general agreement about which ones are easier and which ones are harder and why.
- Groups may decide to cluster excerpts as easiest, more difficult, most difficult.
- As the group finishes the task, they should make some notes of the features they talked about, in order to share their thinking with the whole group. (Some of these features may be about the text, some about them as readers, some about the task assigned.)

For the last 10 minutes, small groups:

- Report on what they noticed and talked about that made text easier or more difficult. Tell them again not to worry about terms or language—for example, passive voice, dependent clause, internal definition. *Just describe what came up.*

- Facilitator or notetaker posts what the small groups report.

- The whole group then looks for *common themes or features that came up as contributing to text difficulty.* These might include the following:

  > Language: Vocabulary difficulty (unfamiliar, abstract, polysyllabic, technical words)
  >
  > Sentence length and complexity
  >
  > Conceptual difficulty: The conceptual understanding required to comprehend the text, e.g., the degree of abstractness; the amount of prior knowledge needed to understand the text
  >
  > Idea density and difficulty: The number of ideas in the text and the difficulty of these ideas

  The discussion should conclude with some recommendations from the group about how to use this awareness of factors affecting text difficulty to support a Reading Apprenticeship classroom.

by readability formulas. Such formulas, of course, were designed to provide teachers with ballpark estimates of the ease or difficulty of particular texts by assigning grade levels to them. Our students are familiar with the readability labels on commercial texts and on editions of novels for use in schools. But they are often surprised to learn that these grade levels are the result of quantitative analysis, literally a factor of average number of syllables in words, words in a sentence, and sentences in a paragraph for a text excerpt. More qualitative analysis of text features such as concept density, discourse structure, discipline-based vocabulary, and relationships among ideas in the text is not involved. Often, it is these qualitative features interacting with a reader's background knowledge, motivation, and purpose that make a text easy or difficult for a particular reader.

In the text-leveling activity, we ask prospective teachers to go deeper than a quantitative analysis with text excerpts to discover what makes some texts more difficult than others. We have several goals here. One is to increase their awareness of the factors affecting text difficulty and how to ameliorate these both with assigned and student-chosen texts. Another is to help them understand that "simpler" texts (with low readability levels) are often more difficult to understand because they lack elaboration of ideas or concepts. This point was illustrated earlier in relation to adapting texts for English learners. Simplified texts also limit the strategies readers apply—for example, they need only to look for main ideas and supporting details. These texts generally do not help English learners or struggling readers to develop more sophisticated strategies of critical reading. A third goal is to model this inquiry into text difficulty as a classroom activity appropriate for use with middle and high school students. (See Exhibit 8.2 again for complete directions for the activity.)

Working in small groups, the preservice teachers read short (one- to two-paragraph) excerpts on the same topic in a subject area. For our inquiry, we have taken science excerpts on amphibians and social studies excerpts on the American Revolutionary War from *Qualitative Assessment of Text Difficulty: A Practice Guide for Teachers and Writers* (Chall, Bissex, Conard, and Harris-Sharples, 1996). A small group takes an envelope containing eight to ten excerpts, each on a separate strip of paper, so that they can move them around, ultimately arranging them in an agreed-upon order of easiest to most difficult. These excerpts have been leveled by the authors, according to a qualitative method of assessing difficulty (which takes into account some of the text and reader-linked features described earlier), but the purpose of our activity here is less to match the texts to scales determined by the authors than to engage prospective teachers in identifying factors beyond word and sentence length that affect ease or difficulty of understanding a particular text. Readers of this book may wish to design their own such exploration, by seeking out a range of text samples in particular subject areas that represent an easy-to-difficult continuum. Teachers can be enlisted to find texts with a suitable difficulty range. We have found that using text samples on the same topic facilitates the discussion of factors affecting difficulty. Some key factors that thus emerged are described as follows.

Language

Easier-to-read selections contain concrete language, mostly familiar to the reader. A life sciences excerpt judged very easy to read contains this description, "The female frog lays lots of eggs. Each one has a ball of jelly around it. The eggs float in clumps on the water." In the easier texts, where more specialized vocabulary is used, the passage itself provides a definition. On the same topic, a slightly more difficult passage contains this description, "Frogs, toads, and salamanders are *amphibians*. Amphibian comes from a Greek word that means 'double life.' Amphibians begin their life cycle as water animals. They develop into air-breathing animals as they grow up."

Traveling up the difficulty levels in other texts on amphibians, more complex and abstract vocabulary appears, often without explanation. In a selection at the ninth-grade level, eggs and tadpoles of frogs and toads are described as "very vulnerable to predators." At the eleventh- to twelfth-grade level, eggs of amphibians are described as "covered with a gelatinous substance," and in a passage rated above sixteenth grade level, genetic amplification and replication are briefly described with references to transcription and coding. In the easier passages, the language is descriptive and explanatory. As the text difficulty increases in these life sciences excerpts, the language becomes either more abstract or more technical. The following sentence was rated at a reading level of eleventh to twelfth grade: "The moist skin of frogs and other amphibians contains mucous glands that assist in maintaining moisture."

Sentence Length and Complexity

Whereas traditional readability formulas take sentence length into account, the inquiry into factors affecting text difficulty allows prospective teachers to go beyond length and look closely at sentence structure as well. They notice familiar language patterns, close to speech, in the easiest selections, and more abstract, formal patterns, with levels of subordination, in the more difficult passages. In a collection of expository social studies excerpts on the Revolutionary War, these sentences come from one rated at fifth- to sixth-grade reading level, "During the nearly two centuries of British rule, the colonists' attitude toward England gradually changed. The early colonists had regarded themselves as English people who happened to live across the ocean from their mother country." The first sentence speaks of change, and the second sentence builds on it, clarifying the colonists' early attitude toward Britain. Contrast this incremental style with the information-loaded phrases in these sentences from a text rated at thirteenth- to fifteenth-grade level, "Beginning in 1740 a series of crises undermined the stability of these established political and social orders. Religious turmoil, war with France, and an economic cycle of boom and bust struck in rapid succession." More than the length of the sentences in this example, the number of ideas and concepts that are rapidly introduced increase the demands this text makes on a reader.

Conceptual Difficulty

As we noted with vocabulary, the content of the easier passages is more concrete and the topics are likely to be familiar to younger readers. So, for example, in the third-grade selection on amphibians, descriptions tap into experiences or objects familiar to children. Each egg has "a ball of jelly" around it, the eggs float "in clumps on the water," and tadpoles hang onto plants with "suckers." At higher difficulty levels, terms and descriptions presume more abstract understandings and background knowledge on the part of the reader. An excerpt rated at eleventh- to twelfth-grade level describes how adult amphibians "have lungs adapted for air breathing and are therefore no longer dependent on water for gas exchange. (It can occur through the skin when amphibians are in water.)" The reader is expected to already understand adaptation, gas exchange, and the role of lungs in breathing. In fact, to understand the information about how amphibians can live on land, the reader must apply these concepts to new information on adaptations in amphibians.

Idea Density and Difficulty

In this inquiry, prospective teachers recognize that factors such as vocabulary and conceptual difficulty are closely, even inextricably related. Multisyllabic science terms like *oocyte, ribosomal,* and *chromosome* require conceptual understanding beyond vocabulary definition. In the social studies excerpts, terms like *fanning the flames of revolution, propagandist, stigmatizing,* and *the authority of religious institutions* also require conceptual understanding deeper than word meanings. As the difficulty level of a text increases, the reader must take in and apply numerous abstract concepts in order to construct meaning with a text. And, as in the following thirteenth- to fifteenth-grade level social studies excerpt, each abstraction is meant to trigger a host of associations necessary to read the passage with deep understanding. These trigger concepts are in italics. "Between 1776 and 1820, the *citizens* of the new United States created a *republican institutional order.* While fighting a financially draining war against Great Britain, they devised *effective state constitutions and governments.* Subsequently, they organized themselves into a *strong national union* and began the *expansion* into the trans-Appalachian West." Texts for younger readers generally rely on connections to the reader's experience to support comprehension. Texts for older readers expect them to bring fully formed abstract understandings to bear on the information or ideas provided. In addition, readers are expected to deal with a density of ideas in which explicit relationships are not explained, often with discipline-specific meanings. For example, in this excerpt on amphibians, rated at sixteenth grade and higher, amplification is quite science-specific and is followed by a number of equally complex scientific concepts: "Amplification of ribosomal genes has been observed in other species. Amplification of nonribosomal genes—of structural genes coding for specific proteins, for example—has not yet been seen, despite intensive and critical search." Students' personal experience of amplification, for example in sound systems, will not be sufficient to understand this text, and in fact, may lead to misconceptions about the science involved.

Related to idea density is a phenomenon in textbooks that might be described as gratuitous information. Especially in the social studies texts designed for primary grade students, participants in this inquiry noticed inclusion of narrative information that was probably intended to catch readers' interest but could conceivably distract them from understanding the point of the selection. For example, in this passage, rated third-grade level, the movement of important artifacts to the new republic is clear, but its purpose is not: "When the British were coming to Philadelphia, the Liberty Bell was taken down from its tower. It was hidden under the floor of a church so that no enemy soldiers could find it. The Congress had to move from Philadelphia to another city—and another—and another. Always, the Declaration of Independence went with them. The Declaration was taken to many different places. Once it even spent the night in a barn."

Participants in the inquiry noticed that tangential stories about people and places often appeared in texts written for young children and hypothesized that textbook writers presume that stories are the main vehicle for children's learning about their world. They questioned this assumption, and discussed the value of inviting students to examine texts to see what information is critical and what might be interesting, but largely irrelevant to understanding the point being made.

Engaging Students in Inquiry About Text Difficulty

We recommend that new teachers explore with their students what makes the texts in their classes easy or difficult. Initially students may focus on difficulty pronouncing words or understanding vocabulary. Skilled facilitation of discussions of text difficulty, though, can help students see that text difficulty varies and is affected by factors such as background knowledge, knowledge of organizational patterns typical in particular subject areas, abstractness of concepts, and difficulty of ideas and their relationships (often implied rather than explicitly stated). In a Reading Apprenticeship classroom, students can learn to recognize factors that make a text difficult for them. Especially by grappling with difficult text in a supported social setting, students can increase their ability to read for understanding. Drawing on the knowledge distributed in a classroom is key to building understanding of discipline-specific concepts, a task well beyond vocabulary definition. Although some students will need more explicit skill instruction—for example, to recognize common Latin or Greek roots in scientific terms—embedding such instruction in authentic, curriculum-related reading is far preferable to consigning low-performing students to remedial reading instruction divorced from subject area content.

Increasing Students' Agency as Readers

In Reading Apprenticeship classrooms, a central goal is increasing students' agency as readers. They may lack such agency for a variety of reasons, from limited English facility to inexperience with academic texts to difficulty connecting school learning to their lives. For students who find reading a challenge, or even painful, it is vital that they be engaged in productive, supportive literacy experiences. For these students especially, teachers need to know how to make their own and other students' invisible reading processes visible and accessible. These students need to have texts that interest them on topics that are linked to the curriculum. They need to have scaffolded instruction in reading these texts, always with a focus on making meaning. As their skills and confidence improve, they need to work with more challenging texts, and they need to learn useful strategies to make sense of text in a supportive, collaborative environment. Looking closely at how texts in particular subject areas work should be a regular part of classroom life, and the teacher should help students who struggle with text know that recognizing when comprehension breaks down is an important first step in understanding a text. These students also need to know that everyone struggles with some texts. In a supportive and engaging Reading Apprenticeship classroom, they can learn how to monitor their own reading for comprehension and take action to remedy problems as they come up. Learning these "fix-up" strategies in the context of authentic reading of subject area texts in a socially interactive classroom is especially important for students whose problems with reading have placed them at risk for developing personal, social, and academic literacies.

References

Allington, R. *What Really Matters for Struggling Readers: Designing Research-Based Programs*. Needham Heights, Mass.: Allyn & Bacon, 2001.

Allington, R., and Cunningham, P. *Schools That Work: Where All Children Read and Write*. New York: HarperCollins, 1996.

Bond, G. L., and Dykstra, R. "The Cooperative Research Program in First Grade Reading Instruction." *Reading Research Quarterly*, 1967, 2, 5–142.

Chall, J. S., Bissex, G. L., Conard, S. S., and Harris-Sharples, S. *Qualitative Assessment of Text Difficulty: A Practical Guide for Teachers and Writers*. Cambridge, Mass.: Brookline Books, 1996.

Darling-Hammond, L. "What Matters Most: A Competent Teacher for Every Child." *Phi Delta Kappan*, Apr. 1996.

Darling-Hammond, L. "Teacher Quality and Student Achievement: A Review of State Policy Evidence." *Educational Policy Analysis Archives*, 2000, 8, 1. [http://epaa.asu.edu/epaa/v8n1].

Darling-Hammond, L. *Access to Quality Teaching: An Analysis of Inequality in California Public Schools.* Stanford, Calif.: Stanford University, 2002.

Englemann, S., Meyer, L., Carnine, L., Becker, W., Eisele, J., and Johnson, G. *Corrective Reading: Decoding Strategies, Student Book B1.* New York: Science Research Associates–McGraw-Hill, 1999.

Greene, J. F. *Language! A Literacy Intervention Program for Delayed Readers, Writers, and Spellers, Grades 1–12.* Longmont, Colo.: Sopris West, 2000.

Greenleaf, C., Schoenbach, R., Cziko, C., and Mueller, F. "Apprenticing Adolescent Readers to Academic Literacy." *Harvard Educational Review,* Spring 2001, 71(1), 79–129.

Hawkes, B. (ed.). *Caught Reading Plus.* Upper Saddle River, N.J.: Globe Fearon, 2000.

Kohl, H. *Reading, How To.* Portsmouth, N.H.: Heinemann, 1989. (Originally published 1973)

Langer, J. *Teaching Middle and High School Students to Read and Write Well: Six Features of Effective Instruction.* Albany, N.Y.: National Research Center on English Learning and Achievement, 2000.

Moje, E., Dillon, D., and O'Brien, D. "Reexamining the Roles of the Learner, the Text, and the Context in Secondary Literacy." *Journal of Educational Research,* 2000, 93, 165–180.

Snow, C., Barnes, W., Chandler, J., Hemphill, L., and Goodman, I. *Unfulfilled Expectations: Home and School Influences on Literacy.* Cambridge, Mass.: Harvard University Press, 1991.

Walqui, A. *Teaching Reading to Adolescent English Learners: Quality Teaching for English Learners, Module Five.* San Francisco: WestEd, 2003.

Walqui, A., and DeFazio, A. "The Selection of Written Text for English Learners." In A. Walqui (ed.), *Teaching Reading to Adolescent English Learners: Quality Teaching for English Learners, Module Five.* San Francisco: WestEd, 2003.

Wilson, S., Floden, R., and Ferrini-Mundy, J. *Teacher Preparation Research: Current Knowledge, Gaps, and Recommendations.* Seattle: University of Washington, Center for the Study of Teaching and Policy, 2001.

Chapter 9

Partnering for Improved Academic Literacy

A University-District Collaboration

Richard D. Sawyer, Diana Bledsoe

In the year 2001, Judy Myers and Diana Bledsoe, administrators in the Evergreen School District (ESD), and Rick Sawyer, an associate professor of secondary education at Washington State University–Vancouver (WSUV), joined forces to address a serious issue: helping high school students become more engaged in meaningful reading approaches across the curriculum. Representing both the professional development efforts in literacy for a large school district and a teacher preparation program for new high school teachers in southwest Washington, they formed a literacy partnership between their institutions to focus on content area reading. This partnership was fully funded through a Bill and Melinda Gates foundation grant awarded the Evergreen district. In this partnership, they decided to use the Reading Apprenticeship framework to inform much of both the form and the content of their work together.

The Partnership

The team decided that it was necessary to work systemically to counter the deeply entrenched notion that literacy is a subject exclusively taught by English teachers. In contrast to this view, there is currently an effort in the United States to prepare all high school teachers to teach reading across the curriculum. This need is recognized both by districts that are engaged in teacher professional development and by teacher preparation programs. Washington State, for example, has recently moved to require a content area reading course for secondary preservice teachers as an initial teaching credential requirement. The Evergreen School District and Washington State University–Vancouver, then, decided to build strategically on an ongoing partnership to respond to this new certification demand. Although the partners shared the same underlying goal—to promote teachers' knowledge about content area reading—their specific motivation and histories in terms of the project differed. In WSUV's preservice program, Rick had been facing problems long endemic to teacher preparation in general. For example, teaching interns frequently had difficulty understanding why and how the teaching of reading applied to them in their classes. If they did see a need to teach reading, their approaches often focused on the mechanics of reading, decontextualized from the cultural-historical contexts of reading. Their lack of knowledge about how to teach reading in meaningful ways was underscored by their active questioning of the need to change their teaching. Historically in the secondary program, interns often distanced themselves from the goals of the content area reading course. The history and biology interns simply did not see the connections between their subject and reading instruction. This lack of understanding had often been reinforced by a number of contexts, such as their mentor teachers' lack of understanding about why and how to teach reading and their own personal issues about content knowledge and classroom management. Interestingly, even the English interns often distanced themselves from this course. Given their love of reading and their appreciation of literature, they were often skeptical about taking a content area reading course in the education department. The interaction of these beliefs jointly held by the mentor teachers and the interns further limited how English and other academic teachers could collaborate at a school to learn about new approaches to teaching reading.

The Evergreen School District was motivated to enter into this partnership for three primary reasons. First, the district wanted to support teaching interns' applied and theoretical knowledge of literacy by supporting their placements with high school teachers who were using the Reading Apprenticeship framework in various academic disciplines. The ESD believes in the teaching of literacy across the high school curriculum and established this partnership in support of this goal for new teachers and teaching interns. Second, the district sought a mutually beneficial collaboration in their classes between preservice and in-service teachers. The ESD is moving toward a mentoring model of professional development along a continuum from novice to experienced teacher. It viewed the inclusion of interns as an integral part of this continuum, in which participating teachers, including interns, contribute individual strengths in a reciprocal learning community. Finally, through this partnership, they wished to help establish a common language—one less abstract and more classroom-based—between themselves and WSUV. In the summer of 2002, Rick and Diana attended the intensive Strategic Literacy Initiative Institute, where they studied the Reading Apprenticeship framework. This experience laid the foundation for a greater consistency in views between these partners about teaching and learning.

Rick and Diana sought to contribute to the Strategic Literacy Initiative by establishing and studying how a school district–university partnership could promote strategic disciplinary reading among teachers and students. With the other members of the initiative, they examined how the promotion of a metacognitive conversation about reading could become a relational and transformational process. Specifically, they examined how "real" high school classrooms and more academic university classrooms could work together to blur distinctions between theory and practice.

A Closer Look at the Partnership Process

At the heart of the partnership, Rick and Diana formed a learning community consisting of existing teachers working in a teacher-mentor program in the Evergreen School District and preservice teachers working on secondary certification at WSUV.

The partnership plan had four key pieces: (1) A WSUV-ESD team taught a content area reading course. (2) A field placement of interns in an ESD classroom used the Reading Apprenticeship framework. (3) English methods courses were taught by ESD teachers knowledgeable about the Reading Apprenticeship framework. (4) There was a full-time teaching internship for one intern.

Figure 9.1 outlines the WSUV-ESD partnership.

Team-Taught Content Area Reading Course

In the spring semester, 2003, Rick and Diana team-taught a secondary content area reading course to approximately forty students, including both preservice and in-service teachers. The students came not only from English but also from history, biology, and mathematics.

The primary class text was *Reading for Understanding* (Schoenbach, Greenleaf, Cziko, and Hurwitz, 1999), supplemented by a range of theoretical readings. Students took part in many of the activities found in the Reading Apprenticeship framework, including read-aloud and think-aloud protocols, analysis of videotapes of students reading, and preparation of literacy frameworks for the promotion of literacy in their own classrooms. In addition, they analyzed their personal approaches to reading and literacy as a means of beginning to unpack and understand some of their underlying values, assumptions, and approaches to literacy. They then used these individual and collaborative reading analyses as a basis for metacognitive conversations about reading patterns in the classroom. In these conversations, they compared and contrasted content-specific reading strategies.

Figure 9.1. WSUV-ESD Literacy Partnership

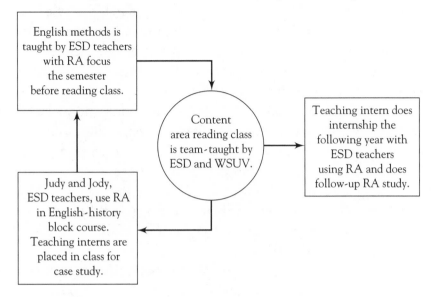

Rick and Diana had a threefold goal in using this framework: to promote the participants' professional development in an experiential and situated way (Sawyer, 2002), to support their efforts to surface and make explicit their own subject-specific reading strategies, and to promote the participants' own sense of learning, because together they would learn new strategies in their collaborative work. In addition, Rick and Diana hoped that their students' experience in the class would foster insights, empathy, and an understanding of learning-centered teaching.

One assignment asked students to complete a case study of a high school student's reading strengths and challenges. Students had a choice of doing this study in an Evergreen School District classroom, team-taught by Judy Wittenberg and Jody Stevens, both teachers who were using the Reading Apprenticeship framework in their ninth-grade classroom. The case study was to include an intervention strategy that would support this student in reading in a particular academic discipline.

As a culminating project, students in the content area reading course wrote a book together in class that integrated their case studies and their literacy frameworks. They worked in content area groups on this project, with each group writing one chapter. The assignment asked for each group to develop a literacy framework in their content area. This framework was to be grounded in theory drawn from their readings and individual studies and include a social dimension, a personal dimension, a cognitive dimension, and a knowledge-building dimension. In addition, their frameworks were to discuss ways to develop their students' metacognitive conversations about literacy in their discipline. On the last night of the semester, students presented their frameworks to the class in a poster session and each received a CD-ROM of the book, which the instructors compiled.

An example from Janet, one of the students in the class who was a practicing secondary mathematics teacher, may help to illustrate the reading frameworks the students developed in their content areas and how these frameworks were related to Reading Apprenticeship. Janet was taking the course as a master's degree requirement. Her example is included here to illustrate how the Reading Apprenticeship framework may apply to an academic discipline that may not on the surface appear to relate to content area reading.

In designing her reading framework, Janet adhered fairly closely to the four dimensions of Reading Apprenticeship. She thought that this framework could help her students learn mathematics and referred to a statement from the National Council of Teachers in Mathematics: "Instead of the expectation that skill in computation should precede word problems, experience with problems helps develop the ability to compute" (Anstrom, 1999, p. 3). Janet developed many language-rich strategies involving her students' speaking, listening, reading, and writing for each of the four dimensions of the framework. For the social dimension, she had her students share how they solved problems through discussions about the problem-solving strategies they used. For example, her students could engage in "number talk" about how they solved problems. This process "involves creating safety, sharing reading processes, problems, and solutions, and noticing and appropriating others' ways of reading," Janet explained. For the personal dimension, she focused on her students' motivation in doing math and their identities as "readers" and "doers" of mathematics. In this process students discussed "different kinds of reading, [such as] decoding of words or numerics, graphs and tables, symbols, and others." For the cognitive dimension, Janet's ideas included scanning, skimming, and chunking. Students engaged in "scanning and skimming prior to more focused reading; this can give them an idea of what the 'complete picture' is, which may give students the parameters within which to work." Janet thought that chunking the text into smaller segments combined with judicious underlining of key in-formation were useful cognitive strategies: "First, the underlined phrases are clarified to understand what is being suggested, which will help to make sense of these chunks. Once these chunks are understood, the rest of the problem may be easier to comprehend." Finally, in the knowledge-building dimension, Janet focused, interestingly, on how her students could begin to visualize mathematics in order to build a knowledge base to support learning. She gave the following example to illustrate when prior knowledge is needed to make sense of a math problem. An English learner in her class read the following problem: "How many bows can you make from five meters of ribbon if a bow takes one-fourth of a meter of ribbon?" Janet explained that although this may seem like a straightforward problem, the student did not know what the word "bow" meant and could not proceed until he could visualize what the problem presented. Janet suggested that graphic organizers, which represent relationships between concepts in a concrete manner, could help students understand the written text and the mathematics problem.

Janet thought that the integration of reading into mathematics instruction could help her students in many ways. It could help them work though problems, learn to communicate their emerging ideas, organize ideas and arguments, support the development of new perspectives, develop problem-solving processes, become more flexible in representing and interpreting ideas, and see mathematics as a life subject. Further, she thought that the metacognitive conversation related to mathematics and reading would help her students make sense of the abstract quality of mathematics, letting them place it into a context of classroom support and emerging meaning.

Field Placement

To support field-based inquiry in an authentic classroom, interns in Rick and Diana's content area reading course were required to conduct the previously described case study of a high school student learning to read academic texts more effectively than he or she had. The graduate students could either select their own classroom placement for this study or be placed into Judy and Jody's class as the site for their case study. This placement was designed to support their inquiry into both their own reading processes and that of their case study participants, because the research protocols the graduate students used mirrored those they experienced in the content area reading course. Although inquiry was woven throughout the course, the students' case study was the primary vehicle for it. This case study then became the basis for the curriculum that the students designed in the end of their casebook chapter.

What was significant about the placement with Judy and Jody was that they were currently facilitating a book study group for in-service teachers with a focus on the Reading Apprenticeship framework and ways to use it in a multidisciplinary classroom in the ESD. These teachers came from a variety of teaching disciplines, including science and history, thus paralleling the teaching disciplines found among the interns in the secondary program. Four preservice teachers asked to be placed in Judy's and Jody's class and worked either in pairs or individually on their case studies.

English Methods Courses

In addition to teaching high school in the Evergreen School District, Judy and Jody taught two English reading and writing methods courses at WSUV. As mentioned, these teachers were knowledgeable about the Reading Apprenticeship framework and used an inquiry approach in their courses. Before entering the content area reading course, all the English interns had taken their methods courses from these two teachers. The content area reading course gave the English interns an opportunity to revisit the Reading Apprenticeship framework, allowing them to deepen and extend their understandings about it through classroom and field-based inquiry.

Internship Placement

The final component of the WSUV-ESD Literacy Partnership was a teaching internship placement in a classroom of two ESD teachers using Reading Apprenticeship in their teaching. Due to placement complications, only one intern in the program, Cait, was given an extended placement with a mentor teacher. Cait was placed with Sheri Walker and Linda Wegner, two veteran teachers who team-taught in a combined English-history class similar to that of Judy and Jody. Cait entered this placement the year after she took the content area reading course. In her placement, Cait had the opportunity to work with Sheri and Linda on a study they were conducting on the impact of Reading Apprenticeship on three high school students in their classes.

The Study

From the inception of their partnership, Rick and Diana had agreed to conduct a study of the contribution of the WSUV-ESD partnership to teaching interns' emerging understandings about content area reading. Specifically, they wished to understand what the teaching interns thought about content area reading in their academic discipline, how the course promoted their learning about teaching content area reading, and more systemically, how the partnership promoted their learning about teaching content area reading.

Rick and Diana collected their data in a variety of ways. Teaching interns took an identical open-response survey related to the research questions both on the first evening of the course and fifteen weeks later, on the last evening. Exhibit 9.1 provides a copy of the survey.

Rick designed the first draft of this survey before the course began. The design was improved during a detailed discussion by participants at a Strategic Literacy Initiative Teacher Education Consortium meeting, which Rick and Diana attended before the study began. The survey was given to all the students of the class to determine general learning themes. In addition, follow-up interviews were given to four interns as the basis for more in-depth case studies. Exhibit 9.2 provides the text of the interview.

Both the survey and the interview asked interns to discuss the role of reading in their content areas, meaning-making strategies their students could use in the different content areas, resources to support learning about reading, their future plans for content area reading, and the impact of the course on them as teachers. The interview and survey items were constructed to gather data from at least two perspectives for each research question in order to deepen or problematize responses. For example, the items about reading strategies and about the role of disciplinary reading may be viewed in tandem to present a level of triangulation.

Additional interns were selected as a focus of more detailed case studies; two are described in this chapter. The intent of the case studies was to allow for a deeper exploration of the themes emerging from the initial survey data. Whereas the survey data presented descriptive themes, the brief case studies presented more analytical understanding of survey findings. Finally, specific

Exhibit 9.1. Literacy Survey for Teaching Interns

Your name: _____

Date: _____

Content area? _____

Years in teaching? _____

1. What do you think the role is for literacy in your content area?

2. Describe your past experiences integrating literacy into your content area. What are some specific literacy strategies that you use?

3. What are some literacy strategies that today's adolescents use in the classroom?

4. What are some activities adolescents engage in outside the classroom related to literacy?

5. What are some literacy strategies that you used as an adolescent?

6. What are some specific strategies students can use to learn your subject?

7. What do you think that the relationship is between literacy and writing in your content area?

8. What do you think that the relationship is between arts-based education and literacy in your content area?

9. What specific resources-approaches-activities have facilitated your learning about the connection between literacy and your content area?

10. Do you intend to use literacy strategies in your classes in the future? If so, please describe.

11. How does your learning about literacy (and learning to integrate literacy strategies in your content area and teaching) relate to you as a teacher?

Exhibit 9.2. Sample Interview for Interns

Interviewee: _____

Date: _____

Interviewer: _____

Location: _____

1. Please describe the experience you had in your participating teacher's class last spring.

2. What were some examples of RA that you saw in that class?

3. How was your content area involved?

4. Was there more than one content area involved?

5. How were you engaged in RA in the class?

6. Tell me a little about the study that you did.

7. What supported your learning about RA in the class?

8. What supported your learning about RA outside the class?

   Prompts:

   Your classmates and their presentations

   Your study

   Class readings

   Your book chapter

   The class activities

9. Are you using-studying RA now? If so, how?

10. If you had any recommendations for our partnership, what might they be?

coursework (the interns' case study and an in-class book chapter they wrote) was analyzed as examples of interns' learning outcomes.

The English Interns

From the start of the semester, the English interns strongly believed that literacy was a central component of their subject. Few clear differences emerged between their views about the importance of content area reading from the beginning to the end of the semester. For example, in the beginning of the semester one student wrote, "Literacy is essential for English. If you can't read, you can't write." Although the interns never wavered in their view of the role of literacy to their subject, by the end of the semester their discussion of the reading strategies students could use in an English course involved a much richer and diverse repertoire, and many of these strategies were related to the Reading Apprenticeship framework. It is important to note again that Judy and Jody had previously exposed the English interns to Reading Apprenticeship in two English methods courses that they had taught. For example, at the beginning of the semester, one student wrote that reading strategies would include "reading for pleasure, class reading, reading aloud with buddies (in front of class), vocabulary word lists, and so on." At the end of the semester, she wrote, "Read-aloud, think-aloud . . . reading strategies like character studies, improvisation, and fortune line. In English, we usually write about reading. But literacy is more than just reading. It's about *understanding*."

The English interns gained a greater sense of control and intentionality in their teaching by taking part in classroom conversations that discussed reading from a learner's perspective. One mentioned, "[It] makes teaching-learning more intentional." Their views were similar to those of the interns in history and science in beginning to examine teaching through the eyes of both a learner and a teacher (with the roles between the two blurred). One stated, "[It] helps [me] to reach kids where they are and help them in relevant ways."

The History Interns

The history interns underwent a dramatic transformation in the course and partnership. Engaged themselves in read-aloud and think-aloud protocols in the class, they began to appreciate parallels between the Reading Apprenticeship framework and methodologies that historians use to understand and interpret history. With an emphasis on having students unpack textual meaning in a classroom context, Reading Apprenticeship reinforces "historical thinking" as an authentic and primary way to learn history in secondary classrooms. To think historically, high school students read and critique primary and secondary source documents from a variety of perspectives found during the historical time period, while applying historical meanings to their own lives in the current time period. In this process, the students are accessing all four dimensions of the Reading Apprenticeship framework.

Interns in the content area reading course found that explicit classroom discussions not only about history but also about *how* they were thinking about it (and from whose perspective) could make history come alive for their students. One intern wrote at the end of the semester, "Reading Apprenticeship is important for reading primary and secondary documents. You must use reading skills to think critically about the subject area." Another said, "[Reading skills are a] basis for civic competence. [RA provides] critical skills for 'learning' history with lots of textual evidence." And a third mentioned that RA "teach[es] students to communicate effectively with literacy... [through] a think-aloud technique."

The most remarkable change was in the interns' understanding of reading strategies that their students could use in history. At the beginning of the semester, one student said that the best way for students to learn to read in high school history was to "read, read, read, and then write." At the end of the class she mentioned these strategies, "Think-aloud, reciprocal teaching, questioning before reading, note taking." Another student at the beginning of the semester wrote that the best strategy was "engaging in essay writing to better understand words." At the end of the semester he mentioned read-aloud and think-aloud protocols and more visual representations of knowledge. Another student, who left this question blank at the beginning of the semester, echoed the thoughts of the previous student at the end of the semester. Further, she wrote that the Reading Apprenticeship framework gave her "a great foundation for teaching literacy in the classroom. [I now] have the knowledge of how to create an environment where students will be able to increase their reading ability and feel comfortable while doing it."

The Biology Interns

While the English interns embraced literacy as a key component of their subject, the science interns, like the history interns, were initially more skeptical. However, over the course of the semester they too underwent a dramatic shift in their thinking. Initially they were unsure about the connection between literacy and their subject matter. Their responses often focused on the importance of their remaining current in their fields to present up-to-date information to their students. Their discussion of reading strategies for students included using flash cards, playing games, writing up lab work, and scanning headings. In contrast, by the end of the semester, their responses were much more specific. Two themes predominated: some interns thought the role of literacy in science was to support student agency and learning; others stressed ways in which the Reading Apprenticeship process itself reinforced the scientific process.

For example, at the beginning of the semester one student wrote, "It is vital that science teachers keep abreast of current research in their field in order to be able to pass this knowledge along to their students. It is important because science is not *static*." . . . At the end of the semester she focused on the personal dimension of reading. She stated: "Literacy is the foundation of the science curriculum. . . . Literacy is the tool used to understand the natural world. . . . It provides the essential factor of student motivation (the personal dimension)." Other responses by interns focused on how the methodology of Reading Apprenticeship was mutually reinforcing with a scientific methodology. One student wrote at the beginning of the semester that the role of literacy in science was to support "the transfer of knowledge and techniques and the archiving of information and events." Reading strategies he gave at the beginning of the semester included "students' reading papers [written] by others to learn information and procedures." At the end of the semester he thought that Reading Apprenticeship's emphasis on student "introspection and thinking" were valuable strategies. This student did his final project on how as a teacher he could use the Reading Apprenticeship framework to have high school students think aloud about and critique the scientific methodology used in scientific studies. He wrote at the end of the semester, "It's . . . exactly what I wanted to develop as a teacher-learner. I've learned things that I should have learned in high school and earlier. The class brought to life many things that I've been trying to develop on my own for many years." This intern began to blur the boundaries between teaching and learning as he himself underwent a paradigm shift in his own thinking.

Supporting Their Development

The question of what specifically *supports* teacher learning is in many ways more important than *what* teachers learn, because knowledge about learning processes can build capacity for future learning. Keeping with the theme of metacognition, the interns in this study had the opportunity to talk about their own learning. Specifically, they were asked to discuss what resources, contexts, or people in their class and placements supported their learning about how to integrate literacy into their content area. Their responses were remarkably similar, regardless of content area. They consistently mentioned the following:

- The *Reading for Understanding* text (Schoenbach, Greenleaf, Cziko, and Hurwitz, 1999)
- The case study assignment
- The class chapter assignment
- The Reading Apprentice framework and learning from peers
- Empathy for student reading strengths and weaknesses

When asked the same question about support at the beginning of the semester, interns either left the item blank or mentioned individualistic ways of learning (for example, finding an expert, reading a book). In contrast to more individualistic ways of learning, at the end of the semester the interns all mentioned items that involved collaboration with their peers in and outside class. The only exception was the first response, to read the class text. However, it was discussed in class using the Reading Apprenticeship framework. These answers underscore an important goal for teacher preparation courses: that the courses model collaborative and social ways of teaching and learning.

Case Portraits

Interestingly, none of the students in the class mentioned the WSUV-ESD partnership itself as a primary support of their learning in the class. The following case studies (presented as portraits) gave Rick and Diana the opportunity to begin to tease out the relationship between the partnership and their students' learning. These two portraits focus on the role these interns thought the partnership played in their learning. Both of these interns did their case study in Judy and Jody's classroom in the Evergreen School District. As mentioned, these two teachers had also taught two of the English methods courses at WSUV. One of the case study interns, Cait, took methods from them. The other study intern, Pauline, was in science, so she did not.

Pauline, a Science Teacher

Pauline entered the teacher education program after a successful career in business. Although passionate about teaching biology, she approached her lesson planning and classroom research methodically and thoroughly. She decided to do her case study in Judy and Jody's classroom even though the two taught in a different content area. Pauline chose to work with Judy and Jody in order to be able to study students already exposed to Reading Apprenticeship.

Pauline conducted case studies of two students reading a page about the water cycle from a ninth-grade science text. She stated in her paper that her purpose in doing the study was to "discover the challenges students encounter when reading science texts and to devise strategies to increase their science comprehension." She first had the two students list three things they would like to improve about their reading. Then, modifying a think-aloud procedure and a general questioning procedure used by the Strategic Literacy Initiative for assessment (Strategic Literacy Initiative, 2002), Pauline used the same data collection process for each student. (See Exhibit 9.3 for a copy of her read-aloud–think-aloud protocol.) Basically, she gave all students the page from the biology textbook, had them review the read-aloud–think-aloud protocols they'd been using in Judy and Jody's class, and asked them to help her understand what they were thinking as they read the text. She took notes and prompted them as necessary. After the students finished she asked them separately to circle any words or phrases they found difficult in any way. She then interviewed them about their reading. Finally, she had the students complete a short written assessment.

Pauline's study is fascinating because of both its findings and its methodology, which actually supported her participants' learning during their interviews. Pauline summarized her findings as follows:

> Tom was able to activate a great deal of prior knowledge (schema) to comprehend the science text. He was able to monitor his own reading and comprehension, demonstrating active metacognitive

Exhibit 9.3. Pauline's Read-Aloud–Think-Aloud Protocol

1. Give the student a copy of the page from the biology text-book.

2. Review with the student the RA/TA skills she has been practicing in _____'s class.

3. Provide pencils and highlighters for the student to use to highlight key points, or to circle or underline words or phrases the student is unsure of.

4. Ask the student to help me understand what he is thinking while reading the text.

5. Write notes to myself as the student begins the RA-TA (in lieu of audio-video recorders).

6. Prompt the student as needed but attempt to remain unobtrusive. Examples of prompts:

   Would you tell me what you are thinking right now?

   Does this remind you of anything you've seen or read or felt before?

   You stopped (slowed down) when you got to this word (sentence); would you tell me what you were thinking?

7. Reassure the student as necessary.

8. After the student is finished reading, ask the student to circle any word or phrase she was unsure of or found difficult in any way. Ask the student to remember what she did when she got to that point in the text.

9. Ask general questions about the text the student just read. Examples of questions:

   Did you like this text? If so, what did you like about it? If not, what didn't you like about it?

   Did this reading seem easy or hard to do? If so, why? What made it easy and what made it hard?

Exhibit 9.3. Pauline's Read-Aloud–Think-Aloud Protocol (cont'd.)

What do you think about being asked to read this piece? Does reading this have any purpose or value for you as a student? As a person?

Why do you think a science teacher might ask you to read this particular piece? What does the teacher think you will gain from it? What do you think about that?

Written Assessment Protocol

Ask the student to complete the short written assessment. The assessment is identical to one developed by the Strategic Literacy Initiative (2002).

1. What kinds of thoughts were happening in your mind as you read this?

2. What did you do that helped you to understand the reading?

3. What questions or problems do you still have with this piece?

4. In your own words, write one or two sentences that tell the most important ideas in this piece.

5. This piece was
(circle one):   Easy   OK   Too hard

6. How well would you say you understood this piece?
(circle one):   Very well   OK   Didn't understand

Closing the Interview

Discuss students' written responses. Thank them for their time, effort, and helping me to become a better science teacher.

thinking. In addition, Tom could create an understanding of an unfamiliar word by relating the text to the picture (knowledge-building dimension). He was able to distill meaning as he was reading and identify significant concepts. In the future Tom may have difficulty comprehending science text in which he cannot activate prior knowledge, or in understanding text that is especially dense and lacks illustrations.

Pauline identified three broad reading strategies for Tom. She wished to try to increase his reading speed (which he himself gave as a needed improvement), create an environment supportive of him as a learner who relies on visuals, and encourage him to make applications of his summaries.

Pauline found that both students were highly capable of verbalizing their thoughts during the read-aloud–think-aloud procedure. She attributed this skill to their prior experience with Reading Apprenticeship. Doing the study, she was struck by a particular insight: "Although both students possess average narrative reading skills, my research suggests they have widely disparate science literacy skills, primarily because of a difference in the amount of prior knowledge each one could activate."

She discovered that Mary was a very different reader than Tom was and that she especially had problems learning "the language of science." She stated, "Mary made many more comments about the text as she was reading, for instance, 'Wow, that's a lot of water. . . . So the water goes back again, a cycle.'" Pauline thought that "Mary was able to make the most sense of the text by relating it to her life. She was unable to activate as much prior knowledge as Tom and was challenged by the vocabulary." Pauline developed a number of ways to support Mary's reading, including teaching vocabulary in the context of scientific processes and encouraging Mary to read more science-related fiction and biographies.

Cait, an English Intern

Cait had also been placed in Judy and Jody's classroom at Evergreen High School. Because Cait was preparing to be an English teacher, she decided to have Matt, her case study participant, read a literature text. She let him select his own text from a small library that Jody and Judy keep in the class. He selected *The Rifle*, by Paulsen.

Cait had initially planned to use a think-aloud protocol with Matt. However, after getting to know him for a few minutes before asking him to read, she decided to change her approach. Instead, she had Matt read aloud to her before discussing his reading. She used follow-up prompts that she herself had used in the content area reading class. The focus of these questions ranged from asking for recall to pronunciation and comprehension problems to sense-making strategies while reading the text.

Cait gained a number of insights into Matt's reading comprehension strategies. She discovered that he was initially motivated to read at the beginning of a text but became easily discouraged, especially when reading in a group format, possibly because of his relatively slow reading speed. Reading in a group often reduced his confidence. While he struggled with certain words, such as "trajectory," he knew how to use contextual clues to aid in understanding. He made a number of personal connections to the text, usually in relation to specific objects, such as rifles. He also often asked questions of the text, using these questions as a guide in his reading. Perhaps one of the strongest insights that Cait had as a new teacher was her identification of reading strategies that Matt used and could actually talk about. Focusing on his existing reading strategies—even though he was a struggling reader—allowed Cait and some of her peers in the class to question deficit approaches to teaching and to try learning-centered approaches to teaching. The study also underscored for Cait how important it is to continue to teach reading to students, even in high school.

Cait was also struck by the theory-practice connections that she could make while doing her study. Doing her case study in the high school classroom of the same teachers from whom she had taken her graduate-level methods course allowed her to make connections between Judy and Jody's classroom practice and their university theory. Cait found that she could "read" Judy and Jody's curriculum not only descriptively (what was happening) but also analytically (underlying meanings for their actions). This experience brought to life for Cait a number of relatively abstract program themes: the importance of planning, the value of inquiry, the resonance and recursive nature of theory-practice connections. In the interview, she said, "Everyone should take Jody and Judy's methods courses."

After taking her content area reading course, Cait began her internship in Sheri and Linda's classroom in the Evergreen School District. Sheri and Linda too are knowledgeable about the Reading Apprenticeship framework. Linda studied Reading Apprenticeship in California with the Strategic Literacy Initiative and is a district literacy coach. Sheri became involved with Reading Apprenticeship through professional development offered by the Evergreen district and receives coaching support from Linda. Cait became very enthusiastic when talking about her placement in a classroom with like-minded mentors. In her internship she discovered a community of learners. Working with these two teachers, Cait became engaged in an inquiry project quite similar to the one that she herself had conducted in Judy and Jody's classroom the previous semester. She said that it was exceptionally validating to enter Sheri and Linda's classroom as a professional, knowing about the Reading Apprenticeship framework as well as how to do inquiry related to it. The three of them are currently conducting a study on the reading habits of three students in one of their classes.

When asked directly about what specific activities and contexts supported her in learning about how to begin to use the Reading Apprenticeship framework in the classroom, Cait initially mentioned the case inquiries in class: "When we looked at the case study about LaKeisha and it showed how she was reading and talking to the text . . . that was great because it was an example for me.

I have to see it to believe it." She was also asked to discuss what the WSUV-ESD Literacy Partnership contributed to her learning to use the framework. Given her involvement in every facet of the partnership, Cait's answer was an important one. She stated,

> It's given me a lot of ideas. . . . I think I have an exceptional placement. I don't think that everyone gets this kind of placement. I am blessed to be with Linda and Sheri . . . because of their own knowledge of Reading Apprenticeship and education in general and how they go about learning for the kids and teaching. It's so much how this program is run. It just kind of all melted together and it's just totally making sense. And how the two of them are working together is amazing. . . . This is not the norm in schools today.

The Veteran ESD Teachers

As mentioned, the focus of Rick and Diana's study was on the impact of the Reading Apprenticeship framework and the WSUV-ESD partnership on the interns' perceptions about their teaching. However, the ESD teachers also contributed informal thoughts to this study. The following question informed this more informal addition to the study: "What were some of the perceptions of veteran teachers who themselves were attempting to incorporate RA into their content area teaching when they had an intern in their class who was also currently learning about the Reading Apprenticeship framework in a content area reading course?"

Three themes about the meaning of this collaborative process emerged from their thoughts. These themes are offered here as a backdrop to the earlier discussion about the value of the Reading Apprenticeship framework to the interns' emerging practice. The veteran teachers . . . explained that working with the interns accomplished the following for them:

- *Promoted consciousness of the importance of focusing on the teaching-learning cycle in the design of academic curriculum.* When in-service and preservice teachers participated in professional conversations, they generated intentional lesson designs focusing on literacy integration in the core content. This process promoted collaboration in planning and executing lessons using the RA framework, followed by discussion and evaluation of the process. Both parties benefited from the careful analysis of the individual literacy needs of the students, as well as the needs of the class as a whole, when planning the core curriculum of the course.

- *Supported intern-teacher reciprocal learning about practice as the interns conducted their case studies.* A significant outcome of having the preservice interns working side-by-side with in-service teachers was the co-learning that happened by both. Gathering evidence to support the planning for teaching is not something secondary educators normally do. A partnership relationship truly set the stage for such activity. Our case study took relatively little time to conduct, yet, as demonstrated by Pauline's efforts in Judy and Jody's class, it yielded valuable information about student understanding during the collaboration. The case study will ultimately be useful to other staff as well. This finding was echoed by Judy when she stated how much she wished to read the case studies: "It would be helpful to be able to have access to the case studies completed by the student interns. I could serve my students better." The ESD is now considering the learning opportunities that the interns' case studies offer for staff and faculty.

- *Created an atmosphere of professionalism.* Participation in a collaborative partnership during the internship allowed for professional growth for all parties. A hallmark of professionalism is the creation and dissemination of new disciplinary knowledge to inform the field. Engaged in collaborative inquiry, the interns and the veteran teachers were profoundly professional. Instead of implementing a centralized district or state mandate to teach in a particular way, the teachers created new understandings and knowledge about teaching in ways directly tied to student learning. In contrast to mediocre forms of teaching internships, these interns were able to work together with veteran teachers in a collaborative way and share their ideas and thinking. One veteran teacher mentioned that her intern helped her to understand the Reading Apprenticeship framework in a new way. This was truly a validating and authentic learning situation for this teaching intern.

Discussion and Future Plans

Inquiry was layered throughout the partnership process. For example, interns engaged in inquiry as they took part in metacognitive conversations about their own reading strategies in different subject areas. Interns also engaged in inquiry as they did case studies of reading strategies that high school students used in different subject areas. And inquiry was modeled by mentor teachers in some of the interns' placement classrooms.

Given this focus on inquiry, it was somewhat alarming that at the end of the semester, approximately one-fifth of the students in the content area reading course continued to question the role of inquiry in their practice. Even though they had understood and found insights into the inquiry approach in the class itself, they expressed a degree of reluctance and uncertainty in using an inquiry approach with their students in the future.

Even Pauline and Cait had to be directly asked about the value of inquiry before they mentioned it. But although they did not mention it without prompting, they had, more significantly, begun to integrate inquiry into their practice, continuing a strong inquiry stance toward their practice after the course ended. The following semester Pauline, for example, devised a new study related to English learners (ELs). Drawing from her findings from the reading study about the importance of visuals, diagrams and illustrations, to some readers, she redesigned a standardized assessment her EL students had to take, making it more visual and less dependent on written English. As she put it, she wanted to "reduce the rival constructs in the tests" (that is, language and scientific concepts). She found that her EL students increased their scores on the revised test and mentioned that her internship school was interested in using it with other EL students. The following semester Cait also continued her inquiry stance. For her master's thesis she began to design a research study that built on the study that she was undertaking with her two mentor teachers on the Reading Apprenticeship framework.

Perhaps the partnership's impact could most clearly be seen on Cait and Pauline and the other two students who did their case studies in Judy and Jody's classroom. In terms of discussing the value of the partnership to their learning, again, both Pauline and Cait had to be prompted. But once they were asked directly, they both implied that their omission was an omission of the obvious, given the central role to their learning that the specific components of the partnership played. Pauline recognized that her two case study students were verbal and could readily think about their thinking related to reading. Her being in Judy and Jody's class gave her inquiry an authentic context that she found coherent and mutually supportive of goals and approaches in her teacher preparation program.

Both Rick and Diana considered the literacy partnership a success, although in need of nurturing and development. The partnership took a small step toward replacing school-university structures that isolate and limit teachers with ones that unite and support them. As Lortie stated a number of years ago, collaboration supports teachers in developing "an empirically grounded, semantically potent common language" (Lortie, 1975, p. 212) that is needed to enlighten practice. This particular partnership modeled and supported collaborative, inquiry-based teaching and learning. However, the interns' views of the value of inquiry were more implicit than explicit, more unstated than stated.

Next year, in 2005, the WSUV-ESD Literacy Partnership will continue to grow. The teachers in the ESD who have taken part in the book study groups will attend a three-day summer institute to study Reading Apprenticeship in greater detail. Judy, Jody, and Linda, for example, will be among the instructors of this institute. As more teachers in the ESD become familiar with the Reading Apprenticeship framework in different academic disciplines, there will be a larger number of mentor teachers for the WSUV interns, who will continue to study the framework in their content area reading course. In addition, the ESD intends to prepare all teachers at an alternative high school to use the framework in their classes. This future development will then become the site for additional inquiry, because the current plan calls for the placement of one or more interns to study collaboratively with the mentor teacher the relationship of the Reading Apprenticeship framework to the discipline. Finally, faculty at WSUV hope that more graduate students will do their culminating research projects on how the framework contributes to learning in different academic disciplines. Given that the Reading Apprenticeship framework with its emphasis on metacognitive conversations can promote language-rich classrooms, such classrooms can offer graduate students diverse possibilities for sustained and thoughtful inquiry as they begin their teaching careers.

References

Anstrom, K. *Preparing Secondary Education Teachers to Work with English Language Learners: Mathematics.* Washington, D.C.: NCBE Resource Collection Series, 1999.

Lortie, D. *Schoolteacher: A Sociological Study.* Chicago: University of Chicago Press, 1975.

Sawyer, R. D. "Situating Teacher Development: The View from Two Teachers' Perspectives." *International Journal of Educational Research,* 2002, *37*(8), 733–753.

Schoenbach, R., Greenleaf, C., Cziko, C., and Hurwitz, L. *Reading for Understanding: A Guide to Improving Reading in Middle and High School Classrooms.* San Francisco: Jossey-Bass, 1999.

Strategic Literacy Initiative. *Curriculum-Embedded Reading Assessment.* Unpublished professional development material. San Francisco: WestEd, 2002.

Chapter 10

Translating Preservice Inquiry to the Classroom

Dilemmas for New Teachers

In Chapter Four we described an inquiry project for preservice teachers to learn from and with their adolescent students how to support them as readers in specific disciplines. In this chapter, we report on our own collaborative inquiries with new teachers who were formerly our students in the preservice program. Dave studied how these new teachers view the role of inquiry in their own classroom practice while Jane explored the extent to which they were incorporating Reading Apprenticeship ideas and practices in their own classrooms. Our goal in both of these inquiries was to learn how to prepare and support new teachers better. Basic to both of these studies was the belief that teacher inquiry—the process and its products—can move us closer to the schools we want, with teachers acting as knowledgeable decision makers, even change agents.

In this chapter we share our initial findings on questions about inquiry-based learning in general and Reading Apprenticeship in particular. Our questions addressed the following issues:

- The role of inquiry in new teachers' classroom practice and their changing questions about practice during their first few years as teachers

- The aspects of Reading Apprenticeship that new teachers incorporate in their classrooms

- Tensions that may arise when new teachers try to create

Reading Apprenticeship classrooms in the current climate of high-stakes testing and accountability

In sharing the findings of our studies, we include the voices of our students as new teachers, responding to the dilemmas framed in our questions. With their help, we trace the path to our conclusions for strengthening literacy instruction in the teacher preparation program. We invite our fellow teacher educators listen to these voices and to reflect on the conclusions we offer.

Inquiry in New Teachers' Thinking and Practice

To advocate, as we do, an inquiry stance among new teachers is to convey a vision of teaching as a decision-making enterprise. Teacher inquiry is action-oriented, geared to improve teaching and learning. But not all new teachers find themselves in settings where they can use inquiry to inform their teaching. As teacher educators, then, we wrestle with a tension between preparing new teachers for schools as they are (with limited teacher control of curriculum and instruction) and preparing them for schools as they should be (with teachers as knowledgeable decision makers, even change agents). Our decision to focus on inquiry reflects our hopes for schools as they should be.

To investigate the role of inquiry in new teachers' thinking about and practice of content area reading, Dave surveyed graduates from three consecutive years of his reading in the content area class. Approximately half the graduates of each year responded—a total of around thirty-five teachers. The survey asked teachers to describe any examples of inquiry related to literacy instruction. Their responses provide one window into how new teachers translate this habit of mind into their own practice.

One general distinction emerged between first-year teachers and more experienced teachers. First-year teachers connected inquiry to thinking about the challenges the profession posed for them, whereas their more experienced colleagues (that is, those in their second or third years) were more likely to focus inquiry on students and their learning. For some more experienced teachers, their thinking about students took on a new or reconfirmed generosity. Bernadette, a third-year teacher, wrote, "Students want to learn. They want to be educated. They want to enter the world of reading and academic success." Nancy, a third-year teacher, said, "I continue to be amazed at how creative and interested children are in solving problems." The more we encourage teachers to inquire into middle and high school students' reading, the more we can invest new teachers with this generous and optimistic view of their students as willing and able learners. Such inquiry can help orient teachers to identify and build on student abilities rather than identify and remediate presumed deficiencies.

More experienced teachers described new understanding about student learning and explained how that understanding translated into evolving practice. Through inquiry, Margot, a third-year English teacher, noted that her "students see reading as burdensome in class," an understanding that shaped her goals and practice. She continued, "My goal is not to make students become avid readers. Instead my goal is to help students develop reading skills. So I have conversations with students about academic versus pleasure versus life (taxes, contracts) reading. I allow them to be bored with the story rather than becoming frustrated. I try to make them aware of struggles, point out successes, and share my own challenges with reading." Joy, a third-year English teacher, realized that her tests were often not revealing her students' knowledge, which made her appreciate "the need for multiple assessments, something that in the past I had interpreted merely as 'making learning fun.'" When these teachers paid attention to their students' learning, they were able to use it to inform their own teaching. Their responses show that the more preservice teachers can learn from focal questions about their students' learning, the more able they will be to shape classroom experiences that foster their students' development in reading. As these teachers demonstrate, the more we help preservice teachers develop good questions about their students as readers, the more we can help them design curricula informed by students' abilities and building on students' strengths.

All of the teachers interviewed highly valued inquiry to inform their teaching, but they practiced it to greater or lesser degrees. Teachers are always thinking about their practice, often in the form of questions. The difference between this type of routine thinking and inquiry into practice is the sustained and systematic look at those questions. In a Reading Apprenticeship environment, teachers learn to seek relevant information from their students to answer the questions. They learn to see students as resources for improving their own practice. For example, Carla, a science teacher, wrote: "There are so many questions I ask every day about my students, the curriculum, how I teach, and so on, that it is often overwhelming. However, having one question to center on has helped me have a focus in what I am doing in my classroom. Right now it is helping students understand how to read and understand what they read in science."

Other second- and third-year teachers found inquiry to be a natural part of their professional lives. Ben, a social studies teacher who investigated how his students "read the world" as part of his master's project, stated: "My questions are at the heart of the educational project as well as the heart of the 'project' of socially transforming the world together." And Dan, a social studies teacher participating in an action research project, concluded, "The practice of inquiry in my teaching is almost as routine as developing lesson plans. It is absolutely necessary, in my opinion, for good teaching. It is critical if an educator is to investigate something as complex as the racialized achievement gap."

Some teachers found value in raising questions even if they were not moving to answer them systematically. Eliza, a second-year English teacher, wrote, "Getting clear about the questions I am most interested in has helped me greatly this year . . . and has made teaching over the past year and a half more doable." Repeating a theme that other teachers sounded, she continued, "It can feel overwhelming when all you are aware of is that things are not how you want them or how you think they should or could be. I've found that classifying my questions helps me relax into the process of learning as a teacher to remember that I don't have to have all the answers this minute." Annette, a third-year teacher, best summed up—albeit grudgingly—the value of inquiry while acknowledging the difficulties mentioned by others:

> As much as I hate to admit it, and for all its faults, I feel the browbeating of inquiry into our skulls is something I do, and something I appreciate. It isn't fun, it isn't always effective, but it has taught me an approach to dealing with all that I do with optimism and possibility—rather than bitching in the lunchroom, I ask questions, I wonder. I'm often frustrated but I do love that there are questions rather than stereotypes and rancor. . . . Having at least a dozen mini-inquiry projects rattling around in my head at the same time makes me crazy, but it keeps me thinking.

Most tellingly, Simon, a third-year English teacher, summed up how his thinking about inquiry and his professional preparation have changed. "When people ask me about [my teacher preparation program], I tell them that it did not prepare me for my first year of teaching, but it did prepare me for a career of inquiry. In my second and third years, I began to see the value in the program's approach." Simon's statement provides a caution for teacher educators. We do not want to prepare teachers for only their first year. However, in preparing them for many years, we do not want to leave them feeling like Simon—unprepared for their crucial first year in the profession.

Evidence of Reading Apprenticeship as a Framework in New Teachers' Thinking and Practice

The prevalence of questions in these teachers' reflections on practice is an encouraging indication that teacher education can nurture professional dispositions that translate to the real world of practice. During their first year, the teachers in Dave's study either reported little time for inquiry, despite their belief that it is important, or asked questions at the technical "what works" level. Teachers in the second and third year of teaching, however, were more likely to find some way to build inquiry into a regular part of their practice and asked questions that were more focused and specific as well as more likely to look at student learning rather than whether certain teaching techniques worked. They came to see inquiry as a critical means of improving their practice, from day-to-day instructional planning to their own professional development.

Translating Inquiry Learning as Teachers into Inquiry Learning for Students

Our awareness of first-year teachers' concerns with "what works" and their need to develop and implement huge amounts of curriculum in too little time prompts us to look closely at how preservice teachers understand and appropriate Reading Apprenticeship. How do they translate RA from their experience as learners in a preservice reading course to their practice as new teachers of adolescents? How can new teachers provide developmentally appropriate inquiry experiences for middle and high school teachers? Can they keep the focus on the learning that inquiry produces, and see the activity—for example, think-aloud—as a scaffold for that learning? In other words, can new teachers focus on concept as well as technique?

The role of inquiry in middle and high school RA classrooms prompted Jane's investigation into the thinking and practice of graduates from her content area reading course, which is organized expressly around the Reading Apprenticeship framework with numerous opportunities for inquiry into teachers' and students' reading. As students in her course the year before, these first-year teachers had experienced and valued apprenticeship in their own learning as readers. They talked repeatedly about the value of sharing reading processes with each other, the motivating influence of reading and reflecting on a text with another, a growing sense of agency about "hooking" adolescents into reading and supporting them to improve as readers, and the importance of tapping students' expertise as readers in the instructional context. With the backdrop of this positive preservice experience, she interviewed five graduates of her class who had gone on to teach middle or high school English to find out how, if at all, they translated the RA framework into discipline-based reading instruction with their students. In what ways did these new teachers—Sally, Barbara, Erin, Theresa, and Pamela—see themselves learning from and with their students about how to develop academic literacy?

During Jane's class, the five women had identified learning from others and seeing others as resources for making meaning with text as a significant insight, one that they planned to carry with them into their own teaching. As these teachers made their invisible reading processes visible to themselves and each other, they developed a strong motivation to create similar opportunities for students in their own middle and high school classrooms. Sally described the personal connection that kept her reading *The Math Gene* by Keith Devlin for the cross-disciplinary journal project. She went on to explain how she would use what she learned to engage her own students in texts that might be challenging. She planned to teach her students to "take their time to read difficult texts . . . stop and summarize or question . . . use adhesive note tabs to mark the text. Helping the students to make personal connections with the text and critique-question the author will help them to better understand and engage while reading. Most importantly, in order to help students get motivated to read a book, I will try to keep an open dialogue about why the book is important, why they think they should read the book."

In her cross-disciplinary log, Barbara contrasted her ease of reading a literary memoir with the challenge of reading Howard Gardner's *Intelligence Reframed*. Aware of how much she had learned about herself as a reader in this activity, she anticipated providing a similar literacy experience for her students: "I can see many benefits of this process for students: the chance to see how other people read and what works and doesn't work for them, the chance to question their own reading habits, and the chance to recognize and clarify what their own reading preferences are. The process is the first step toward helping students become better readers."

As these responses from their preservice year indicate, these teachers saw the value of Reading Apprenticeship to support learning from texts in various disciplines. They saw how in an RA classroom, expert readers mentor apprentices, making invisible reading processes visible and accessible. In the cross-disciplinary journal project, they experienced being experts reading in their own discipline and novices reading outside their disciplines. They came to see themselves as readers with both strengths and challenges. They wanted to help their own students to see themselves in a similar way. A goal they shared was to help students develop confidence and skill in content area reading.

During their first year, the teachers indicated that they were able to accomplish some of the goals they had set for their students as readers, whereas others were more difficult to achieve.

One challenge faced by all five of the teachers was overcoming student resistance to reading and ultimately fostering strong engagement with books. Usually they instituted extensive in-class reading, often through silent sustained reading (SSR). In addition, most of the teachers paid attention to the cognitive and knowledge-building dimensions of reading—for example, including instruction on comprehension strategies and building discipline-specific vocabulary and schema.

Tapping Both the Social and the Personal Dimension to Build Reader Identity

During Jane's course, the teachers had explored their own reading, analyzing their processes and identifying areas of confidence and of uncertainty. Often, insights about themselves as readers came from classroom or e-mail dialogue with a partner. These exchanges also allowed them to expand their repertoire of strategies for working through difficult or boring text. In Jane's classroom, the metacognitive conversation helped them see a range of reading processes across various disciplines. Preservice teachers who experience their own reading ability as variable and situation-specific and who learn valuable approaches to texts from trusted peers will likely want their students to learn the same about themselves as readers and through similar means.

But herein lies a new dilemma. In RA classrooms, students learn from and with the teacher and each other how to become skilled academic readers. But these new teachers were wrestling with how to start and sustain the metacognitive conversation in settings where students didn't know how to talk to each other in safe, respectful ways, much less how to learn from each other. They wondered how they could help students develop a reader identity in schools focused on reading achievement measured by tests and in classrooms where students resist reading as they have experienced it in school. In some instances, these new teachers decided to leave out conversation and collaboration on reading preferences and processes, feeling overloaded already with the demands of improving students' reading achievement.

For all five of these first-year teachers, there was a clear focus on building students' reader identities and increasing their stamina. All of the teachers dedicated class time to SSR in books of the students' choice, and most had students keep metacognitive logs in which they periodically described their reading process—for example, points of engagement, moments of confusion, and strategies used to repair comprehension lapses. These teachers were well aware that their students needed to engage with books in order to find uses for literacy in their lives, both in and out of school. Erin said of her students, "They really need to have reading defanged." To this end, she focused class attention on SSR and described her pleasure in recognizing students' growing ability to read independently for increasing periods of time. As students warmed to SSR, they guarded the time allotted, often reminding classmates slow to settle down that this was distracting them. Erin began to see the perseverance students were developing as they read books of their own choice begin to pay off in a willingness to stay engaged with assigned novels.

Theresa, though less successful at establishing SSR as a valued part of class, described a similar goal of helping students connect to books. Frustrated by student resistance to reading, she once responded to a complaint about "reading again in here" with the promise, "We're never *not* going to read in here." Theresa was optimistic that once engaged with books, students would learn how various kinds of texts operate. But to bring her students to various types of texts, she first needed to help them connect with at least one. Her challenge was to overcome their resistance and create a classroom community in which various reading processes and problems could be acknowledged and shared to the benefit of all. A serious obstacle that she reported was the absence of a climate of trust in the classroom that made it difficult to share confusions or insights with reading without fear of ridicule. As a result, the students would attend to her modeling a think-aloud but would not engage in think-alouds with each other, sharing confusions as well as understandings.

Theresa described herself as an impatient reader: quick to get through uninteresting text and likewise to "devour" something she enjoyed. Her confidence as a reader may help explain her difficulties in planning how to support students as readers. Her own experience had allowed her to become immersed in enjoyable books and otherwise get through boring or difficult texts. The challenge for her was to anticipate students' difficulties with a text, help them get through it, and see that they were readers. She also wanted them to acknowledge that they all had strengths and weaknesses as readers and could learn from each other, but this goal was elusive. Theresa reflected on her experience in the cross-disciplinary reading, noting that because she was currently "helping my class work through a difficult text that I have chosen, I can now empathize with their lack of agency." She had concluded that for the next reading event in her class, she would let her students choose their own books, feeling they would have an easier time making meaning if they were able to choose books that interested them.

Several of the teachers found that students' metacognitive logs provided a window into their reading processes. In reading their students' entries, the teachers learned about their reading interests, challenges, and needs. Pamela described her students' willingness to share book recommendations, and Erin felt that her students were becoming more interested in each other's reading tastes and processes. She planned to have them share their metacognitive logs when next she taught the academic literacy class.

Creating a classroom climate in which students can share their confusions as well as their understandings is critical to Reading Apprenticeship. Faced with a classroom culture where competition and criticism were the norm, some of our new teachers, like Theresa, backed away from inviting their students into the inquiry-driven metacognitive conversation. These teachers found ways to work around students' lack of positive communication and interaction skills, usually by restricting the conversation about reading processes to individual students and the teacher. In much the same way, many teachers worked around students' perceived reading inabilities by reading aloud from the text or lecturing on the text content. But here is the problem with this approach: when teachers work around students' inability to engage in classroom conversations or their inability to read content area texts, they inadvertently prevent students from learning how to do either.

Consequently, we realize that we need to assist Reading Apprenticeship teachers to do the hard work needed to create safe classrooms in which conversations about how and why we read, as well as what we read, can take place. We do not want them to "teach around" reading by lecturing, providing notes, or otherwise compensating for students' perceived inability to read course texts.

Helping Students Learn and Control
a Range of Cognitive Strategies

The teachers had developed confidence using a variety of cognitive strategies and learning by doing in Jane's class, and then themselves employing in their classrooms reciprocal teaching, question-answer relationship, and other tools for reading academic texts. But often such strategies become ends in themselves rather than means to student agency in reading challenging texts. When strategies are a means and not an end, they are internalized and used flexibly by students, as appropriate, with any given text and task. Some of Jane's students reported a confusion between strategies as ends rather than a means to learning in the schools where they worked.

Barbara's case illustrates the problem. In her cross-disciplinary reading log, Barbara had described the impact of "realizing strategies that I knew about, but haven't used in a while. The strategy of summarizing what I have just read in my head shortly after reading it had been growing rusty at the bottom of my mental toolkit. It was good to activate those muscles again, and become a more active reader." Now in her own classroom, Barbara was intent on having students become active readers with powerful cognitive strategies to support their understanding, but she described her dilemma. In her department, faculty agreed to teach students a structured, socially interactive process: reciprocal teaching (RT), which builds strong questioning, clarifying, summarizing, and predicting skills (Palincsar and Brown, 1984). Barbara valued RT as a socially mediated way for students to experience the cognitive processes (predicting, questioning, summarizing, clarifying) that she eventually wanted them to use independently. RT for her was a means to an end. A decision in the English department, though, to foreground the use of RT in the final exam for the academic literacy class seemed to shift the emphasis. Demonstration of skill in participating in an RT dialogue on a short story appeared more important than using RT to support students' understanding of the story. Barbara was concerned that the scaffolding might have become the learning, with predictable student focus on "doing" RT right rather than internalizing its cognitive strategies (Jay, 2002). This reminded us that we want teachers to have the knowledge and the confidence to challenge inappropriate (counterproductive) practices in their schools.

A technique that she saw her high school students using with more control and effect on their comprehension was talking to the text—that is, marking up a text with questions, connections, and responses that help students engage and check their understanding (Jordan, Jensen, and Greenleaf, 2001). Her students were using this technique on their own to construct an understanding of a text. This less structured way of interacting with the text seemed more compatible with Barbara's literature comprehension goals and more natural for her students.

In contrast, Sally was seeing a formulaic use of talking to the text among many of her middle school students. She wanted them to use it to support comprehension but was concerned that it had become a word-focused marking-up of the text, rather than a targeted way of engaging, noting problem areas, and recognizing connections. Similarly, she had become aware that students saw metacognition as "what we do in the logs" rather than the thinking about their reading that they share by writing in the logs. So the idea of internalizing the process hadn't sunk in. Her dilemma was finding a way to scaffold students' learning and help them internalize these reader moves.

Schema: Building New Knowledge on What Students Already Know

In our preservice courses we challenge the temptation to treat students as academic blank slates, a temptation that may be intensified by curriculum and school contexts that privilege the teacher (or the text) as the source of knowledge. However, all students bring knowledge to our classrooms, and finding out what schema students bring to academic learning from outside of school or from other subject areas can provide a base on which to build new knowledge. But this takes skill and persistence, not to mention class time.

Pamela described her attempts to blend teacher or text-driven vocabulary study with student-initiated vocabulary development. She wanted students to become aware of new terms that came up as they read and take responsibility for learning them, especially when the terms were critical to understanding the text. At the same time, she felt a need to develop some common vocabulary understandings, identifying a tension between teacher-prescribed content learning—in this case vocabulary—and text schema.

Sally found building appropriate schema a challenge as she worked with a mixed group of sixth-, seventh-, and eighth-graders in an academic literacy class. Yet she was convinced that this knowledge area is critical; in fact, she felt that without more extensive vocabularies on essential topics, her students would not be able to make effective use of the cognitive strategies she was helping them develop. She was committed to helping students develop positive attitudes toward reading, but struggled to find ways to help them connect with reading, given sometimes weak or inappropriate schema.

Making Room for the Metacognitive Conversation

Although all five of these new teachers were intent on creating a safe place for reading and fostering a positive learning environment, another piece of the social dimension in an RA framework seemed missing—providing students with access to each other's and the teacher's reading processes. Ironically, this social interaction around reading processes and problems had been one of the most powerful learning experiences for these new teachers themselves in the inquiry activities of Jane's course. Yet none described providing this experience to their students. The metacognitive conversation they described was between individual students—in their reading logs—and them. But this conversation, at the heart of a Reading Apprenticeship classroom, should include student-to-student talk as well as student-to-teacher talk. The concurrent internal and external metacognitive conversations build student awareness of reading processes and fuel student growth in academic literacy. How can we prepare new teachers to scaffold this collaboration so that their students benefit from the social dimension as readers in the same way that they themselves do?

To increase engagement and efficacy in reading, the teachers made class time for reading a priority, but class time for talking about and learning from each other's reading processes was less frequent. For us as teacher educators, this discrepancy raised the dilemma of how much to put the metacognitive conversation into the foreground in our content area reading classes. On the one hand, overemphasizing the metacognitive conversation may leave new teachers without strategies for making it a reality in their classrooms. On the other hand, overemphasizing strategies can leave teachers without deeper understandings of literacy and learning in the disciplines.

Implications of Jane's Study for Reading Apprenticeship in the Preservice Course

We were struck by the degree to which the new teachers were incorporating key features of RA as an instructional framework in their classrooms. As a group, they were applying their learning from the cross-disciplinary reading journal and other inquiries into readers and texts from the preservice course. They valued and sought ways of understanding how their students work to make meaning with text. However, we saw less evidence of how their students shared their reading problems and processes with each other.

As teacher educators thinking about these findings, we gained a new appreciation for the importance of how we frame our content area reading courses. We want our preservice teachers to understand and value all four dimensions of the RA framework with the metacognitive conversation as a dynamic link. We also want our teachers to feel confident in planning and implementing instruction based on this framework. We see encouraging evidence in the personal, cognitive, and knowledge dimensions. We see more work ahead of us to prepare new teachers adequately to cultivate literate possibilities in the social dimension. We want the preservice teachers with whom we work to understand that their metacognitive conversations with each other as students in our courses are a model of how they as teachers can apprentice adolescents into a shared inquiry into reading, so that the different processes, problems, and perspectives the students bring to texts are part of the instructional content.

Rethinking the Metaphors of First-Year Teaching

These two exploratory studies of new teachers, inquiry, and Reading Apprenticeship raise a number of questions of concern to teacher educators. How can first-year teachers who have no time, who seem to exhibit only a technical inclination for reflection, or who appropriate surface features of Reading Apprenticeship without seeming to appreciate its conceptual framework (especially the importance of metacognitive conversation) evolve into teachers who incorporate active, persistent, and careful inquiry into their teaching, as part of their pedagogy and part of their professional development? Although these two exploratory studies do not trace the development of individual teachers as inquirers over time, one (Dave's) does examine a group of teachers in different years of their professional practice who share the same education and a similar set of values about teaching and learning. And both studies look at the challenges to inquiry-based teaching during a teacher's first year. In consequence, it seems reasonable to assume that some teachers do move through a period during their first year when they value inquiry but practice it in limited ways, when teachers are enthusiastic about implementing learning activities with their students that resemble in form the activities in which they engaged with colleagues in their preservice coursework, but fail to provide the same access to the social dimension of reading or student-to-student metacognitive conversations. As a result, we ask ourselves: How can teacher educators build a bridge between inquiry in teacher education and inquiry after several years in the profession, a bridge that holds out hope for first-year teachers, a bridge that honors the unique context of first-year teaching without settling for "survival" as the only goal, a bridge that allows new teachers to see their students as bringing strengths to reading in the same way, though different in content, that their colleagues in their preservice reading courses brought strengths to reading various genres in different disciplines?

Teacher educators tell teachers that inquiry should be part of their teaching and offer models such as Atwell (1998), who used the metaphors "creationist" and "evolutionist" to describe her changing stances as an inquiring, reflective teacher. We have mentioned Atwell's metaphors in an earlier chapter. As a creationist, she studied her creation—the curriculum—to prove its superiority. As she became an evolutionist, she found that "the curriculum unfolds now as my kids and I learn together. . . . What I learn with these students, collaborating with them as a writer and reader who wonders about writing and reading, makes me a better teacher" (p. 3). Actually, this nicely describes the stance of teacher as coinquirer with students in a Reading Apprenticeship class. The difficulty for first-year teachers is that neither metaphor for inquiry serves their unique circumstances. They are still creating their curriculum, often at a breakneck pace to keep up with the demanding teaching loads put on first-year teachers. No wonder new teachers implement curricula that on the surface provide the same strategies as activities from their preservice reading course without the scaffolding to support metacognitive conversation. They are not ready to let the curriculum evolve—something that presupposes the ability to draw on a rich, well-developed storehouse of knowledge about content and teaching strategies. Seen in this light, "what works" questions or implementing strategies-based curricula adapted from their preservice course might generously be considered part of a "realist" or "survivalist" metaphor for first-year teacher inquiry.

The work of teacher educators is to acknowledge first-year teachers' questions and practice as part of a developmental continuum that leads toward more evolutionary inquiry about students' literacy, to acknowledge that getting a classroom to "work" may not be an entirely inappropriate goal for the first year. By acknowledging the potential of "what works" questions, teacher educators can help teachers to refine their questions and deepen their inquiry. By contrast, presenting a model of inquiry that dismisses new teachers' "what works" questions is more likely to lead first-year teachers into believing that inquiry is beyond the work of a classroom teacher.

Another metaphor for first-year teachers' inquiry might be "experimenter." Whereas more experienced teachers inquire into student learning, first-year teachers' inquiry usually involves trying out a variety of strategies to meet multiple goals: improving their students' skills, promoting content knowledge, and maintaining a safe and productive environment in the classroom, for example. Rather than thinking of themselves as survivalists, these new teachers are more likely to find inspiration in the metaphor of experimenter. To consider themselves experimenters, they must do more, however, than try out one strategy after another. They need to collect data about these strategies—documenting their practice and capturing student learning processes and outcomes—so they can reflect *in* action during teaching and *on* action after the school day and school year (Schön, 1983, 1987). Analyzing data from teaching, whether hours or months later, is what distinguishes active, persistent, and careful inquiry from helter-skelter scrambling to find something that works. Teacher educators can play a powerful role in providing preservice teachers with the disposition to view their first year as contributing to their learning from inquiry about practice if they conceive of the year as one in which they will experiment or test hypotheses and collect data for later reflection. Such a disposition might help new teachers recognize gaps between their experiences as learners and their practice as teachers.

Those of us who care about nurturing inquiry as part of teaching cannot count on waiting until after teachers have "survived" their first year to incorporate inquiry. Sadly, many teachers leave after one year in the profession. Nor can we count on the teachers who do survive to incorporate inquiry if part of what they learned in surviving is merely to keep their curriculum working or that research is for those not involved directly in teaching. Our dilemma as teacher educators is how to work with preservice teachers in ways that honor the particular difficulties of the first year without preparing them only for survival.

Finally, we want to prepare teachers and invite our colleagues in teacher education to frame their inquiry not only to deepen their understandings of teaching and learning but also to recognize and question assumptions in schools that may work against powerful, connected reading and learning. Two pressing areas of inquiry strike us: the conflation of high-stakes testing with the goals of teaching and the general preference for control over interactive learning in secondary classrooms.

References

Atwell, N. *In the Middle: New Understandings About Writing, Reading, and Learning with Adolescents.* (2nd ed.). Portsmouth, N.H.: Heinemann, 1998.

Jay, J. K. "Meta, Meta, Meta: Modeling in a Methods Course for Teaching English." *Teacher Education Quarterly,* Winter 2002, 29(1), 83–102.

Jordan, M., Jensen, R., and Greenleaf, C. "Amidst Familial Gatherings: Reading Apprenticeship in a Middle School Classroom." *Voices from the Middle,* 2001, 8(4), 15–24.

Palincsar, A., and Brown, A. "Reciprocal Teaching of Comprehension-Fostering and Comprehension-Monitoring Activities." *Cognition and Instruction,* 1984, 2, 117–175.

Schön, D. *The Reflective Practitioner: How Professionals Think in Action.* New York: Basic Books, 1983.

Schön, D. *Educating the Reflective Practitioner: Toward a New Design for Teaching and Learning in the Professions.* San Francisco: Jossey-Bass, 1987.

Chapter 11

Teacher Preparation for Academic Literacy

Summary and Recommendations

Why is it necessary to rethink preparation for content area teaching? What are we hoping to achieve with the Reading Apprenticeship approach? We began this book by describing a fictional new teacher, Mark, whose frustration in addressing the reading needs of his middle school mathematics students was limiting both his instructional repertoire and his students' access to a rigorous mathematics curriculum. The authors of *Reading for Understanding* describe this kind of mutual impasse as hitting the "the literacy ceiling" (Schoenbach, Greenleaf, Cziko, and Hurwitz, 1999, p. 5). In this volume, which is a teacher education and professional development complement to *Reading for Understanding*, we propose ways to equip prospective teachers with understandings and tools to help them and their adolescent students break through the literacy ceiling. Mark's situation is a cautionary tale, and we can move beyond it. In organizing our content area reading courses around Reading Apprenticeship, we seek to enlarge preservice teachers' thinking about:

- The nature of reading
- The role of reading in content area learning
- The resources adolescents bring to reading in academic texts
- The role of teachers in improving students' capacity to learn from academic texts

Our summary recommendations speak to key considerations in accomplishing this goal, specifically developing the expertise to teach reading in the disciplines effectively as part of teaching the disciplines. We recap key themes explored in this book such as the power of inquiry to drive teachers' learning about literacy and about students, the importance of placing the metacognitive conversation in the foreground of reading processes as well as products, and the need for teachers to make instructional decisions informed by deep understandings of literacy and learning and their students' rich cultural and linguistic diversity. In Chapter Four we described teaching as the learning profession. The learnings we advocate here for teachers at the beginning of their careers are also appropriate for experienced teachers seeking better ways to help all their students successfully engage with challenging academic texts.

Building a Larger Vision of Reading

Prospective teachers need to understand reading as a complex and interactive process. When we engage them in inquiry activities designed to surface their own reading processes and learn about those of others, we invite them to begin a metacognitive conversation, one that they sustain through their preservice experience and carry into their own teaching. Rather than seeing reading as a free-standing technical skill, these teachers come to understand the complex mental activity and developmental process that reading is. And as prospective teachers experience their own struggles to understand certain texts—for example, in specialized disciplines other than their own—they come to understand that reading ability is not fixed; everyone struggles with some texts. This experience can help them problematize the notion of reading difficulties, and more importantly, to look beneath labels such as "struggling" or "limited" applied to students as readers.

Seeing That Teaching Reading in Our Disciplines *Is* Teaching Our Disciplines

Of special relevance to their role as teachers is the insight that they *learned* how to be expert readers in their chosen discipline. Their challenge as teachers will be to function as expert-mentor to novice-apprentice, helping students to learn to read in discipline-specific ways. In addition to having knowledge of effective reading strategies, they must have a deep understanding of the demands subject area texts place on readers and the reading processes suited to comprehending them (Greenleaf and Schoenbach, 2004). Making these understandings visible to students involves engaging them in metacognitive conversations, conversations about how we read in particular disciplines. In such classroom engagements, teachers help demystify reading, making their own and their students' invisible reading processes visible and accessible to each other. Making time in the classroom for such conversations about the processes we use to make meaning and to repair comprehension when it breaks down enhances students' capacity to read for understanding. As students develop greater agency in reading to learn, their potential for solid content area learning increases.

It is also important for teachers to provide extensive content area reading experiences, with appropriate instructional support, because the knowledge and strategies needed to learn from such texts develop through interaction with them. This is perhaps the most important critique of isolated instruction in basic reading skills for students identified as needing intervention; without access to disciplinary texts and support in learning from them, such students remain outside the mainstream curriculum.

Seeing the Resources Students Bring to Academic Reading and Learning

In our courses, we engage prospective teachers in inquiries into student reading, helping them learn from students both vicariously (via SLI's student literacy cases and classroom video cases) and in person (for example, through the inquiry into student reading practices described in Chapter Four and the student diversity dimensions exercise for teachers of English learners described in Chapter Five). It is important for preservice teachers to recognize and understand the various resources students bring to learning and reading in an academic setting, to move beyond a deficit model of reading, especially for students identified as struggling or otherwise underperforming. To do this, teachers must have access to student thinking—hence, again the rationale for supporting the metacognitive conversation in the social dimension. At the same time that these teachers learn to see students as resourceful readers, they learn how to anticipate and address problems that students are likely to have with content area texts. The teacher thus needs to know both the demands of reading in that discipline and the abilities and needs of the diverse classroom of students as readers.

Understanding the Teacher's Role in Students' Reading to Learn in the Content Areas

With Reading Apprenticeship framing our content area reading courses, we share a view of teaching as responsive and interactive. In an RA classroom, the teacher takes the leadership to create a community of learners with inquiry at its heart. The teacher's key responsibilities are to initiate and sustain the ongoing metacognitive conversation about reading and to provide extensive opportunities for engagement with a variety of texts linked to the content area curriculum. This means that the teacher needs in-depth knowledge about how reading operates in the specific discipline and about how to guide students to read in particular ways to learn in that discipline. Rather than compiling a collection of strategies, we have focused on helping new teachers learn and routinely implement content-appropriate high-leverage strategies that tap the social, personal, cognitive, and knowledge-building dimensions in their classrooms.

Part of teachers' work with strategies is to model their own reading processes for students; this is followed by scaffolded instruction that gradually shifts the strategy control, and decisions about when to use particular strategies, to the student.

From Preservice Learning to Classroom Practice of Reading Apprenticeship

Ultimately, a measure of our success will be the extent to which the teachers in our classrooms go on to teach in ways that allow their students to succeed beyond narrow assessments of reading ability. Their task is daunting, particularly for those who will take it upon themselves to work with so-called struggling readers, constrained by prescribed curricula and facing punitive consequences for their students' test scores. A natural response to this situation might be to equip preservice teachers with all the available strategies and hope that these cover all possible teaching scenarios. In this book, however, we have advocated a different approach. We know that language proficiency depends on a deep understanding of principles and structures, not on attention to surface features. So too with teaching, and specifically with teaching adolescents to read in particular disciplines. In the same way that learning a language is essentially a cognitive process, we believe that learning to teach in general, and especially, learning to teach reading must consist of many thoughtful and purposeful opportunities to think about literacy and ways to become literate in the various disciplines. As such, we see inquiry as playing an integral role in preservice courses. We hope that the examples of projects that we have described in this book and our discussions of what we have learned from our efforts will help other teacher educators to think about ways to engage new teachers in purposeful literacy inquiry as a basis for learning how to teach for understanding. Our goal is ultimately to support new teachers with powerful understandings of reading, with a view of students as resourceful, and with strategic approaches designed to ensure that all students engage productively with academic texts.

Finally, we also hope that, in the same manner in which teacher educators and professional developers invite teachers to carry out carefully designed Reading Apprenticeship inquiries, in turn they rely on reflection on their own practice as a way to further their ability to prepare teachers for the challenges of modern-day classrooms. It is, after all, inquiry about our efforts to introduce our students to Reading Apprenticeship that brought us, the authors of this volume, together in the first place and allowed us both to learn from one another and to draw support and inspiration for our efforts. We hope that our readers will take the sharing of our collaboration in this book as an invitation to join us in the conversation.

References

Greenleaf, C., and Schoenbach, R. "Building Capacity for the Responsive Teaching of Reading in the Academic Disciplines: Strategic Inquiry Designs for Middle and High School Teachers' Professional Development." In D. Strickland and M. Kamil (eds.), *Improving Reaching Achievement Through Professional Development* (pp. 97–127). Norwood, Mass.: Christopher Gordon Publishers, 2004.

Schoenbach, R., Greenleaf, C., Cziko, C., and Hurwitz, L. *Reading for Understanding: A Guide to Improving Reading in Middle and High School Classrooms.* San Francisco: Jossey-Bass, 1999.

Appendix A:
Understanding Metacognition

Literacy Autobiography

Cathleen D. Rafferty

Anyone who works with preservice or in-service teachers on content reading–literacy has faced the dual challenge of responsibility and application resistance. Teachers often question taking responsibility for their students' ongoing literacy development and they also have difficulty seeing how various strategies might be applied in their respective content areas. Much of this resistance seems related to a firm commitment to teaching content and concerns about lack of time and expertise to support literacy. In addition, a large number of teachers—both preservice and in-service—have not spent enough time examining their own literacy approaches and strategies, even in their own content areas. As a result, they lack an in-depth understanding of the literacy demands their students will face. These elements often result in powerful resistance as teachers struggle to understand why they—and not someone else, like the English teacher—must provide additional literacy-based assistance to their middle school and high school students in their content area classrooms.

I too have struggled to help teachers understand both the how and the why of content literacy, but the Teacher Education Consortium–sponsored Strategic Literacy Initiative (SLI) summer institute I attended several years ago gave me new insights into this long-standing dilemma. My SLI experience resulted in a major redesign of the course I teach for secondary credential candidates at Humboldt State University, a change that has resulted in more credential students embracing their responsibilities and working to modify various strategies for application with their students. Of course, this has meant dropping some previously used projects, assignments, and readings in order to accommodate the changes, but I was so enthused about these new ideas that I willingly made the revisions and have been quite pleased with the results. This shift in my own classroom practice resulted from many conversations with counterparts teaching in other credential programs, my introduction to the Reading Apprenticeship model, and a closer examination and understanding of my own reading and metacognitive approaches captured in a metacognitive log. (See Chapter Two of this volume for insights from other teacher educators incorporating RA into their preservice courses.)

At my institution, the required secondary reading course includes credential candidates from all content areas, including art, industrial education, languages other than English, music, and physical education. Teaching this course to such a diverse audience is quite challenging primarily because teachers (either preservice or in-service) must carefully examine their own beliefs, experiences, successes, failures, skills, processes, and approaches to reading and learning in order to be of assistance to others. If an *apprentice* is defined as one learning a trade under a skilled master, then in a Reading Apprenticeship model the *masters*, or the teachers themselves, must have at least a basic awareness of their own reading development. Better still, they should have an understanding of their own degree of executive control, or metacognition, so that they are better positioned to make their own reading and learning processes visible and available for their students.

To convey more completely the literacy autobiography assignment that is detailed in the following paragraphs, I will first provide some description of my approach to the course that was recently renamed Content Area Literacy. My course retains many traditional elements often found in a content reading–literacy course, such as vocabulary development strategies and various reading-to-learn strategies that can be implemented before, during, and after instruction. The recently revised course, however, begins with a unit entitled, "Getting to Know Yourself and Your Students," in which the credential candidates experience and reflect on a variety of self-assessment inventories that require them to think about the following: the types of textbook adaptations they would have preferred teachers use versus their actual experience with textbooks in school, their own strengths and preferences as aligned with Gardner's theory of multiple intelligences, their own metacognitive tendencies, and their preferred learning styles (Gardner, 1983). Individually and collectively these self-assessments begin the process of the credential candidates' close examination of themselves as readers-learners and provide part of their required analysis for the literacy autobiography project. (We also use this information—combined with subject area and gender—as a way to form diverse interdisciplinary learning teams that will be used throughout the semester for discussion groups and in-class presentations, but that's another story.) What I am doing here is consciously addressing the social and personal dimensions of literacy with my credential candidates, modeling this as an important focus in their work with adolescents using literacy to learn in various content areas.

Finally, we work to expand the definition of text in order to move from the traditional narrow focus on textbooks. Given the wide range of subject area majors—from English to art, music, and physical education—and types of text they frequently use, it is vital that we establish early and revisit often the idea that text may range from a textbook to an Internet site to a work of art or a piece of music. It can be printed, auditory, or visual. Together, the self-assessments and expanded definition of text provide a foundation on which credential candidates then further reflect upon themselves as readers-learners through a literacy autobiography. Again, the focus here is to model how these credential candidates can begin to think of ways to apprentice their own students in different content area disciplines and their accompanying text types.

The Literacy Autobiography Project

The literacy autobiography is the first part of a two-part project entitled "Getting in Touch with Your Inner Reader." The primary purpose of both project components is to have credential candidates closely examine themselves as readers and learners. Part Two, the metacognitive literacy journal project, is similar to the cross-disciplinary reading experience with metacognitive logs described in Chapter Three. In fact, my project description credits David Donahue's original work and Jane Braunger's adaptation as the genesis for my version, which subsequently refers students back to their literacy autobiography.

Specific directions for the literacy autobiography state the following: "As a prospective teacher, you know how important it is for your students to be able to interact with a variety of texts. However, you might feel that you don't know enough to be able to help your students understand content area texts in your subject area. By analyzing and reflecting on your own strengths (and areas to improve) as a reader-learner, you will be better positioned to understand and provide assistance to your students."

The project description and scoring rubric are both available on the course Web site, which is initially discussed on the first day of class and provides credential candidates with additional project guidelines and parameters. The rest of the directions are shown in Exhibit A.1.

After students receive this detailed project description, we spend some time in class exploring ideas, questions, and potential examples that would fulfill the project requirements. When students process the rubric requirements, they seem more comfortable with pursuing alternative formats, such as the examples provided in the note shown at the bottom of the scoring rubric (see Exhibit A.2). For example, in a recent class, one student asked whether

**Exhibit A.1. Literacy Autobiography
Project Description**

This project does not have a required format. Following you will find some questions and suggestions to consider as you begin to compose your literacy autobiography. An autobiography can be defined as the biography of a person narrated by himself or herself. In this case, you are writing your own biography about how you became literate, what literacy means to you, how literacy influences your life, and so on. Additional questions to consider are these:

- What are my characteristics as a reader?

- What strategies do I use when I read? (Remember the STAEI, MAI, MI, and Walker inventories?)

- Do my reading strategies change depending on what I'm reading or for what purpose? (For example, do I read narrative differently from how I read expository or informational text?)

- What role does reading and literacy serve in my personal and public life?

- Besides traditional notions of school-based literacy, what other literacies have been important to me?

- What role will reading-literacy play in my future education and career goals?

- What goals do I want to set and work toward to help myself develop as a reader-learner?

- Which particular elements from coursework to date have the most relevance for my own reading-learning and implications for my future teaching? Why?

Of course, there are dozens of other questions and ideas that you can consider while writing your literacy autobiography. Be creative and try to tell your story in an engaging manner. A scoring rubric for this assignment is attached.

creating a piece of artwork might fulfill the project requirements. I suggested that we peruse the rubric to brainstorm ways that a piece of art might accomplish this. Another student wondered about poetry or song lyrics, and I commented that in the previous year a student had done a live performance of his original composition that conveyed his story in a most entertaining fashion. After class, one student said he had an idea to write a dialogue between two men in a bar and asked if something like that could work for this project. Time and again we revisited the rubric to determine how a format other than a standard paper might fulfill project requirements. Although this process did take some time (in class, during office hours, and via e-mail), it helped to confirm for all of us that this project and accompanying rubric provided a variety of options for credential candidates to explore and examine their own literacy histories. In addition, because I was able to convey a variety of options and formats to students in other sections of the course, both their comfort level and excitement about pursuing this project increased.

Recent literacy autobiographies have been particularly compelling, with a number of students—several of whom self-identified as "risk takers"—choosing alternative formats: poetry, a diary or journal, a screenplay dialogue, a performance of an original song accompanied by acoustic guitar, a collage, a three-point perspective piece of art, and an illustrated comic book version of literacy development. The next section provides examples of several of the literacy autobiographies and highlights the credential candidates' learning associated with this project.

Literacy Autobiography Examples and Insights

Selecting examples to help convey the power of this project was particularly difficult because I received so many high-quality submissions from my students. Further, the range and number of nonstandard formats has increased.

**Exhibit A.2. Literacy Autobiography
Scoring Rubric**

1. Includes reflection about yourself as related to your literacy development and how these insights have implications for your future role as teacher.

2. Provides evidence of inclusion of some of the self-assessment inventories from the course Web site (STAEI, MAI, MI, Walker) and responses to questions on the assignment sheet.

3. Has been proofread for coherence and mechanics, such as grammar, spelling, and punctuation, and is long enough to be coherent and to fulfill the project's requirements.

Note: If the format is more creative than a standard written product, it should be accompanied by a brief written explanation to provide a point of entrée for the reviewer. Previous creative examples have included poetry, original song lyrics performed live or on audiotape, interpretive dance, original art, and so on.

Total points:
Comments:

The first example I present here is a standard paper from a math major (Dustin). The second is a "Dear Journal" format from a science major (Sasha). A third example, penned and illustrated by an English major (Chris), is a variation of Joyce's *A Portrait of the Artist as a Young Man*, while the final example is a beautifully detailed three-point perspective sketch of a classroom viewed from a desk in the back of the room, created by an art major (Rich) who is self-described as learning-disabled. (It should be noted that these are the students' actual names, and their work is shown here with their permission.)

Math: Dustin

"For as long as I can remember, I have loved to read—that is, until I got into college—but let me start at the beginning." Dustin's opening line captured my attention immediately, possibly because I have a math phobia and here is a math major telling me that he loves to read. It created a kind of cognitive dissonance and I was immediately drawn into his story that describes a print-rich environment and a mother who provided lots of support and encouragement. Dustin's fortunate early years' experience, which was echoed by many of my credential candidates, reflects the type of environment we wish for all of our students. However, his story did have a few dark moments:

> It wasn't until college where my pleasure reading virtually stopped. It was difficult enough to finish all the assigned reading in order to complete the weekly problem sets. During my college years I really began to despise reading. Quite frankly, I can say that I hated it. I did not understand the reading. I began to read very slowly, struggling for meaning. I often had to reread a passage over and over again and still would not grasp what it was saying or what I was supposed to be getting from the passage. . . . Much of the time it felt that I might well have been reading a foreign language. Furthermore, I read so much during the school year that I would not touch a book during the summer.

Unfortunately, Dustin's description closely matched what many credential candidates had to say about reading. For many, however, their dislike began at a much earlier age—usually middle school or high school—and was attributable to required reading of textbooks and often, their lack of skills for working with various types of expository texts. As Dustin noted in his analysis of his love-hate relationship with reading:

> I believe that my ease and love of reading for the majority of my life was due to the fact that I understood what I was reading, could

comprehend the reading, and actually was interested in the reading. The last point is what I feel is the most important point. As my interest in the subjects of my reading decreased, I began to read less, even in my pleasure reading. Here I believe was my downfall. Even if I did not like the subjects I read in school, I still should have kept an active pleasure reading life in which I chose a book that really caught my interest. I feel that being able to keep an interest in reading leads to easier reading and comprehension and understanding; however, high school and college textbooks are often very dry and boring, producing a lack of interest in students, which leads to a lack of comprehension and understanding. As a teacher, I want to make sure that my students understand *how* to read different texts, especially math texts. I do not want them to fall into the same trap as I did.

Dustin's insights, which resulted from the opportunity to examine his personal literacy history and were echoed by many of his peers, attest to the power of having credential candidates reflect on their own growth and development as literate individuals. Dustin concluded by noting that he did not learn how to and was not taught how to employ different reading strategies depending on the text and purpose for reading. Clearly, however, from his closing comments, he had some definite ideas about ways to assist his future students.

It is up to teachers to help all students learn to read to understand in an interesting way so as not to turn off students to reading. . . . Students need to be taught ways to monitor their understanding of the materials and methods to use in reading specific texts. It is also important for teachers to show students how to "read to learn" by actually demonstrating these strategies. In math, I hope to engage students by using charts, graphs, pictures, and other illustrations as a supplement to their reading. . . . I believe that if I had been taught this in high school and college I would not have struggled as much with reading.

Science: Sasha

"Dear Journal, For one of my classes I have been assigned to reflect on the ways in which I read, gain and retain information, and learn. I'm a little lost, but journaling always seems to provide an opportunity for understanding. Hopefully you can help shed some light on this assignment." So began Sasha's literacy autobiography, which took the form of a journal written across several sessions. In it, she "thought on paper" or had a conversation with herself as she used this type of writing to help herself process various questions and project components. In one portion of the journal she reflected on the types of books she read by examining her bookshelf and then connecting various book categories (for example, self-help books) with different multiple intelligence strengths, such as intrapersonal.

In another section of her journal, Sasha reflected on a reading we did early in the semester that emphasized the importance of various text features such as vocabulary, pictorial or graphic aids, and various organizational text patterns and how readers-learners can use them for better understanding the content and concepts. As a science major, Sasha noted the importance of lists because they helped her to "recognize important from less important concepts, organize information, and simplify and summarize concepts."

When Sasha considered various approaches that she could use to assist her future students, she acknowledged that learning how to learn is critically important and that teachers must remember that students learn in different ways. She further acknowledged that "it will be a constant struggle not to teach in only the same way that (I) learn . . . and that I would like to give a variety of different types of reading assignments." This acknowledgment of student differences is a critical insight for all teachers. It also seemed linked to Sasha's closing statement in which she noted both the power of writing and reflection—RA's personal dimension—and the importance of providing students with options for assignments:

> I think it's about time to call it a night. You have definitely helped
> me to clear some things up. I have a better understanding of the

roles that different types of literacy have in my life, my strengths and weaknesses as a learner, and the beginning thoughts on what this means as far as my future goals as a teacher. One of the main things I have realized is that although in some ways structure is important to me, when I am allowed to be a little creative with an assignment, it becomes much more enjoyable, exciting, and beneficial. Thanks for listening to me.

English: Chris

Chris began his illustrated version of "A Portrait of a Reader as Young Man" with the following Preface statement: "As a teacher, I know that my students will be at various places on their journeys as readers. Some, I am sure, will barely be able to link letters together to form a word, while others will have surpassed me as critical consumers of literature and culture. However, I think I will have something to offer all of my students because I, too, have been on the journey of finding myself as a reader, have reflected upon it, and continue to read that path critically and with awareness."

What followed this portion of the Preface was an illustrated narrative that began with learning to read before entering school and culminated with examples from his undergraduate education as an English major and as a secondary credential candidate. Both the age-appropriate drawings and printing-writing across Chris's development as a reader-learner provided powerful insights into major events that shaped this young man's commitment to his future students (see Figure A.1).

Both the illustrations and explanations in his literacy autobiography attested to the mentoring or apprenticing influence that teachers can have on students. It is entirely possible that Chris could have been a successful science teacher, given his interest and previous performance in that area. However, he turned his attention to English because of positive role models and an increasing interest in the elements-aspects of that content area over another.

Given his highly developed metacognitive awareness as a reader-learner, it could be argued that a student like Chris might

Figure A.1. Chris's High School Reading

Mr. Ford was a really good teacher. I m really glad that he was my first English teacher in high school. He told me on quite a few occasions that he saw himself in me. He made me like reading and writing even more than I had had before. He helped me to like poetry. I think he understood that not everyone liked reading as much as he and I did, so he did stuff like reading all of <u>Great Expectations</u> out loud to our class and acting out the poems we were reading.

I don t know how I knew, but by the time I had made it to Mr. Ford s class I knew that I wanted to be a teacher. I thought that I wanted to be a science teacher, but there was something about Mr. Ford that I wanted to fold into myself. I wanted to be like Ms. Harris, my science teacher, too, but there was something special about how Mr. Ford touched us. He made reading and writing a very personal matter.

At the end of my freshman year, Mr. Ford recommended that I go into English honors and after a grueling test, which I later found was an old AP test they used to assess us, my thoughts started to turn away from science. Reading was becoming, it seemed, increasingly important to me.

* * *

I sat there writing my response to the daily prompt, or, perhaps, I was taking a test; I can t remember. Her hand came from behind me and placed the corrected essay on my desk and Ms. Pettrone leaned in to whisper a message to me. I hope you are thinking of becoming an English major, she said, with a smile.

My mind broke from whatever task I was working on before Ms. Pettrone had blessed me with her whisper, and I erupted into thought. Had I been considering that? I thought I wanted to be a science teacher! This stuff does make sense to me . . . even the grammar.

* * *

A variety of factors, which came together during my sophomore year of high school, turned my mind toward the study of English. The most important factor was Ms. Pettrone s surprising recommendation. I had loved the biology that I studied my freshman year and the idea of it had pushed me closer to science as a career, but then I discovered, to my horror, that I dislike chemistry. It wasn t that I did poorly in the class; I just thought that it was boring. At the same time, I realized that I wanted to try to end my contact with math as soon as possible; I found that both algebra and geometry left a bad taste in my mouth.

have difficulty connecting with struggling readers. It could also be debated that such an in-depth understanding might better equip a teacher, as Chris noted in his opening statement, to assist all students in their journey to becoming readers. Given that Chris also continued "to read that path critically and with awareness," the latter scenario seems more likely than the former, but it is incumbent upon us, as teacher educators, to continue to monitor all of our credential candidates to help ensure that they are well-equipped to meet the needs of all students. Chris himself underscored the importance of this vigilance: "Hopefully, I can translate my experiences into a way to help others move into a more comfortable place, so that some day they will be able to help others be better readers. I hope to foster a critical literacy in my students that will help them transform their lives, and, in turn, create a better world. I have this hope because I have seen what a happy, beautiful life my own literacy has helped create for me."

Art: Rich

The final example from the credential candidates contained the fewest number of words but conveyed an extremely cogent message about Rich's literacy background (see Figure A.2).

After I had examined this beautifully detailed three-point perspective drawing, I talked with Rich to encourage him to present his drawing in class. I explained that he could both educate us about some art-related concepts and provide us with an example of how visual literacy can be a powerful learning tool. To my delight, he agreed, and what follows is a synopsis of the key elements of his literacy history as portrayed in his drawing.

One immediately notices that the perspective is from a student seated at the back of the room (again see Figure A.2). According to Rich, this was both his location of choice and where he was often assigned to sit once some teachers understood that he didn't read, write, or participate in discussions very often or well. There are no windows or light and there is a name on the board with disciplinary

Figure A.2. Rich's Classroom Experience

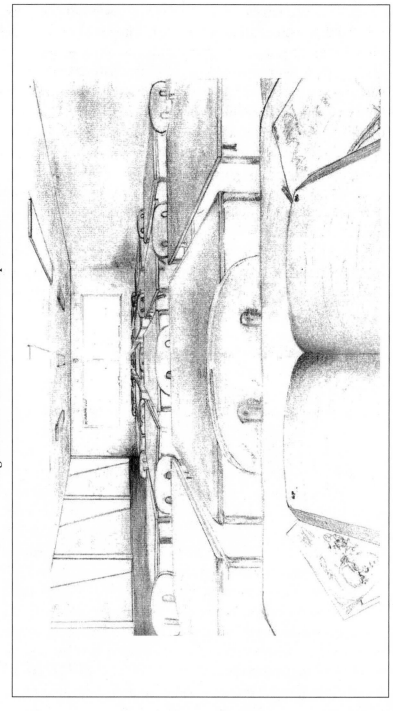

checkmarks behind it (Rich's, of course). There is also a clock prominently placed in the center, indicating that he was watching it for the release it could provide and that it was a constant source of irritation because it seemed to move so slowly. Both the book on the desk in front of him and the chalkboard (except his name) are blank to convey that there was no meaning for him. What was meaningful is captured on snippets of paper that protrude from within the textbook and underneath it—his sketches—surreptitiously drawn and easily hidden if the teacher ever decided to venture to his back-row world.

Rich's in-class presentation-explanation resulted in gasps, expressions of sympathy, and a productive discussion about ways that teachers can use alternative assignments to meet students' learning needs. For example, Rich himself observed that being permitted to draw his literacy autobiography allowed him to convey more of his story than words alone could have done. Other credential candidates acknowledged that providing options both promotes creativity and helps to support various learning styles, while some expressed surprise that a student such as Rich could be "ignored" for so long over his educational career. Still others had friends or acquaintances with similar experiences. All, however, noted that they had a moral and professional responsibility to reach out and try to assist all the students in their classroom—a powerful testimony and foundation that was established early in the semester and upon which we would continue to build throughout the academic year.

Conclusion

As these examples convey, the literacy autobiography project resulted in some cogent insights for these secondary credential candidates. They gained a deeper understanding and appreciation for elements and factors that influenced—both positively and negatively—their own literacy development and also benefited from interacting with their peers regarding their experiences. They acknowledged that all teachers have a responsibility, albeit different perhaps, to learn about and then find ways to support their students' literacy needs. Most importantly, however, the literacy autobiography—the first part of a larger project designed to put these preservice teachers "in touch with their inner readers"—sensitized them to the challenges they would face later in the project, when they would more fully understand that literacy development is a lifelong process that involves all dimensions of the Reading Apprenticeship model. Who we are as readers, learners, teachers, and human beings is part of an ongoing story that benefits from examination and self-reflection and analysis to help us help our students.

Reference

Gardner, H. *Frames of Mind: The Theory of Multiple Intelligences*. New York: Basic Books, 1983.

Appendix B:
Reading in Mathematics

Inquiry with Preservice Teachers

Virginia Draper

Think-alouds make visible the activities that mature readers do to understand a text. In addition, they bring to light the attitudes and prior knowledge that can facilitate—or impede—those activities. For instance, think-alouds reveal that good readers often predict what will be coming next in a text, and if their predictions are off the mark they are willing to revise their predictions and reread if needed. Think-alouds also tell us that good readers usually draw on their previous experience with the genre of the text and prior learning. And when they realize they need some information or context they do not have, they often consult a friend or a reference book.

In sum, when we use think-alouds to inquire into the nature of reading, we discover what a complex social process reading is. But because fluent, mature, and motivated readers of familiar texts usually employ successful reading strategies intuitively, they may well be unaware of how they actually construct meaning. Thus, they may be puzzled about how to teach others to read texts in their field. However, less experienced readers, including those faced with unfamiliar genres or texts, need to become aware of and consciously use strategies if they are going to do anything more than run their eyes across a page. When teachers and preservice teachers do think-alouds together, they not only become more aware of these strategies but get a chance to explore where and why some of their students become confused or meet roadblocks and what they can do to help students negotiate those blocks.

For all these reasons, I introduced think-alouds early in the ten-week reading in the content areas course I taught in Winter 2002 at the University of California, Santa Cruz. The class had thirty-five credential students—twelve from English, nine from social science, seven from science, and seven from mathematics. During the first five weeks, we did think-alouds with an excerpt from a social studies textbook ("Totalitarianism in the Modern World" [Krieger and Neill, 1994]), a poem ("Old Man" [Sanchez, 1990]), and samples of scientific writing on similar subjects written for readers from grade four through college.

But halfway through the course, some of the mathematics students told me that they were having difficulty connecting what we were learning about reading to what students need to do to become competent in math. My math students knew the challenges of reading a poem—and how difficult it might be to teach someone to read poetry—but what, they wanted to know, did that kind of reading have to do with reading in math? Though some of their assignments (for example, *Infotext: Reading and Learning* [Feathers, 1999]) contained references to mathematics, and the course reader included *Teaching Reading in Mathematics: A Supplement to Teaching Reading in the Content Areas* (Barton and Heidema, 2000), our in-class inquiries had not included any texts from their field. So unlike the students in English, social studies, and science, the math students had not had the chance to explore reading in mathematics with others outside their field. And as Donahue (2003) points out, cross-curricular inquiry can be very informative and provide valuable practice for preservice teachers.

In a similar reading in the content areas course, Donahue paired mathematics teachers with English teachers and asked them to read two books together, one from each field, and to keep a reading log that focused on why and how they read. Reflecting on his students' work, he concluded that when teachers engage in inquiry with those "outside their discipline, they can learn how to translate and then share the process of understanding as expert readers in a discipline with colleagues who are novice readers in that discipline and who, in many respects, resemble their students" (p. 36). And equally important, he noted, "By working with colleagues, they will also practice apprenticing their expertise in ways that respect not only the experience and knowledge but also the dignity of novice readers" (p. 36).

I initiated a similar inquiry in my class by inviting students to engage in a think-aloud activity using sample test items for the mathematics part of the California High School Exit Examination, which I found on the California Department of Education Web site. The think-alouds were done in small groups that included students from the four disciplines, with each group facilitated by one of the mathematics students. (See Exhibit B.1 for a detailed description of the activity.)

The math students' reflections on this activity indicated that while listening to the think-alouds of their classmates, most of whom had far less experience doing math than they did, they discovered how individuals less adept in the field read and misread, and how negative and self-defeating attitudes block successful performances. One English teacher, who said she was math-phobic, almost refused to engage in the think-aloud, but was willing to persist when she realized she could help her math colleagues understand and work with students who had similar blocks. To help her get beyond her phobia—which made her a less-than-fluent reader of math problems—people in her group suggested that she use strategies, like talking to the text, posing questions, or asking a friend, strategies that we had identified earlier to help students gain access to a poem or a textbook. For instance, when she did not understand the meaning of *quartile value* in one of items, she needed to ask someone rather than give up. Thus, though they noted that often there is a single correct answer in mathematics (compared, say, to the proliferation of interpretations a poem invites), some strategies are equally effective in courses across the disciplines.

Exhibit B.1. Inquiry into Reading in Mathematics: Doing Think-Alouds with Items from High-Stakes Tests

Prepare Materials

Select mathematics problems for the think-alouds. Include both word problems, which usually have a narrative context, and algebra problems without a narrative context. Select enough problems so that everyone in small groups will get a chance to do a think-aloud. (I had five people in each group, so I selected ten items from the "Sample Test Items for Mathematics," which were then available from the California High School Exit Examination on the Web site of the Standards and Assessment Division.) You may also want to select sample items from your state's exit examinations or other high-stakes tests. Make enough copies for everyone in the class. Also make copies of the answer key on a separate piece of paper.

Form Heterogeneous Groups, Each with a Mathematics Teacher-Leader

Have students get into groups of four to six, with at least one math teacher at each table who will be the facilitator of the inquiry. Ideally, others in the group will come from different disciplines. (In my class of thirty-five students we had seven groups of five because we had seven math teachers. And I asked students from the other content areas—English, social studies, and science—to spread themselves among the seven groups.)

Pose the Inquiry

- What kinds of reading strategies do the math questions on the California High School Exit Exam require?
- How can math (and other) teachers assist students to acquire these strategies?

- Is reading in math the same as reading in other subject areas?
- Do readers need to acquire strategies specific to mathematics to be good readers of mathematics problems?

Give Each Person a Set of the Problems

Give out the problems without the answer sheets.

Explain the Procedures

For example, you might say something like this: "By using think-alouds you will discover what strategies you use to solve these problems, where you experience roadblocks, and what you do when you meet them. You will also explore what prevents comprehension and why you do or do not come up with the correct answer."

Before beginning, the math teacher-leaders scan through the problems and decide which ones they want the others to use for the think-alouds. They select as many as there are people in the group, and pick a combination of those that use words and those that are mostly or only mathematical symbols.

The leaders then decide which problem to work on first, second, third, and so on. Then they ask for a volunteer to go first. This person will try to solve the problem thinking aloud. In other words, instead of working silently, this person will let others know when he or she is confused, puzzled, relieved, or gets an insight. This person will also note when doing things like this:

- Accessing prior knowledge
- Setting purpose
- Predicting or changing predictions
- Creating mental images

**Exhibit B.1. Inquiry into Reading in Mathematics:
Doing Think-Alouds with Items from High-Stakes Tests
(cont'd.)**

- Posing questions
- Defining words in context
- Looking back or rereading
- Summarizing
- Making analogies
- Fitting material to personal experience
- Reflecting on attitudes or reactions
- Drawing pictures or taking notes

While the person is thinking aloud trying to solve the problem, the others in the group, including the math teacher, will listen and take notes. When the first person has solved the problem, or perhaps given up (but that person must not give up until having worked for at least three minutes), those who were listening will compare notes.

- What strategies did the person use? What strategy or strategies helped to solve the problem? Did any strategies get in the way?
- Did she use strategies that only mathematicians might use? Should she have used some strategies that only mathematicians might use?
- Where and why did she experience a roadblock? What did she do?
- Did she come to a permanent roadblock? Why?
- What new strategies would you like to help her acquire? How might you do this?
- Would everyone in the group have approached the problem in the same way?

After discussing the first person's process, the math teacher should ask for a volunteer to solve a second problem while thinking aloud. Again, the others listen, take notes, and then discuss. They then keep going until everyone in the group—including the leader—has had a chance to work on a problem while thinking aloud. Then, they discuss what they have learned about reading in math. How is it similar or different from reading other texts, such as a poem, a social studies or science textbook?

Reflections

You could have all your students write about this activity in a notebook including what they learned, insights they had, questions or issues that remain, and implications for their own practice or career. You could ask them to share the questions or what seemed most exciting to them with the whole class. Reflections could then be posted on the class Web site.

In addition, the class realized that concepts such as fluency and motivation also apply to reading mathematics and that readers' prior knowledge of genre, content, and vocabulary very much influence their ability to understand and do what they are asked. For example, students with little or no experience in expressing inequalities and with negative numbers struggled with one item: "Ten less than a number, x, is greater than twice the number. Which of the following inequalities represents this information?" To help students get the right answer, the math teacher had to explain not only how to express inequalities and negative numbers but the differences between "less" and "minus."

They also discovered that there were often two or more ways to solve a problem. For example, another item read: "Maria rode her bike 1¼ miles. How many feet did she ride on her bike? (5,280 feet = 1 mile)." To find the correct answer, students could multiply

5,280 by 1.25 or by ¾. Or they could multiply 5,280 by ¼ or by .25 and add the answer to 5,280. People usually chose the process that seemed easiest or most efficient, based on prior knowledge and experience.

In their groups, the math teacher-leaders began to uncover and explain expert ways of reading math to their less experienced colleagues, most of whom had not worked a math problem in years. Reflecting on this activity at the end of the course, one mathematics student wrote: "It helps to see what is important when reading math texts and what I have done [to read and solve math problems], but never really articulated, which I should do now for my students so they can see how people read mathematical texts and problems."

The think-aloud activity in this class led Dora (pseudonym), one of the mathematics teachers, to initiate her own inquiry with her seventh- and eighth-grade ELD students and share what she discovered with us. To the next class she brought copies of mathematics problems, explained the challenges that she and her students were facing, and invited us to help her out.

Dora's students had been in California less than a year, and after observing them as a student teacher for a month or so, she had estimated that half could do "high-level math" if the texts were in Spanish, their native language. But she came to realize that simply translating the problems into Spanish wouldn't be sufficient, because to read and understand some of the story problems, students needed some cultural knowledge that many of them did not have. For instance, a lesson on figuring percentages included the following problem:

> Faaiz and Tat Ming go to a restaurant for dinner. Their meals total $13.75.
>
> a. The local sales tax is 5%. How much tax will be added to the bill?
>
> b. They want to leave a 15% tip based on the bill and the tax combined. How much should they leave? Explain.

    c. If Faaiz decides he should pay $2.75 more than Tat Ming because he ordered the more expensive dinner, how much should each pay? Explain.

To illustrate the challenges her students faced in understanding this text, Dora explained that few of her students had been to restaurants in the United States, so the social context that initiated the need to do the percentages was unfamiliar to them though it would be familiar to most native-born, middle-class American students. In addition, many did not know about local sales tax and that it was added to bills. And most did not know about the social custom of tipping. So before they could even see the need to figure percentages and begin doing that, Dora had to explain quite a bit—or get other students in the class to tell their peers—about eating out in American restaurants.

Our discussion of this math problem also brought to light a difference in ways we interpret texts in different fields. When reading a story, memoir, even a social studies text, readers would expect the names of the characters, Faaiz and Tat Ming, and also perhaps their genders, to be significant. Good readers of literature would draw on prior knowledge to guess each one's cultural background; they might appropriately raise questions about their relationship and ages and predict that this information would be forthcoming. But in a math problem such as this the cultural backgrounds, genders, and ages of the characters are irrelevant, and trying to figure these out could be distracting.

A math problem, then, can be seen as a particular genre, and students familiar with the genre will know which kinds of reading strategies are appropriate and which are inappropriate. Barton and Heidema (2000, p. 50) identify some of the appropriate strategies when they suggest that math teachers help students read word problems by completing a "KNWS Worksheet." On the worksheet students record:

What facts do I *know* from the information in the problem?

Which information do I *not* need?

What does the problem ask me to find?

What *strategy*-operation-tools will I use to solve the problem?

This kind of guide might have helped Dora's students, especially in the third part of the problem, with its complex syntax and verbs in the conditional, which her students found particularly difficult to understand.

Once students figured out what the problem asked them to find, Dora noted that some needed help identifying the mathematical processes called for. For instance, first they needed to reduce the first part, "The local sales tax is 5%. How much tax will be added to the bill?" to something like this: "What is 5% of $13.75?" Then they needed to translate that into a multiplication problem, such as $13.75. × .05.

For the second part ("They want to leave a 15% tip based on the bill and the tax combined. How much should they leave?"), they needed to realize that though the problem contains only one question, to find the answer there are actually three questions that require three operations. The first question is: "What is the total of the bill and tax combined?" To get this sum they need to add the answer they got for the first part to $13.75. The second question is: "What is 15% of that total?" To get this they need to figure the percentage. And the third question is: "What is the sum of the total bill and the 15% tip?" To do this they need to add the answers for the first and second questions.

In sum, what Dora showed us is that students may be able to figure percentages when asked "What is 5% of $13.75?" or when the problem is given only using numbers, such as $13.75 × .05.

But their computational abilities may be compromised if comprehension of story problems requires a cultural literacy and syntactic maturity they have not yet acquired. To respond to these kinds of problems successfully, students need to draw upon not just their mathematical abilities but also their reading comprehension abilities. And when teaching mathematics involves such problems, math teachers need to be astute and informed teachers of reading.

In addition, if becoming competent in math requires not only learning how to figure percentages (or do some other operation) but understanding how percentages are used in common events in the United States, then math teachers are also teachers of cultural literacy. And schools need to make sure there is sufficient classroom time for teachers to teach and students to learn these literacies.

Unfortunately, at Dora's school there was a policy that bilingual students had to cover exactly the same material as the other students in the same amount of time. In her reflective notebook, she wrote:

> I disagree with the curricular decision to expose the bilingual Math A students to the same amount of material as the English-only Math A students. I understand the reason behind the decision . . . so they will be "ready" to move on to algebra or Interactive Mathematics Program 1 next year . . . but the cold truth is that rushing them through the material is not preparing them for next year. . . . When the pace of the class is slow enough, they understand what they are doing and they complete the work. When the pace of the class is too fast, they get lost and just copy someone else's work at the end. This is teaching them how to cheat in algebra or IMP 1.

These two classes, when we explored reading in mathematics, came to mind when the chair of the education department asked me if I thought the department should continue to have credential students from all subject matters in this class. She noted that the English teachers had had substantial instruction on teaching reading (they had read some of *Reading for Understanding* [Schoenbach, Greenleaf, Cziko, and Hurwitz, 1999] in their Fall methods course). The social studies teachers, she continued, ought to have instruction in reading as part of their methods courses, and the department was planning to add that to the next year's curriculum. So, she speculated, it was really only the science and math students who might be unaccustomed to thinking about reading and whose subject matter teachers did not introduce reading theories and research to them.

However, the think-alouds and the inquiries they inspired in my course showed that inquiry into reading is most fruitful when teachers from different subjects are in the class together. Teachers (and the students in this course were no exception) are appropriately "in love" with their subject areas, and because they are usually quite adept at reading the texts for their own fields, they often fail to understand what it takes to become engaged in them. By working with those outside their fields, they become more aware of what it means to be a novice or awkward reader in their discipline. So although at the beginning of the course two-thirds of my students thought that teaching reading was mainly the responsibility of language arts teachers in elementary and high schools, by the end of the course they all realized the value of attending to reading in the context of their own courses. Equally important, they began to develop a shared vocabulary, set of concepts, and strategies to talk about and teach reading that apply across the disciplines.

Perhaps most important, they gained insights into the challenges students face when reading expository prose and the importance of helping students to read those kinds of texts. Most of the English teachers thought their job was to help students read poetry and fiction and had little interest in teaching them how to read expository texts (even though it is exposition that they ask students to write). And a social studies teacher said she only wanted students to learn how to skim and not to read for comprehension. But the inquiry into reading mathematics helped them see that they had a shared mission. I believe that improving reading can best be accomplished if it is a whole-school effort, and this effort is greatly enriched when teachers are aware of the similarities and differences between subject areas. As Donahue noted, it gets the teachers "to pay attention not only to *what* but also to *how* and *why* they read in their discipline" (2003, p. 37).

Students need to learn the *how* and *why* in order to understand and interact with the *what*. When students become competent and confident readers, they are less dependent on teacher talk for the *what*, and through reading they can access a variety of sources and become inquirers themselves.

References

Barton, M. L., and Heidema, C. *Teaching Reading in Mathematics: A Supplement to Teaching Reading in the Content Areas.* Aurora, Colo.: Mid-Continent Research for Education and Learning (McCREL), 2000.

Donahue, D. "Reading Across the Great Divide: English and Math Teachers Apprentice One Another as Readers and Disciplinary Insiders." *Journal of Adolescent and Adult Literacy,* 2003, 47(1), 24–37.

Feathers, K. *Infotext: Reading and Learning.* Portsmouth, N.H.: Heinemann, 1999.

Krieger, L. S., and Neill, K. "Totalitarianism in the Modern World." In *Issues of the Modern Age.* Lexington, Mass.: D.C. Heath, 1994.

Sanchez, R. "Old Man." In C. Tatum (ed.), *Mexican American Literature.* Orlando: Harcourt Brace Jovanovich, 1990.

Schoenbach, R., Greenleaf, C., Cziko, C., and Hurwitz, L. *Reading for Understanding: A Guide for Improving Reading in Middle and High School Classrooms.* San Francisco: Jossey-Bass, 1999.

Name Index

Subject Index

Reading for Understanding: A Guide to Improving Reading in Middle and High School Classrooms

Ruth Schoenbach, Cynthia Greenleaf, Christine Cziko, and Lori Hurwitz

Paper / 240 pages

ISBN: 0–7879–5045–9

Published in Partnership with WestEd

"These authors do not take sides between authenticity of text and task at one end of an instructional continuum and ambitious, explicit instruction at the other end. Instead they transform the apparent contradiction into a sort of resonant complementary, showing that these two seemingly opposite notions actually support one another quite remarkably. In a policy world in which forced choices have become all too common, it is refreshing to see contradictions transformed into synergies."—P. David Pearson, John A. Hannah Professor of Education, Michigan State University

This book introduces the nationally recognized Reading Apprenticeship™ instructional framework, a research-based model with a proven record of success in increasing the engagement and achievement of adolescent readers, including many considered "struggling" or disengaged students. Filled with vivid classroom lessons and exercises, the book shows teachers how to "apprentice" students to reading in the disciplines. This approach demystifies the reading process for students so they can acquire the necessary motivational, cognitive, and knowledge-building strategies for comprehending diverse and challenging types of texts. The book also presents a detailed description of the pilot "Academic Literacy" curriculum, a year-long course in which a group of urban ninth-grade students made an average of two years' gain in rewarding comprehension. In addition it shows how Reading Apprenticeship™ strategies can be embedded in science, math, English, and social studies classrooms, thus serving as a useful guide for teachers working across the curricula in grades 6–12.

Building Academic Literacy:
Lessons from Reading Apprenticeship Classrooms, Grades 6–12

Audrey Fielding, Ruth Schoenbach, and Marean Jordan, Editors

Paper / 192 pages

ISBN: 0–7879–6556–1

Boost the Engagement and Achievement of Adolescent Readers

Featuring pieces by five practicing teachers, this book shows how the Reading Apprenticeship™ instructional framework can be adopted to diverse classrooms and teaching styles. Filled with insights and guidance on strengthening adolescent literacy, the book includes instructional tips, lesson plans, and classroom exercises for enabling students to become independent, strategic, and competent readers serving as a vital resource for English/language arts teachers in grades 6–12. The book also includes extensive resources and tools for implementing Academic Literacy course units, as well as examples of classroom practices using selections from *Building Academic Literacy: An Anthology for Reading Apprenticeship* (Fielding and Shoenbach, 0-7879-6555-3), making this an invaluable teacher companion to the related student reader.

"Whenever we read books about teaching, we ask ourselves, 'But what does that look like in the classroom?' *Building Academic Literacy: Lessons from Reading Apprenticeship Classrooms* answers the question of what 'Academic Literacy' is, why it matters, and how teachers can develop these key intellectual habits in their students. This book, and its companion anthology, provide me with the guidance and resources that I need."—Jim Burke, author, *The Reader's Handbook* and *The English Teacher's Companion*